300 Years
of
Carolina Cooking

Published by

The Junior League of Greenville, Inc.

1970

Tricentennial Edition

For Additional Copies of
300 Years of Carolina Cooking
Send $4.50 per copy (plus 50-cents postage per copy)
(S. C. Residents Please Add 18-cents Per Copy Sales Tax)

To: The Junior League of Greenville, Inc.
P. O. Box 8703 Station A
Greenville, South Carolina 29604

Contents

Cookbook Committee

Mrs. Newton Stall, Jr. . . . . Chairman
Miss Choice McCoin . . . . Editor, Assistant Chairman
Mrs. William B. Ellis III . . . . Recipe Solicitation Chairman
Mrs. William W. Kehl . . . . Testing Chairman
Mrs. Walter G. King . . . . Typing Chairman
Mrs. William H. Richardson, Jr. . . Game Section Chairman
Mrs. Robert J. Stephenson III . . Indexing Chairman
Mrs. John C. Dunson . . . . Promotion Consultant
Mrs. E. Calhoun Haskell, Jr. . . . . President, Junior League
    of Greenville, Inc.

Mrs. Robert E. Buck III . . . . Vice-President, Junior League
    of Greenville, Inc.

Mrs. Ralph Bailey
Mrs. C. D. Bessinger
Mrs. David E. Cromwell
Mrs. John Edwards
Mrs. James A. Harris, Jr.
Mrs. William H. Johnson, Jr.
Mrs. William H. McCauley II
Mrs. David Quattlebaum
Mrs. Charles W. Rosson

Mrs. Louis T. Runge
Mrs. E. E. Stone IV
Mrs. Heyward M. Sullivan
Mrs. Gordon R. Vinson
Mrs. Ben Brockman
Mrs. James W. Knox
Mrs. Walter Clark
Mrs. R. Burnett Pamplin

Preface

"The object of this League shall be to train its members for effective participation in the community through a program of education and volunteer service."

From 1929 until 1970 The Junior League of Greenville, Inc. has matured from The Junior Charities with 20 members to The Junior League of Greenville, Inc. with over 130 Active members, 225 Sustaining members and 40 Provisional ones.

During these years The Junior League has continually trained its members for effective community service and raised funds to . . .

. . . begin a baby diet kitchen

. . . employ a trained social worker as first director of Family Service

. . . establish the Youth Service Center, now grown to the Special Services of the County School District.

. . . assist the Hearing Society, now United Speech and Hearing

. . . aid the Visiting Nurse Association

. . . establish the Youth Concert Series

. . . produce Children's Theatre plays

. . . sponsor Music Appreciation Hours

. . . produce puppet shows yearly

. . . found the Parent Youth Association with Area III PTA

. . . participate in the Arts Festivals

. . . conduct art classes at the Greenville Museum of Art

. . . initiate the Corrective Reading Program

Funds from the sale of these cookbooks will be used in the Greenville community to finance new and needed programs of the same high calibre demonstrated in past projects.

Acknowledgments

The *300 Years of Carolina Cooking* Committee is deeply grateful to:

The many contributors without whom this book could not have come into being;

The Junior League members who have worked diligently on all phases of the preparation of the book;

Mr. J. C. Keys, Jr., Mrs. W. H. League, Mr. Ralph Bailey, Miss Laura Smith Ebaugh, Mr. Ralph Benoy, Jr., Mr. Arthur Frahm, Mr. Jack Morris, Jr., Mr. Robert True, Mr. Harris Milligan, Mr. Wilton E. Hall, Jr. and Mrs. Fred S. Brown, for their special contributions.

Foreword

South Carolina's reputation for gracious living, charming manners and good food dates back to the early plantation days of the Colonial period and the delightful resort life of Upper South Carolina following the American Revolution. This Tricentennial cookbook, reminiscent of those early days yet usable in the new technological South, is a welcome addition to this year's publications. In this excellent book, one will find not only the traditional recipes of the early days, such as red rice, creole shrimp, hopping john and scores of others but also up-to-date recipes for salads, canapes, soups, sauces, etc.

Recall as you enjoy this book that the food of today is a result of the adaptations made by our early ancestors to their new environment where strange vegetables, fruits and grain grew, unknown game and fowl abounded in the forests, and unheard of fish swam in the streams or lived in the ocean. As the men cleared the forests, built the homes, and earned the living, the women prepared food for the family. These women were remarkable and ingenious in their adaptations. They learned much from the Indians

about the preparation and use of the unfamiliar grain — corn. They experimented in cooking the strange game and fowl the men brought from the forest. From their experimentation and inventiveness, delectable dishes were created which have made the state famous. Today South Carolinians are still famous as game cooks and so in this book you will find how to cook venison, wild turkey, birds the hunters bring in and fish from the seacoast, lakes and rivers. In 1694 rice was brought in from Madagascar. Tea came in from China — both became basic parts of all Carolinian meals. Recently they have added to their tea and rice taste highly seasoned oriental dishes and delicious salads. Of course, Carolinians continue special recipes utilizing the native products which have become famous and have passed for three hundred years from mother to daughter.

We of today owe these early cooks a debt of thanks for this heritage. Fortunately today's housewife no longer faces the trials of the early pioneer women. She can be an even better cook than her grandmother if she makes up her mind to do so, decides she can cook and accepts her cooking not as a chore but as an imaginative adventure which she can enjoy and can share happily with her family.

Modern technology has provided this modern cook with all the gadgets needed to make cooking easy. The corner grocery or supermarket is filled with everything a good cook needs from all over the world. There she can find spices, herbs, vegetables, meats, condiments and fish such as her grandmother never dreamed could be. Through modern transportation she can have a fresh Maine lobster or Maryland oysters within hours after they came from the water.

Domestic help she may not have, but with labor saving devices, a joy in her cooking and careful planning, she can do well without it. This Tricentennial cookbook will help all cooks who enjoy good food and take pleasure in preparing it for their family and friends.

The Junior League of Greenville, Inc. hopes these kitchen tested recipes will be helpful to all who read them.

Laura Smith Ebaugh

Hors d'oeuvres and Party Foods

Artichokes à la Roquefort

1/4 pound butter
1/4 pound Roquefort cheese

2 cans artichokes, drained
(Artichokes may be cut in
1/2 or 1/4 if large).

Melt butter and cheese, mixing well. Add artichokes and heat. Serve in chafing dish as hors d'oeuvres.

Mrs. Roger W. Smith
(Mary Jane Peter)

Mrs. Keith's Anchovy Puffs

1/2 cup margarine
1 cup flour
Anchovy paste

1 3-ounce package
cream cheese

Blend margarine and cream cheese and mix with flour. Chill. Roll very thin and cut with 2-inch biscuit cutter. Spread with thin layer of anchovy paste and fold over. Bake in 400 degree oven for 10 minutes. Serve hot. Yields about 50.

Mrs. Calvin Prince
(Lucy Kelly)

Asparagus and Bacon Hors D'Oeuvres

1 loaf thin sliced very fresh
   white bread
1 pound bacon

1 jar salad dressing or
   mayonnaise
1 can green asparagus tips

Cut edges off bread. Cut bacon in long strips, about 3 strips to each piece of bacon. Spread bread with dressing, and then place an asparagus tip on bread and roll it up carefully. Wrap thin bacon strip firmly around bread and asparagus. Place in pan and cook under broiler, watching constantly. When bacon is done, serve hot. Recipe can be doubled according to number of guests.

Miss Blanche James Carroll

11

Bacon Crisps

1 pound very thin sliced bacon   1 package Waverly Wafer
                                   crackers

Wrap 3/4 strip of bacon around cracker until completely covered. Place on broiler pan and broil slowly, turning until crisp and brown. Makes approximately 25 crisps.

Mrs. Dan Hair
(Elizabeth Harris)

Bacon Tidbits

Sliced bread   Sliced bacon
Condensed mushroom soup

Cut crust off bread. Cut each slice into two triangles. Spoon a dab of soup into the center of each and fold up corners. Wrap bacon (cut in half lengthwise and again widthwise) around each and secure with tooth pick. Bake on cookie sheet at 400 degrees for 15 to 20 minutes or until crisp.

This is a good and easy hors d'oeuvre.

Mrs. J. N. Strausbaugh
(Lucy Wilson)

Cheese Straws

1/2 pound (2 cups) finely   3 cups flour
  grated New York State   2 teaspoons baking powder
  sharp cheese   2 heaping teaspoons salt
1/2 pound (2 cups) finely   1/4 teaspoon red pepper
  grated medium sharp   (more if desired)
  New York State cheese   2 sticks real butter

Sift flour, baking powder, salt and red pepper into the cheese. Add melted butter. Mixture will be stiff. Shape into curls, using the star shaped disc on cookie press, or shape as desired. Cook on ungreased cookie sheets in moderate oven until light brown, about 12 or 15 minutes. Makes about 180 curls.

Mrs. H. T. Williams
(Catherine Hudson)

12

Cheese Rice Krispies

2 sticks butter
2 cups sharp cheese, grated

2 cups plain flour
2 cups Rice Krispies

Melt butter and mix in cheese. Mix well. Then mix in flour (mix this very well). Add Rice Krispies. Drop by spoonful on ungreased cookie sheet, and bake in oven at 375 degrees for 10 minutes.

Mrs. Ralph Bailey
(Pappy Godbey)

Cheese Biscuits

1/4 pound sharp cheese
1 cup plain flour
1 stick margarine
Dash red pepper

1 1/2 teaspoons corn meal
Salt (according to saltiness
 of cheese and margarine)
5 dozen pecan halves

Mix all ingredients thoroughly and roll on floured board to 1/4 inch thickness. Cut with round cutter. Place a half pecan in center and bake at 350 degrees. Do not get too brown as they darken more when cooling. They will keep well in covered tins or jars. Makes 5 dozen.

Especially good for luncheon.

Mrs. H. B. McBee
(Ava Ferguson)

Cheese Biscuits

2 cups sharp cheese, grated
1 cup flour
1/2 cup butter
1 teaspoon dry mustard

1 teaspoon salt
1 teaspoon red pepper (less if
 not desired hot)

Mix well. Chill. Roll out and cut into rounds or shape into logs. Wrap each log in waxed paper and freeze until ready to use. Bake at 375 degrees until light brown. A pecan half may be pressed into the top of each biscuit, if desired.

Good with cocktails.

Mrs. J. M. Gregg
(Martha Norment)

Frances's Poppy Cheese Sticks

1 pound corn oil margarine
8 ounces Italian type Parmesan
   cheese
2 Tablespoons poppy seed

1 teaspoon celery salt
1 teaspoon paprika
1 large loaf thin sliced bread

Melt margarine thoroughly in top of double boiler, and mix cheese, poppy seed, celery salt and paprika on foil. Trim edges from bread and cut each slice into 1/2-inch strips. Using a basting brush, lightly brush each strip on both sides with butter, stirring butter each time. Then roll strip in cheese mixture and place on cookie sheet which has been lightly but evenly greased with Crisco. Bake in 325 degree oven for 15 to 20 minutes until golden brown, being careful not to burn. Remove from pan with spatula and cool on paper towels.

Mrs. W. C. Cleveland
(Alice Burnett)

Cheese-Sausage Balls

3 cups Bisquick
1 pound hot sausage

10 ounces Kraft Cracker Barrel
   cheese grated

Add all ingredients and mix well. Form small balls. Bake on ungreased cookie sheet for 12-15 minutes at 350 degrees.

These may be frozen before being cooked and stored until needed. Baking time is 10-15 minutes longer, if cooked straight from freezer. Yields about 125.

Mrs. Doris S. White
(Doris Sexton)

Hot Cheese Hors D'Oeuvres

1 pound cheddar cheese
1/2 pound raw lean bacon
1 medium onion

12 slices bread, approximately
   (crust trimmed and cut into
   four squares)

Grind together cheese, bacon and onion. Spread mixture on bread squares. Amount of bread depends on thickness of spread. Bake in 300 degree oven (not under broiler) approximately 20 minutes (or until bread crisp and cheese melted).

Mrs. William Kehl
(Libby Adams)

14

Cheese Olive Balls

1 stick butter
1 jar Kraft Old English cheese
Red pepper, salt, garlic
  (optional)

1 cup flour
Approximately 50 olives,
  drained dry

Mix and season to taste. Roll olives in mixture to cover. (Dip hands in flour before rolling into balls.) Make balls. Freeze. To cook, put on cookie sheet and bake at 450-500 degrees until they are brown.

Mrs. J. W. Norwood III
(Jackie Torkington)

Cheese Puffs

1 stick margarine
1 3-ounce package cream cheese
1/4 pound sharp cheese

1 loaf unsliced Pepperidge
  Farm bread
2 egg whites, beaten stiff

Cut crusts from loaf of bread. Cut the loaf in cubes, about 1 inch square. In the top of double boiler melt margarine, cream cheese and sharp cheese. When the mixture thickens fold in the beaten egg whites. Dip bread cubes in cheese mixture and bake on ungreased cookie sheet 10-15 minutes in 375-400 degree oven.

Mrs. Brown Mahon
(Carolyn Cartwright)

Sausage Wheels

1 box Jiffy pie crust mix

1 pound hot sausage, softened

Half crust mix and roll out; spread half of the sausage thinly over the mix; make long roll and trim edges; wrap in wax paper and chill. Repeat for second halves. Cut in thin slices and bake at 350 degrees until brown and sizzling. (The thinner, the crispier.) Makes 2 rolls — about 60 wheels.

Mrs. Paul C. Gault
(Mary Bennett)

Red Cheese Ball

1/2 pound natural cheddar cheese, finely grated
1 3-ounce package cream cheese, softened
1/4 cup pitted ripe olives, coarsely chopped
3 Tablespoons sherry (plain or dry sherry)

1/2 teaspoon Worcestershire sauce
Dash onion salt
Dash garlic salt
Dash celery salt
Dried chipped beef

Several days ahead or day before: In a large bowl, with electric mixer at medium speed, beat cheeses with olives, sherry, Worcestershire sauce, and salts until thoroughly combined. Shape into ball, wrap in foil, and refrigerate. About 30 minutes before serving, remove foil from cheese ball. Round up ball with hands and roll it lightly in dried chipped beef until completely coated. Makes about a 3-inch ball. Serve with crackers.

Mrs. C. D. Bessinger, Jr.
(Jane Prevost)

Cheese Ball

2 large packages cream cheese
1 1/2 cups grated sharp yellow cheese
1 small onion, minced
2 Tablespoons Worcestershire sauce

1 1/2 Tablespoons garlic salt (or to taste)
1 teaspoon lemon juice
1/2 cup grated pecans

Let cream cheese soften. Then mix together first 6 ingredients and form into ball or log. Roll in pecans until completely covered and refrigerate until firm.

Mrs. Thomas Mitchell
(Lynn Carroll)

Chili Dip

1 large onion, chopped
1 1/2 pounds ground meat
Salt to taste
1 teaspoon ground cumin

1 teaspoon chili powder
1 pound can chili (all meat)
1 pound grated American cheese

In large skillet, brown meat. Add onion; cook over low heat until tender, but not brown. Add remaining ingredients. Cook, stirring occasionally, until all cheese melts. Serve in chafing dish over low heat with corn chips or tortillas. Makes approximately 1 quart – 20 servings.

Mrs. K. D. Adcock
(Judy Liggett)

Cheese Spread

Button of garlic
1 8-ounce package
  cream cheese
1/2 cup mayonnaise
1 Tablespoon butter
1 Tablespoon onion juice
1 teaspoon lemon juice

1/2 teaspoon Worcestershire
  sauce
Salt to taste
1/2 teaspoon sugar
Pinch red pepper
2 pinches paprika

Rub button of garlic inside mixing bowl. Mix together remaining ingredients. Serve on crackers.

Mrs. Frank P. McGowan, Jr.
(Gena Bryant)

Chip Beef Dip

2 packages chipped dried beef
  (scald to remove salt)
2 cans cream of mushroom
  soup, undiluted

1 large can mushrooms
1 package garlic cheese roll
1 package toasted almonds,
  sliced

Chop beef. Mix all ingredients over medium heat. Serve hot with crackers or melba toast. (Excellent brunch or lunch dish, served over toast.)

Mrs. William D. Workman III
(Marcia Moorhead)

17

Hot Clam Dip

2 8-ounce packages
  cream cheese
2 cans minced clams, drained
1/4 cup chopped onions
1/8 teaspoon red pepper

1 Tablespoon Worcestershire
  sauce
2 Tablespoons lemon juice
1/8 teaspoon black pepper

Cream the cream cheese at room temperature. Add other ingredients and a little of the clam juice for proper consistency. Serve hot.

Miss Elizabeth Arnold

Crab Dip

8 spring onions
1 can all white crabmeat
  (De Ming's, if possible)

1/2 pint sour cream
1 large package
  cream cheese

Chop onions including green tops very fine. Be sure crabmeat has no shell in it. Mix sour cream and cream cheese. Add onions and crabmeat. Serve as dip or spread.

Mrs. A. Welling LaGrone
(Martha Dunson)

Hot Crab Dip

8 ounces cream cheese
1 Tablespoon milk
1 can crab meat, flaked
2 Tablespoons finely chopped
  onion (or dried onion)

1/2 teaspoon cream style
  horseradish
1/4 teaspoon salt
Dash of pepper

Bake at 350 degrees for 15 minutes or until bubbly. This may be frozen before baking.

Mrs. Charles W. Bazemore
(Nancy MacCalla)

Shrimp Dip

1 5-ounce can shrimp (reserve
 juice)
1 large package cream cheese
1 1/2 teaspoons mayonnaise

1 teaspoon lemon juice
1 teaspoon onion, grated
Worcestershire sauce

Let cheese stand at room temperature until soft. To this add mayonnaise, lemon juice, grated onion and Worcestershire sauce. Grind and add shrimp and blend until smooth. Add a little of shrimp juice (2 teaspoons) if needed.

Mrs. P. C. Fant, Jr.
(Sally Lowe)

Garlic Dip

1 package Good Seasons Garlic   1 pint sour cream
  Cheese Dressing Mix

Mix together — let stand several hours for best flavor. A small package of cream cheese may be added also to make it go further.

Mrs. Donald Harrison
(Barbara Farr)

Shrimp Dip

1 3-ounce package softened   1 package Good Seasons Italian
  cream cheese   Salad Dressing Mix
1 cup sour cream   1 can shrimp, finely chopped
2 teaspoons lemon juice   Salt and pepper to taste

Blend all ingredients. Chill at least one hour. Serve with fritos.

Mrx. Braxton B. Comer
(Charlene Holloway)

Shrimp Cocktail Dip

1 8-ounce package cream   1 jar shrimp cocktail
  cheese

Mix together with electric mixer. Serve with chips, etc. Serves 8.

Mrs. Donald Harrison
(Barbara Farr)

Vegetable Dip

1 cup mayonnaise
2 teaspoons tarragon vinegar
Salt and black pepper
1/4 teaspoon curry powder or
   more to taste

1/4 teaspoon thyme
2 Tablespoons chili sauce
Chopped onion (small)
1 teaspoon onion juice

Mix and chill and serve with fresh vegetables (cauliflower, celery, carrots, etc.) Better if made the day before using.

Mrs. J. H. Sitton
(Nancy Morris)

Cocktail Meatballs

Meatballs

1 pound ground chuck
1 egg, beaten
1 Tablespoon cornstarch

2 Tablespoons minced onion
1 teaspoon salt
1/4 teaspoon pepper

Sauce

1 12-ounce bottle chili sauce
1 8-ounce jar grape jam

Meatballs: Combine all ingredients and shape into small meatballs. (approximately 1 teaspoon per meatball.) Makes about 50.

Sauce: Combine in pot and bring to a boil. Stir. Drop in meatballs and cook for about 7 minutes. Serve in a chafing dish. The flavor from this sauce will surprise you.

Mrs. Gladney McGee
(Elizabeth Williams)

Marinated Mushrooms

3/4 cup salad oil
1/4 cup olive oil
1/4 cup tarragon vinegar
Onion

Pod of garlic
Parsley
Canned button mushrooms

Mix ingredients except onion and mushrooms in blender and add salt to taste. Pour over canned button mushrooms and slice onion on top. Let stand for several hours or overnight.

Mrs. K. D. Adcock
(Judy Liggett)

Cocktail Meatballs with Curry Sauce

Meatballs

1 pound ground beef
1/2 cup grated soft bread
  crumbs
1/4 cup milk
1/4 cup sherry

1 egg slightly beaten
2 Tablespoons grated onion
1 teaspoon salt
1/4 teaspoon pepper

Sauce

1 can mushroom soup
1/4 cup sherry

1/2 teaspoon curry (or to
  taste)

Mix meatball ingredients well and shape into small balls using 1 level teaspoon. Melt 4 tablespoons bacon drippings in large heavy skillet. Add a single layer of meatballs and cook slowly for about 10 minutes or until done. (These can be frozen). Combine sauce ingredients and heat until piping hot. Pour over meatballs in chafing dish.

Men love this!

Mrs. William Kehl
(Libby Adams)

Peanut Sticks

1 pound peanut butter
  (medium size jar)
1 loaf day old sandwich bread

3 Tablespoons safflower
  or corn oil

Mix oil and peanut butter thoroughly until mixture has a creamy texture. Trim sides and ends of bread. Cut slices into 4 strips and toast. Roll in peanut mixture. Pulverize sides and end pieces which have also been toasted. Roll peanut sticks in crumbs thoroughly. Place sticks on paper towels to drain for an hour. Place in tins and keep cool. Yields 5 to 6 dozen.

Mrs. J. Robert Rhodes
(Grace Pepper)

Rumaki

1 8-ounce can water chestnuts
1/3 pound chicken livers, cut
   into thirds or halves
8 slices bacon, cut in half

1/2 cup soy sauce
1/4 teaspoon ginger
1/4 teaspoon curry powder

Cut chestnuts to fit into livers. Wrap chestnut piece in liver; then wrap with bacon. Fasten with toothpick. Marinate 1 hour in marinade mixture of soy sauce, ginger and curry powder. Preheat broiler. Broil 7 minutes each side, 4 inches below burner. Serves 16.

Mrs. Thomas C. Gower, Jr.
(Ducky Grier)

Tuna Fish Balls

1 small can tuna
3/4 cup bread crumbs
1 cup grated sharp cheddar
   cheese

1/3 cup mayonnaise
1 teaspoon minced onion
Dash oregano
Crushed Post Toasties

Mix all ingredients except Post Toasties. Make into balls the size of a quarter. Roll in crushed Post Toasties. Heat before serving in 325 degree oven. Serve hot.

Mrs. William D. Workman III
(Marcia Moorhead)

Liver Paté

2 cans consommé
1 1/2 pound liverwurst
2 small (3-ounce) packages
   cream cheese

1/2 cup Madeira wine
1 Tablespoon brandy
1 envelope plain gelatine
2 Tablespoons cold water

Mix liverwurst and cream cheese; add half brandy and wine. Heat consommé and add to gelatine that has been soaked in cold water and remaining wine. Pour half gelatine mixture into pyrex pie plate and put in refrigerator to set. Press liverwurst mix on set gelatine, not quite to the edge, and pour remaining consommé, wine, and brandy over it. Let set.

Mrs. L. Jerome Alexandre
(Margot Edwards)

22

Braunschweiger Paté

1/2 pound red Braunschweiger
1 teaspoon onion juice
3 Tablespoons mayonnaise
5 shakes Tabasco sauce
1 Tablespoon Worcestershire
  sauce

1 teaspoon dry mustard
Salt to taste
1 large package soft
  cream cheese
1 small jar caviar
Parsley

Blend all ingredients except cream cheese, parsley and caviar. Form mold high and mound-like (takes time, and usually must be placed in freezer for 5 to 10 minutes to keep from melting.) Thin cream cheese and "ice" mold. Spread caviar over it and place in refrigerator to harden. Garnish with parsley and serve with crackers.

Mrs. Robert A. True
(Prudie Fogel)

Shrimp Delight

11 ounces (1 large and 1 small
  package) cream cheese
12 ounces (1 package) frozen
  shrimp, preferably small ones
1 small or 1/2 medium onion
2 Tablespoons butter or
  margarine

2 Tablespoons white wine
  (optional)
1/2 teaspoon Worcestershire
  sauce
Dash red pepper
Pecans or parsley

Melt margarine in skillet. Add *frozen* shrimp. Cook slowly until shrimp defrost. Lift shrimp out and mash or grind. Grate onion and mix with shrimp, softened cream cheese and seasoning. Form into a ball or loaf or mold. Top with ground pecans or chopped parsley. Serve with crackers. Serves 25 to 30.

Mrs. Perry M. Parrott
(Ardis Flick)

Pickled Shrimp

1 quart shrimp (3 pounds)
1 1/4 cups Wesson Oil
3/4 cup white wine vinegar
1 1/2 teaspoons celery seed.

1 1/2 teaspoons salt
2 1/2 Tablespoons capers
Tabasco sauce to taste
1 onion sliced thin

Cook and peel shrimp. Mix ingredients and cover shrimp. Put in large jar and refrigerate at least 4 to 6 hours.

Mrs. Marvin Dukes
(Priscilla Jones)

23

Shrimp Mold

2 cans Blueplate shrimp,
    drained and mashed
1 can minced clams, drained
    (reserve juice)
1 package gelatine
1 8-ounce package cream
    cheese, softened

1 cup mayonnaise
1/2 cup minced onion
1 cup celery, chopped fine
1 teaspoon lemon juice
Tabasco to taste
Salt to taste
Pepper to taste

Soak gelatine in clam juice. Cream mayonnaise and cream cheese. Blend in shrimp, clams, onion, celery, lemon juice, and seasonings. Blend in gelatine mixture last. Pour into lightly oiled mold and refrigerate to congeal.

Mrs. Hugh Z. Graham
(Hessie Morrah)

Bourbon Wieners

1 cup catsup
1 cup brown sugar

1 cup bourbon
3 pounds wieners

Mix catsup, sugar and bourbon. Cut wieners into bite size pieces. Simmer in sauce for several hours. Serve hot in chafing dish. Serves 30. Better when made about six hours before serving.

Mrs. Julian L. Wade, Jr.
(Maggie Echols)

Curry Dressing

2 bouillon cubes
1/3 cup boiling water
1 clove garlic

1 cup mayonnaise
2 teaspoons capers
2 teaspoons curry powder

Dissolve bouillon in water. Add to crushed garlic and blend in rest of ingredients.

Makes a tasty dressing for green salads and a zingy dip for hors d'oeuvres.

Mrs. Robert A. True
(Prudie Fogel)

24

Party Sandwich Spread

2 hard boiled eggs
1 medium jar of olives,
  drained

1 small onion
1 cup pecans
1 pint Duke's mayonnaise

Put eggs, onion, olives and pecans through food grinder. Mix well with mayonnaise. This yields about 1 1/2 pints of spread.

Mrs. William W. Kehl
(Libby Adams)

My Grandmother's Oyster Sandwich Filling

1 pint oysters with liquor
4 soda crackers
1/2 pint heavy cream
1/8 stick butter
Salt
Pepper

Onion Salt
Worcestershire sauce
2 egg whites
1/2 package gelatine (for
  salad)

Put oysters with liquor through grinder. Roll crackers to make crumbs. Put oysters, crumbs, cream and butter in double boiler. Add salt, pepper, onion salt and Worcestershire sauce to taste. Cook until thick. Add stiffly beaten egg whites. Put in square pan and refrigerate 4 to 5 hours. Filling can be used as salad by adding gelatine to egg whites. Serves 8.

Delicious with ham or turkey.

Mrs. A. H. Drummond
(Dorothy Hover)

Vegetable Sandwich Filling

1 large cream cheese
3 small carrots
1 small onion
1 small cucumber

3 Tablespoons Duke's
  mayonnaise
Salt
Red pepper

Grind or grate the 3 vegetables. Drain well. Add mayonnaise to cream cheese and mix well. Add well drained vegetables, salt and red pepper.

Mrs. John Coble
(Alma Presnell)

Vegetable Sandwiches

2 tomatoes
1 green pepper
1 carrot
1 cucumber

1 large onion
1 envelope unflavored gelatine
1 cup mayonnaise
Salt and pepper to taste

Put all vegetables through food grinder. Drain well. Soak gelatine in a little cold water to dissolve. Heat juice drained from vegetables and add about 1/4 cup to gelatine. Combine all ingredients and congeal. Best to make day before using. Take out of refrigerator about 1/2 hour before spreading. May be used for picnic sandwiches or spread on rounds of white bread or melba toast.

Mrs. Thomas H. Coker
(Peggy Holt)

Orange Balls

2 1/2 cups vanilla wafer
  crumbs
1 stick melted butter

1/4 cup undiluted frozen
  orange juice
1 cup confectioners 4X sugar

Mix all. Roll in small balls. Roll in more 4X sugar. Store in tin box. If keeping longer than a week, put in refrigerator. They stay fresh indefinitely. Makes about 60.

Mrs. G. Herman Walker
(Betty Wilson)

Ripe Olive Sandwich

3 small packages Philadelphia
  cream cheese
1 small can (or 3/4 cup)
  crushed ripe olives
Small amount scraped onion
1 cup chopped pecans

Salt
Red pepper
1/2 teaspoon Worcestershire
  sauce
1 teaspoon lemon juice
Miracle Whip

Combine all the ingredients, using Miracle Whip to obtain spreading consistency. Makes 15 large sandwiches.

Mrs. H. T. Williams
(Catherine Hudson)

26

Soups, Salads and Dressings

Potage Creme d'Artichauts
(Cream of Artichoke Soup)

2 9-ounce packages frozen
  artichokes
1 1/2 cans (10 1/2-ounce
  size) mushroom soup

1 cup heavy cream
1/4 cup chicken broth
1/4 cup dry white wine

Cook, drain and chop artichokes. Combine with other ingredients. Chill. Serves 6-8.

Mrs. Ellison McKissick, Jr.
(Noel Parker)

Clam Chowder

2 cans minced clams
4 cups milk
1 cup coffee cream
6 slices bacon
1 medium onion, chopped

1 large potato, diced
Salt and pepper to taste
1 Tablespoon butter
1 teaspoon Worcestershire
  sauce

Cut up bacon and onions and sauté until brown. Pour off grease. Boil potato in small amount of water until done. Pour off water. Add milk, clams, onion, bacon and let simmer a few minutes. Add seasoning and butter. Serves 6.

Mrs. W. Ben Dunlap
(Martha Workman)

Mac's Soup

1 can chicken gumbo soup
1 can pepper pot soup
1 can crab meat, drained well
1 large can Carnation milk

Lemon juice
Dash mace
Salt and pepper to taste
Sherry to taste (optional)

Pour lemon juice on crab meat. Combine all ingredients, adding the milk last and heat. Do not boil.

Good served with crackers or rolls and a salad for a complete lunch.

Mrs. V. N. Shepherd
(Sarah Thompson)

Wright Skinner's Fish Chowder

2 pounds fresh white fish
1/4 pound bacon
5 small potatoes
1 small onion
6 tomatoes

1 quart milk
1 teaspoon flour
3 Tablespoons Butter
1/2 teaspoon pepper
Pinch soda

Pick the fish to pieces. Remove bone and skin. Cut potatoes into dices and bacon into small pieces. Rub the butter and flour to cream. Spread in a granite (or enamel) kettle half of the potatoes, then half of the fish and then sprinkle in the minced onions, the bacon and half of the tomatoes. Add a shake of salt and pepper, the rest of the fish, tomatoes, potatoes and more salt and pepper. Cover with water and let simmer for half an hour. Scald the milk, put soda into chowder and stir. Add the hot milk to the butter and flour; stir smooth and then add to the chowder. Serve very hot. Serves 12-14.

Mrs. Wright Skinner, Jr.
(Virginia Bruorton)

Mrs. Jameson's Soup

1 can cream of mushroom soup
1 can cream of asparagus soup
1 1/2 cups of milk

1 can Harris white crab meat
1/4 cup sherry

Mix and heat all ingredients.
This makes an excellent crab bisque and a real good Sunday night supper in the winter.

Mrs. Byrd Miller, Jr.
(Kitty Parker)

Crab Soup

1 can white crabmeat
1 can asparagus soup
1 can mushroom soup

1 1/2 cups milk
1/2 cup sherry

Heat but do not boil. Serve with Keebler rye toasts and cheese.

Mrs. James A. Harris
(Elizabeth Vipperman)

30

She Crab Soup

2 cans celery soup
1 1/2 cans milk
1/2 cup heavy cream
Cornstarch

1/2 can fresh crab meat (or
1 can canned crab meat)
1/2 cup sherry

Heat and strain soup and milk. Thicken with cornstarch. Add crab and cream. Add sherry after removing from stove. Serves 4-6.

Mrs. E. D. Sloan
(Caroline Young)

Crab Meat Soup

2 cans tomato soup
2 cans pea soup
2 cans consommé

1 Tablespoon curry
1 pound crab meat

Heat soups together. With 1/4 cup water smooth the curry powder. Add to soup. Add crab meat. Serve with sour cream and slice of avocado.

Mrs. J. Cooper Shackelford
(Lib Bennette)

Curried Deviled Eggs in Consommé

Deviled egg half per serving
Curry powder, to taste
3/4 cup consommé per serving

Sour cream
Chives

Devil eggs using curry powder to taste (lots if you are a curry lover). Place one egg half (sunny side up) in bottom of pretty soup bowl. Pour 3/4 cup consommé. Let congeal in refrigerator. Serve with blob of sour cream sprinkled with chives.

Good as first course or for light supper with salad and garlic bread.

Mrs. Jan G. Schipper
(Dottie Norris)

Consommé

1 can Campbell's beef broth
1 can Welch's tomato juice
1 can College Inn chicken
  broth

Juice of 2 lemons
1 1/2 packages plain Knox gelatine
Salt and pepper to taste

Use Campbell's can to measure chicken broth and tomato juice. Heat beef broth. Dissolve gelatine in broth. Mix in remaining ingredients. Refrigerate for 4 to 6 hours, stirring every hour. Serve with lime wedges.

Miss Nelle Griffin

Consommé Solera

2 1/2 cups consommé
1 cup tomato juice
1/4 cup sherry

Chopped chives
Salt and pepper to taste

To the consommé add the tomato juice and seasonings to taste. Heat, and just before serving, add sherry and a sprinkling of chopped chives. Serves 4.

Mrs. James W. Knox
(Katherine Richards)

New Year's Day Tomato Soup

1 small onion
1 Tablespoon butter
3 quarts tomato juice
3 bay leaves
1 cup celery and leaves

6 whole cloves
4 Tablespoons fennel seed
Pinch oregano
Pinch black pepper

Sauté chopped onion in butter; add other ingredients. Bring to boil, reduce heat and simmer for five minutes. Strain and serve with unsweetened whipped cream on top. Serves 10-12.

Serve with ham biscuits, cheese straws, and congealed salad.

Mrs. Edmund A. Ramsaur
(Dorothy Peace)

Tomato Soup Supreme
(Appetizer)

1 small can V-8 juice

1 can red wine

1 can beef bouillon (do
not dilute)

Heat. Add lemon slices and croutons to individual bouillon cups and serve. This is good for an appetizer.

Mrs. Edwin Collins
(Susan Hayward)

The One and Only Onion Soup

14-18 onions

1/4 cup olive or peanut oil

4 Tablespoons sweet butter

Salt and pepper

2 level Tablespoons sugar

8 cups beef stock

8 slices of bread

8 heaping Tablespoons fresh
Parmesan cheese

Slice onions, cutting on bias to avoid rings, and sauté in oil. When onions get clear and tender (never burnt or crisp), add butter. Add salt and pepper to taste and for the secret ingredient, add sugar. Have hot beef stock in saucepan and combine with other ingredients. Trim slices of bread to fit earthen wear cups and toast slightly. Put bread into cup. Fill with soup and a heaping tablespoon of Parmesan cheese. Place covers on cups and put in 375 degree oven for 10 minutes. Serve sizzling. Serves 8.

The 5 Major Sins of Onion Soup

1. *Too* few onions used.
2. We forget the oil, substituting margarine.
3. *Too* much salt used, spoils flavor.
4. We omit the sugar, and this is a real secret.
5. We use stale grated Parmesan cheese instead of grating from a hunk of fresh cheese.

Mrs. Peter J. Gilmore
(Lockie Cox)
Mimosa Inn, Tryon, N. C.

Minestrone

2 teaspoons salad oil
1/8 pound salt pork, cut into
  small pieces
1/2 clove crushed garlic
1 medium onion, diced
1 Tablespoon chopped parsley
1/4 cup tomato paste
1 cup water
2 cups shredded cabbage

1 cup chopped celery
2 carrots, sliced thin
1 can French-style green
  beans, drained
2 1/2 cups consommé with
  enough water to make
  1 quart
1 cup uncooked macaroni
Salt and pepper

Sauté salt pork, garlic, parsley and onion in salad oil until onion is golden. Add tomato paste, mixed with 1 cup water. Cook 5 minutes. Add cabbage, celery, carrots and beans. Add consommé and remaining water, season to taste and simmer 1 hour. During last 20 minutes, add macaroni. Serve with toasted French bread.

Mrs. Caldwell Harper
(Lib Stone)

Gazpacho

4 large ripe tomatoes, peeled
  and chopped fine
1/2 cucumber, peeled and
  chopped fine
1/4 cup chopped green pepper
4 Tablespoons salad oil

1 cup tomato juice
Dash of Tabasco sauce
1/2 teaspoon salt
1 teaspoon grated onion
Fresh ground pepper
1/2 teaspoon fresh lemon juice

Place all ingredients in blender and blend until well mixed and smooth. Chill well. (Soup should be blended slightly again before serving.) Soup should be served ice cold and with bowls of finely chopped cucumbers, tomatoes and scallions. Serves 6.

Mrs. Heyward Mahon Sullivan
(Kay Williamson)

34

Cold Soup

1 can tomato soup

1 can chicken gumbo soup

1 or 2 sliced cucumbers

1 can water

1 or 2 Tablespoons vinegar

1 garlic bud (on toothpick)

Combine ingredients and chill overnight. Remove garlic bud and serve ice cold.

Mrs. James A. Harris, Jr.
(Dolly Martin)

Cold Cucumber Soup

3 white potatoes

1 pint milk

1 cup clear chicken broth

Salt

Pepper

Onion juice

1 large or 2 medium cucumbers

1 cup cream, whipped

Chopped parsley or fresh
fennel

Boil potatoes in just enough water to cover. When done, drain and mash through strainer or blend. Bring milk and chicken broth to boil. Season with salt, pepper and onion juice to taste. Cool. Add finely chopped cucumbers. Chill thoroughly. Add whipped cream and a little chopped parsley or fennel.

Mrs. C. C. Berry
(Willie Scoville)
Berry's-on-the-Hill
Orangeburg, South Carolina

Swedish Soup

1 Tablespoon butter or
margarine

1 Tablespoon flour

1/2 pint coffee cream

2 10 1/2-ounce cans of
bouillon (beef broth)

1 Tablespoon shredded lettuce

Blend butter and flour in top of double boiler. Add undiluted bouillon and lettuce and let simmer for five minutes. Add cream and serve when mixture is thoroughly hot. Do *not* allow to boil. Serves 4.

Mrs. E. George McCoin
(Trudy Cleveland)

Split Pea Soup

10 cups water
2 cups dry split green peas
1 ham bone
1/2 cup chopped onions
1 cup chopped celery with
    leaves

1/2 cup chopped carrots
1 clove garlic
1 bay leaf
1 teaspoon sugar
Dash cayenne

Cut away and set aside any good chunks of ham. Combine all ingredients in a large pan. Simmer, covered, for 3 1/2 hours. Remove ham bone. Put soup, including vegetables, through a sieve. Add ham chunks to soup. Salt to taste, and simmer for 1/2 hour more. Yields about 2 quarts.

Mrs. Eugene W. Stuart
(Claire Hanner)

Lentil Soup

1 pound dried lentils
1/4 pound diced bacon
2 medium onions, thinly sliced
2 medium carrots, diced
2 quarts water
1 cup sliced celery
2 bay leaves

3 teaspoons salt
1/4 teaspoon pepper
1/4 teaspoon thyme
1 large potato, peeled and
    grated (or 1 cup uncooked
    instant mashed potatoes)
1 meaty ham bone

Rinse and pick over lentils; soak overnight. Drain well. In large pot, sauté bacon until golden. Add carrots and onions, and sauté until onions are golden. Add celery, water, lentils, seasonings, grated potato and ham bone. Simmer, covered, for 4 hours until peas are tender and broth thick. Remove ham bone and return bits of meat to soup, discarding bone. Soup keeps a long time in refrigerator and freezes well.

Mrs. Edward D. Sloan, Jr.
(Charlotte Ferguson)

Okra Soup

1 beef bone (beef shank about
  2 inches thick with plenty
  of meat)
1 large onion, chopped
2 pounds fresh okra, chopped
  fine

2 quarts water
2 16-ounce cans tomatoes,
  mashed
Bay leaves
1 teaspoon sugar
Salt and pepper

Cook meat in water with bay leaves and onion for 1 hour. Add okra and cook another hour. Add tomatoes, salt, pepper and sugar and cook for another two or three hours. Season to taste and add more water if desired. A little corn added about last hour of cooking is good. Be sure to stir often. Serves 12.

Mrs. G. P. Apperson, Jr.
(Frances Towles)

"Kitchen Sink" Soup

3 pounds lean stew beef
Several nice marrow bones
1 package Lipton onion soup
2 cans cream of mushroom soup
2 cans bouillon
1 quart water (add more later
  if needed)
5 onions
4 carrots
1 rib celery

3 cans tomatoes
1 can mushrooms (optional)
Salt and pepper
String beans
Butter beans
Peas
Corn
Okra
Potatoes
Tiny egg noodles

Put stew beef and marrow bones in cold water and bring to a simmer. Add onion soup, bouillon and mushroom soup. Peel and quarter onions and carrots, chop celery and add to soup with canned tomatoes and mushrooms. Salt and pepper to taste. Simmer for several hours, the longer the better! A couple of hours before serving, add any or all of the other vegetables. About half an hour before serving, add several cups of cooked noodles. This yields a huge pot of soup and freezes well too.

Mrs. M. A. Johnson
(Motsy Crosland)

Apple Juice Salad

2 small boxes lemon Jello
1 medium can fruit cocktail
(reserve liquid)
1 small can crushed pineapple
(reserve liquid)

7 or 8 whole cloves
1/2 cup broken pecans
1 banana, sliced
6 olives, sliced round
2 cups apple juice

Boil cloves with juice of pineapple, fruit cocktail and apple juice about 5 minutes. Take out cloves and pour into Jello, mix and let cool. Then add all ingredients.

Mrs. James Earle Huffman
(Anne Pettit)

Blueberry Mold

2 small packages black
raspberry Jello
2 small packages cherry Jello
4 cups boiling water

1 can blueberries, drained
1 cup nuts, broken
1 large can crushed pineapple
1/2 pint sour cream

Mix all Jello in boiling water. Add juice from pineapple. Put 1 cup of this in oiled mold. Congeal well. Add blueberries, pineapple and nuts to the rest of the Jello. Put half of this mixture on top of plain layer. Congeal well. Add sour cream. Allow this layer time to set up. Add remaining mixture. Congeal.

Mrs. T. R. Easterby
(Margaret West)

Carrot and Pineapple Salad

1 package lemon Jello
1 cup hot water
1 teaspoon orange rind, grated

1 number 2 can drained,
crushed pineapple
1 cup raw carrot, grated

Dissolve lemon Jello in hot water. Add syrup from the canned pineapple and enough water to make one cup. Add orange rind. Chill until slightly thickened. Fold in the crushed pineapple and carrots. Chill until firm. Unmold. Garnish with mayonnaise and pimento strips.

Mrs. J. M. Shoemaker, Jr.
(Polly Sloan)

38

Cherry Jubilee Salad

1 1-pound can pitted bing
  cherries
1/2 cup currant jelly
3/4 cup cooking sherry

1 3-ounce package black
  cherry Jello
1/4 cup lemon juice
1/2 cup chopped pecans

Drain cherries, reserving 3/4 cup syrup. Combine syrup, jelly and sherry. Bring just to boil; remove from heat. Add Jello and stir to dissolve. Add cherries and lemon juice. Chill until partially set. Add nuts. Chill overnight. Serves 6.

Mrs. A. Neal Satterfield
(Pee Wee Easterby)

Congealed Grapefruit Salad

3 large pink grapefruit
2 packages lemon Jello
1 cup boiling water
1/2 cup chopped pecans

Sliced or chunk pineapple
Juice of 1 lemon
Pinch salt

Cut grapefruit in halves. Get all pulp and juice out, and add it to enough pineapple juice, lemon juice and cut up pineapple to make 1 quart. Add the nuts and salt. Add Jello, dissolved in boiling water.

Scrape the grapefruit shells clean and pour the mixture into them. Put them in a pan in the refrigerator so they won't tilt over and spill. When congealed, cut the 6 halves in half — making 12 quarters.

Top with following Whipped Cream Salad Dressing.

Whipped Cream Salad Dressing

1/2 cup sugar
6 teaspoons flour
3 egg yolks
1 cup pineapple juice

Juice of 1 lemon
12 marshmallows
1/2 pint whipping cream

Mix sugar and flour and add beaten egg yolks, pineapple and lemon juice. Cook in double boiler until thick. Add marshmallows and let melt. Refrigerate. Before serving, add whipped cream. Serves 16.

Mrs. H. T. Williams
(Catherine Hudson)

Frozen Cranberry Salad

1 large can cranberry sauce
1 small can crushed pineapple, drained

1 cup nuts
1 cup sour cream

Combine all ingredients and freeze. Serves 8 or 9.

Mrs. Julian W. Dority
(Jean Eidson)

Ribbon Salad

1 cup fresh cranberries or cup canned whole cranberries
1/3 cup sugar, to be used with fresh cranberries only
2 packages (3-ounces) lemon flavored gelatine
2 cups hot water
1/4 cup lemon juice

1 can (No. 2 1/2) fruit cocktail (reserve liquid)
1 3-ounce package cream cheese
1/3 cup heavy cream
1/3 cup mayonnaise
3/4 teaspoon prepared horseradish

Wash cranberries and put through food chopper using medium blade. Sprinkle with sugar; let stand 1/2 hour. Dissolve gelatine in hot water. Drain fruit cocktail and add 1 1/4 cup syrup to gelatine. Add lemon juice and divide gelatine into three parts, about 1 1/4 cups each. Chill first portion until thick and syrupy. Add undrained cranberries; turn into loaf pan 8 1/2x4 1/2x2 3/4. Chill until firm. To second portion of gelatine, add 1 1/2 cups fruit cocktail. Spoon over cranberry layer and chill until firm. Beat cream cheese, cream, mayonnaise and horseradish until smooth and creamy. Blend 3/4 of this into remaining portion of gelatine, reserving other 1/4 for garnish on top. Spoon gelatine mix over fruit layers. Chill until firm. Unmold and garnish with curly endive. With remaining cream cheese mixture outline a star on top of mold and fill with remaining fruit cocktail. Serves 8-10.

Mrs. Pat Sullivan
(Alice Linder)

40

Cranberry Salad

1 pound can whole cranberry
  sauce
1 package cherry Jello
1 cup boiling water

Dash salt
1/2 cup mayonnaise
1 diced apple
1/4 cup nuts

Heat cranberry sauce. Drain and pour hot juice and boiling water over Jello with salt. Chill in refrigerator until grainy. Whip mayonnaise into Jello and add cranberries, apple and nuts. Chill in refrigerator until firm.

Mrs. Heyward Mahon Sullivan
(Kay Williamson)

Cranberry Salad

1 quart fresh cranberries,
  ground
3/4 cup sugar
8 to 9 ounces crushed
  pineapple
Juice of 1 orange
Rind of 1 orange, grated

Juice of 1 lemon
1/2 cup boiling water
1 3/4 envelopes plain
  gelatine
1 cup chopped celery
3/4 cup chopped pecans

Grind cranberries (in blender or meat grinder). Mix cranberries, sugar, pineapple and let stand overnight in refrigerator. Let gelatine soften in orange and lemon juice. Add boiling water to dissolve completely. Add remaining ingredients and mix thoroughly. Pour in ring mold or individual molds and refrigerate several hours or overnight to congeal. Serves 8.

Lime Dressing for Cranberry Salad

3 Tablespoons lime juice
1/2 cup honey

3 eggs, well beaten
1/2 cup cream, whipped

Cook lime juice, honey and eggs over low heat until thick, stirring constantly. Cool. Stir in whipped cream and chill.

Miss Nelle Griffin

Orange Delight

1 large package orange Jello
1 package miniature
  marshmallows
2 cups boiling water
1 cup chopped pecans

1 8-ounce package cream
  cheese, softened
1 small can pineapple, crushed
1/2 pint whipping cream,
  whipped

Dissolve Jello and marshmallows in the boiling water; cool. Beat in cream cheese. Refrigerate until almost congealed. Remove from refrigerator and beat until smooth. Add pineapple, whipped cream and pecans. Congeal in long, shallow pan and cut into squares to serve on lettuce. Serves 12.

Mrs. Russell Goodale
(Sissy Cannon)

Cucumber — Onion Salad

1 package lime Jello
1 Tablespoon plain gelatine
1 1/2 Tablespoons wine vinegar
  or substitute 1 teaspoon
  lemon juice
2 Tablespoons sugar
2 teaspoons salt
1 1/2 cups hot water

1 medium onion, minced fine
1 large cucumber, diced
1 pint sour cream or 1 cup
  salad dressing (cream
  is best)
1/2 cup celery (optional)
1 carton cottage cheese
  (optional)

Mix all ingredients and chill overnight.

Mrs. T. J. Benston
(Lyda Gerrald)

Pickled Peach Salad

1 package gelatine
1 package lemon Jello
1 package orange Jello
1 large jar pickled peaches
1 small can crushed pineapple
  (not drained)
1 Tablespoon lemon juice

1 Tablespoon orange juice
2 teaspoons ground ginger (or
  less to taste)
1/2 cup chopped celery
1/2 cup chopped nuts (I use
  pecans)

Soften gelatine in 1/4 cup of peach juice. Add 1 cup boiling water and Jello. Cut up peaches and add — then mix in all the other ingredients (including remaining peach juice). Congeal in ring mold. Fills one large or 2 small molds.

Very good with poultry or ham.

Mrs. Cooper Shackelford
(Lib Bennette)

Pear Salad

1/2 envelope gelatine, dissolved
2 Tablespoons cold water
1 small package lime Jello

1 3-ounce package cream cheese
1 lemon
1 No. 2 1/2 size can pears
1/2 pint whipping cream

Cream lime Jello (as comes from package) and cream cheese together. Add the juice of one lemon and the dissolved gelatine. Heat juice from a No. 2 1/2 size can of pears. Add enough water to make 1 3/4 cups, pour over gelatine and cheese and dissolve. Put in the refrigerator, and when it gets ripply like egg whites, beat with a rotary beater and fold in 1/2 pint cream that has been whipped and the pears which have been thoroughly drained and dried and cut up. Pour into mold and let set until firm.

Mrs. F. W. Poe, Jr.
(Dit White)

Raspberry Salad

1 large package raspberry Jello
1 large can fruit cocktail, drained (save juice)
2 cups boiling water
2 bananas

3 envelopes gelatine
1 carton frozen raspberries
1/2 cup chopped nuts
3 cups small marshmallows
1 pint whipping cream

Mix Jello with 2 cups boiling water. Stir to dissolve. Mix gelatine in juice from fruit cocktail. Combine with Jello. Add remaining ingredients except cream. Whip cream and fold into the above. Chill until firm. Serves 12-16. (Strawberries may be substituted for raspberries).

Mrs. Wake H. Myers, Jr.
(Mary Jane Webster)

43

Strawberry Salad

2 packages strawberry Jello
1 2/3 cups boiling water
1 number 2 can crushed
  pineapple (juice included)
1/2 pint sour cream

2 bananas, mashed
2 packages frozen strawberries
  (12-ounce size)
1 cup broken pecans

Dissolve Jello in boiling water. Add other ingredients. Pour into mold and refrigerate. Serves 12-16.

Mrs. Julian L. Wade, Jr.
(Maggie Echols)

Tomato Aspic

3 cups tomato juice
2 teaspoons Worcestershire
  sauce
Pinch of salt
Dash of pepper

Pinch of celery salt
2 teaspoons vinegar
1/2 medium onion, cut fine
1 1/2 envelopes gelatine
1/2 cup cold water

Stir seasonings into juice. Put gelatine into cold water and soak about 5 minutes. Dissolve over hot water. Mix all ingredients and mold.

Miss Margaret Mahon

Aspic Salad

1 package orange Jello
1 1/4 cups hot water
2 Tablespoons vinegar
1 can tomato sauce (small)
Salt and pepper to taste

Good to add:
Celery seed
Onion salt
Horseradish
Olives

Dissolve Jello in hot water. Add sauce and seasonings. Place in molds.

Mrs. Henry E. Barton
(Sarah Guess)

Tomato Salad

1 envelope gelatine
1 cup tomato soup
1 cup water
1 large package of cream
   cheese, softened

1 small onion
1 cup mayonnaise
1 cup chopped celery
1/2 cup chopped olives
1/2 cup chopped pecans

Soften gelatine in small amount of water. In a saucepan combine soup and water and let come to a boil. Stir softened gelatine into this and set aside to cool. Mash cream cheese with a fork and grate in onion. Blend in mayonnaise and then celery, olives and nuts. Mix into cool soup mixture and put into a 1 1/2 or 2 quart mold which has been lightly oiled. Serves 8 generously or 12 adequately.

Mrs. H. William Carter, Jr.
(Margaret Kelley)

Small Aspics of Paté de Foie Gras

2 chicken bouillon cubes (or 1
   can Swanson's chicken broth)
1 can paté de foie gras (or
   Sell's Liver Paste or
   Romanoff's Cocktail Paté)

2 envelopes Knox gelatine
Watercress
Tomato
Ripe olives

Dissolve bouillon cubes in 2 cups hot water (or heat can of chicken broth). Dissolve gelatine in a little cold water and add hot stock. Pour liquid into 6 individual molds to about 1/4 inch depth. Set molds in freezer for 5 minutes. (Time this carefully!) Scrape fat from paté de foie gras (may substitute Sell's Liver Paste or Romanoff's Cocktail Paté). Place a slice or ball in each mold. Cover with more aspic and allow to stand in refrigerator until set, or place again in freezer for 10 to 15 minutes. At serving time, unmold and serve surrounded by watercress and tomato points, alternated with 3 to 4 ripe olives. Serve with melba rounds. Serves 6.

Mrs. A. H. Drummond
(Dorothy Hover)

Asparagus Salad

1/2 cup liquid (from drained
  asparagus plus water)
1/4 cup white vinegar
1/2 cup sugar
1/4 teaspoon salt
1 envelope gelatine

1/2 cup chopped celery
1/2 cup chopped pimentoes
1/2 cup chopped pecans (or
  almonds)
1 cup green asparagus, cut up

Put liquid, vinegar, sugar and salt in a saucepan and bring to a boil. Soften the gelatine in 1/4 cup cold water. Add to boiling liquid and remove from heat. Stir to dissolve completely. Let cool partially. Add remaining ingredients. Mold and refrigerate several hours or overnight. Serves 5 or 6.

Mrs. A. T. Odell
(Kina McGlothlin)

Congealed Broccoli Salad

1 package frozen broccoli or
  one bunch fresh broccoli
3/4 cup mayonnaise
1 can consommé
1 3/4 teaspoons salt
2 Tablespoons lemon juice

4 hard boiled eggs, grated
1 envelope plus one teaspoon
  gelatine
4 Tablespoons Worcestershire
  sauce

Soften gelatine in 1/4 cup consommé. Cook and drain broccoli, then chop fine. Heat consommé, add gelatine and stir until dissolved. Then add other ingredients. Pour into loaf pan or a mold and place in refrigerator to congeal. Serves 10.

I use this more often for a vegetable on a luncheon plate than I do for a salad. In this case I make in a loaf pan and simply slice thickness I want.

Mrs. H. R. Stephenson, Jr.
(Kitty Lawder)

Beet Salad Mold

1 package lemon Jello
1 can (1 pound) whole beets,
  grated
2 Tablespoons lemon juice

4 to 6 Tablespoons prepared
  horseradish
Salt to taste

46

Add water to beet juice to make scant 2 cups liquid. Dissolve Jello in hot liquid and allow to cool. Add ingredients and put in lightly greased molds. Not good unless hot, but suggest smallest amount of horseradish for first making! Serve with mayonnaise and sour cream dressing. Serves 5 to 6.

Men like this.

Mrs. George M. Grimball
(Dot Glover)

Golden Fruit Salad and Topping
Salad

2 3-ounce packages
  orange Jello
2 cups boiling water
1 1/2 cups cold water
1 11-ounce can mandarin
  oranges
1/4 cup grated cheese

1 8 3/4-ounce can apricots
  or pineapple
1 cup white seedless grapes
  (optional)
2 large bananas (can use
  1 banana)

Topping

6 Tablespoons sugar
2 Tablespoons cornstarch
1 egg, slightly beaten
2 Tablespoons butter
  or margarine
1 Tablespoon lemon juice

1/2 pint whipping cream (or
  small carton of Cool Whip
  or 12-ounce package of
  topping mix)
1 cup reserved liquid

Salad: Dissolve Jello in water and let cool until syrupy. Drain fruit. Reserve liquid to make 1 cup. Use apricot juice and any other juice on hand to make 1 cup. (Do not use juice of oranges — other juices have more flavor.) Add fruits to Jello when partially set.

Topping: Combine sugar and cornstarch. Blend in egg and liquid. Cook over low heat until thick, about 5 minutes. Add butter or margarine and let cool. Fold into whipped cream, Cool Whip or prepared topping mix. Put topping on congealed salad in large 12x7 1/2x2 inch pyrex pan and refrigerate several hours. (Put topping on salad after it is congealed or on each portion when ready to serve.) Keeps well for several days.

Mrs. J. V. Christian
(Bobbie Sharp)

Macaroni Salad

1 1/3 cups macaroni — cook
  according to directions
1/2 cup diced cheddar cheese
1/2 cup diced celery

1 small can peas
1 to 2 Tablespoons pickle relish
1/2 teaspoon paprika

Mix all with mayonnaise and French dressing. Salt and pepper to taste. Serves 6-8.

Mrs. Henry D. Prickett
(Erna Pritzlaff)

Boo's Potato Salad

8 medium size potatoes
3 stalks celery
1 bell pepper
Spring onions (optional)

1 small jar pimento
Mayonnaise
Salt

Boil, cool and dice potatoes. Chop celery and bell pepper. Mix potatoes, celery, bell pepper, onions and pimento. Salt to taste and mix with mayonnaise.

Mrs. Gordon Brown Sherard, Jr.
(Ann Cheves)

German Soft Potato Salad

6 medium potatoes, boiled
1 13-ounce can evaporated
  milk
1/4 pound butter
3 Tablespoons vinegar
1 cup mayonnaise

3 hard boiled eggs, mashed or
  chopped
1 teaspoon chopped onion
Olives
Pimento

Peel and mash potatoes. Cream in mixmaster with milk and butter. Add vinegar and mayonnaise. Lastly add eggs and onion. Serve in large bowl, warm and decorated with olives and pimento strips.

This is delicious served with baked ham or fried chicken and is good the next day cold. It should be the consistency of firm mashed potatoes.

Mrs. L. Jerome Alexandre
(Margot Edwards)

48

Instant German Potato Salad

Potatoes   Dry onion soup mix
Bacon drippings

For each cup of left-over diced potatoes, use 2 tablespoons bacon drippings and 1 heaping teaspoon dry onion soup mix. Brown potatoes in bacon drippings, stir in the onion soup mix and serve at once.

Mrs. Philip G. Hill
(Marjorie Ellen Fyfe)

Artichoke — Clamata Salad

1 can artichoke hearts (8   1/8 teaspoon freshly ground
  hearts), drained   pepper
1 small package lemon Jello   1 Tablespoon vinegar
1 2/3 cups Clamata juice   1 teaspoon salt
1/2 teaspoon Tabasco

Garnish

Sour cream dressing   1 small jar caviar (black)

Dissolve Jello in heated Clamata juice. Add seasonings. Adjust Tabasco if you really like it hot. Place one artichoke heart in the bottom of each of 8 individual molds or around a ring mold *upside down.* Slowly pour Clamata mixture over hearts. Mold in refrigerator. Unmold on Bibb lettuce. Top with sour cream dressing, below; dot with a teaspoon of caviar.

Sour Cream Dressing

1 container sour cream   1 teaspoon sugar
Juice 1 lemon (approximately   Dash salt
  2 Tablespoons)

Mix thoroughly and chill in refrigerator for two hours.

Mrs. E. Calhoun Haskell, Jr.
(Pat Corbin)

Caesar Salad

2 large heads Bibb lettuce
  or 1 head leaf lettuce
1 head iceberg lettuce
2 cups herb seasoned Kellogg's
  croutettes
1/4 cup crumbled blue cheese,
  or to taste

1 clove garlic
3/4 cup salad oil
3/4 teaspoon salt
1/4 teaspoon pepper
2 Tablespoons lemon juice
1 Tablespoon Worcestershire
  sauce

Soak garlic clove in 1/4 cup salad oil. Add 1/2 cup salad oil, salt, pepper, lemon juice, and Worcestershire sauce. Combine lettuce, croutettes, and blue cheese, and toss with salad dressing mixture just before serving.

Mrs. Zeke Bowen
(Anne Johnson)

Walton's Grecian Salad

1 head lettuce
3 large tomatoes, cut bite size
4 hard boiled eggs
Chopped onion to taste
24 ripe olives, chopped
Salt and pepper to taste

Phedo cheese to taste (Feta in
  America)
4 strips bacon, cooked and
  crumbled
4 Tablespoons olive oil
3 Tablespoons lemon juice

Combine ingredients, except eggs. Toss with dressing made of olive oil, lemon juice, salt, and pepper. Garnish with sliced hard boiled eggs.

This does not taste anything like American tossed salad. It is quite filling served as luncheon or supper dish in a large quantity or it may be served in a small quantity as salad with a meal. 4 large or 10 small servings.

Mrs. Eugene W. Beacham
(Elizabeth Newman)

Waldorf Date Salad

4 large apples, peeled
  and chopped
3 tall ribs celery, chopped
1/2 cup dates, chopped

1/2 cup pecans, chopped
1/2 cup mayonnaise
2 teaspoons lemon juice

Mix all ingredients and serve on lettuce.
Good with sliced ham and a green vegetable for lunch.

Mrs. A. Welling LaGrone
(Martha Dunson)

South of the Border Salad

2 ripe avocados, peeled and
  diced into bite-size chunks
Juice of one lemon
1/2 cup cottage cheese
1/4 cup sour cream

1 Tablespoon grated onion
6 medium size tomatoes, cut in
  wedges
Salt and pepper
Lettuce

Sprinkle avocado chunks with lemon juice, and salt and pepper liberally. Mix cottage cheese, sour cream and onion to make dressing. Toss avocado and dressing carefully so as not to mash avocado. Arrange tomato wedges on lettuce and top with avocado. Sprinkle with paprika. Serves 6.

Mrs. Thomas W. Miller, Jr.
(Linda West)

Slaw

1 medium cabbage,
  shredded fine
1 onion, shredded
1 cup sugar
1 cup vinegar

3/4 cup oil
1 teaspoon dry mustard
1 teaspoon celery seed
1 Tablespoon salt

Put cabbage and onion in bean pot; top with sugar. Combine vinegar, oil, mustard, celery seed, and salt. Bring to boil. Pour hot mixture over cabbage and cool. Cover and refrigerate for at least 2 days.

Mrs. H. William Carter, Jr.
(Margaret Kelley)

51

Slaw

1 large head cabbage, chopped
1/2 pound cheese, cubed
2/3 cup mayonnaise
2 teaspoons celery seed

1 1/2 Tablespoon vinegar
Salt and pepper to taste
Accent to taste

Mix together all ingredients. Serves 8.

Mrs. I. L. Donkle, Jr.
(Jean McSween)

Sweet-Sour Cole Slaw

3 cups cabbage, shredded

3 Tablespoons salad oil
1/2 cup vinegar
1 teaspoon grated onion
1 Tablespoon sugar

1/4 cup chopped green pepper

Dressing
1/2 teaspoon dry mustard
1/4 teaspoon celery seed
1 teaspoon salt
Pepper to taste

Shake dressing ingredients together and toss with cabbage.

Mrs. Charles H. Lawton
(Caroline Lauchman)

Hot Slaw

1 medium cabbage
1 teaspoon dry mustard
1 teaspoon sugar
1 Tablespoon vinegar

6 Tablespoons heavy cream
1/2 stick Nucoa margarine
2 eggs, hard boiled

Coarsely chop cabbage and cook in salted water until tender (not mushy). Drain thoroughly and mix with mustard, sugar, vinegar, cream and margarine. Just before serving hot add two diced hard boiled eggs.

Mrs. Paul Byrum
(Lila Miller)

Scandinavian Salad

1 can wax beans
1 can green beans
1 can red kidney beans

1/2 cup sugar
1 cup vinegar
1/2 cup oil
1 teaspoon salt

1/2 cup chopped celery
2 scallions (or onions), sliced
   thin

Marinade

1/4 teaspoon Italian Seasoning
   Herbs
Coarse ground pepper

Drain beans. Mix with celery and onion. Mix marinade in a jar. Shake well. Pour over beans. Marinate 24 hours in refrigerator. Drain and serve.

Mrs. William Kehl
(Libby Adams)

Lima Bean Salad

2 packages cooked frozen baby
   lima beans
1 1/2 bell peppers
4 stalks celery

3 cored tomatoes
2 chopped onions
1 large cucumber
1 cup mayonnaise

Chill lima beans several hours after cooking. Chop all vegetables well, add to beans, and fold in mayonnaise. Can be prepared ahead of time but do not add tomatoes until a few hours before serving. Serve as a salad or green vegetable. Serves 8.

Mrs. G. T. Buckland
(Kay Tolbert)

Marinated English Pea Salad

1 can Le Sueur peas, drained
1 small onion, chopped
1/2 cucumber, chopped
2 Tablespoons tarragon vinegar
Salt

Pepper
1 stalk celery, chopped
10-12 olives, sliced
Green pepper, chopped
2 Tablespoons salad oil

Toss and chill and it is ready to serve. 4 generous servings.

Mrs. Richard Taylor, Jr.
(Karolyn Kendrick)

Sauerkraut Salad

1 green pepper
1 large can sauerkraut
  (reserve liquid)
1 cup sugar

1 onion
1 small jar pimento
  (reserve liquid)
1/2 bunch (2 cups) celery

Chop finely celery, onion, pimento and green pepper. Combine all ingredients and let marinate overnight in the refrigerator. Use as a salad, on sandwiches or as hors d'oeuvre served on crackers.

Mrs. Walter G. King
(Mary Louise Bouchillon)

Orange and Onion Salad

Oranges (naval or tangelos)
Bibb lettuce

Onions
French dressing

This salad should be appealing to the eye as well as to the taste, and so do use Bibb lettuce and the brightest select oranges you can find (naval, tangelos, etc.) Arrange Bibb lettuce leaves on individual salad plates. Peel oranges, being careful to remove all white rind, slice, and remove any seeds. Place three or four orange slices on each plate and top with raw onion rings sliced paper thin. Add French dressing. I use Good Seasons Garlic dressing mix, with wine vinegar and half and half Wesson oil and olive oil.

Mrs. James W. Knox
(Katherine Richards)

Fruit Salad

1 small can mandarin slices,
  drained
1 cup coconut
1 cup sour cream

1 cup pineapple chunks,
  drained
1 cup small marshmallows
1 cup nuts, if desired

Fold all ingredients together and serve as salad or dessert.

Mrs. Frank Olechovsky
(Olga Tasker)

54

Fresh Fruit Salad

2 cantaloupes, cut into balls
1/2 watermelon, cut into balls
1 honeydew, cut into balls
1 basket blueberries

1 large bunch seedless
  green grapes
2 sliced bananas

Combine and toss all ingredients together and chill. Serve on Bibb lettuce with cream cheese dressing.

Mrs. I. L. Donkle, Jr.
(Jean McSween)

Dressing for Fruit Salad

1 large package cream cheese
2 or 3 Tablespoons mayonnaise
1 teaspoon poppy seed

1 teaspoon lemon juice
2 teaspoons salad oil

Blend cheese and mayonnaise. Add poppy seed and beat in lemon juice. Very slowly beat in oil. If mixture separates beat in a little boiling water. The result should be the consistency of "runny" whipped cream.

Mrs. I. L. Donkle, Jr.
(Jean McSween)

Frozen Fruit Salad

2 3-ounce packages
  cream cheese
1 cup mayonnaise
1 number 2 1/2 can fruit
  cocktail

1 cup heavy cream, whipped
1/2 cup drained maraschino
  cherries, quartered
2 1/2 cups (24) diced
  marshmallows

Soften cream cheese. Blend with mayonnaise. Fold in remaining ingredients. (For pink color, add red food coloring or cherry juice.) Pour salad mixture into molds. Put in freezer. Serves 10-12.

Mrs. Hugh Aiken, Jr.
(Clairene Harris)

Frozen Fruit Salad

1 average or large size can
   fruit cocktail
1 small can white cherries
1 small can crushed pineapple,
   drained (optional)
1 large or 2 small bananas,
   diced
Pinch salt

2 heaping Tablespoons
   mayonnaise
Juice of 2 lemons
3 level Tablespoons sugar
3 level Tablespoons flour
1/2 pint (or more) whipping
   cream

Mix sugar and flour with juice from one lemon and some juice from the fruit cocktail. Put on the stove and cook slowly. Stir until mixture becomes thick. Remove from stove and let it cool. Mix all other ingredients in a separate container. When the juice has cooled, add all together and stir. Pour into ice trays or freezer containers and freeze. Cut into squares and serve on lettuce. With one large can fruit cocktail this makes 1 1/2 trays.

Mrs. Larkin H. Jennings, III
(Nancy Thayer)

Fruit Salad Dressing

Butter size of an egg
1 egg
1/2 cup pineapple juice
1/2 cup orange juice

1 Tablespoon lemon juice
3 Tablespoons sugar
1 Tablespoon flour
1/2 pint whipping cream

Melt butter in double boiler and cool. Beat egg. Cream flour and sugar into butter. Add juices and cook until mixture thickens. Cool and fold in whipped cream with sugar added to taste. Dressing should be the consistency of mayonnaise.
   Good on fresh fruit or drained canned fruit.

Mrs. T. R. Thackston
(Lottie Tindall)

Poppy Seed Dressing

3/4 cup sugar
1 teaspoon dry mustard
1/4 teaspoon salt
1/2 cup vinegar

1 1/2 Tablespoon onion, grated
1 cup salad oil
1 1/2 Tablespoon poppy seed

Mix first four ingredients. Gradually add onion and oil, and then poppy seed. Refrigerate. Serve over fruit salad. This keeps well in refrigerator.

Mrs. William H. Johnson, Jr.
(Becky Cashwell)

French Dressing

2 teaspoons salt
Pinch ground cloves
1 clove garlic
1/2 large white onion
1 pint oil
1/2 cup catsup

2/3 cup apple cider vinegar
3/8 cup sugar
10 drops Tabasco
2 Tablespoons Worcestershire
sauce

Grate onion, mash garlic, add other ingredients and beat with mixer or put onion and garlic in blender to chop, add other ingredients and blend on low. Yields 1 quart.

Mrs. Ben Brockman
(Margaret Mardre)

Vinaigrette Sauce

3/4 cup olive or vegetable oil
1/4 cup vinegar

Salt and pepper to taste
1/2 teaspoon dry mustard

Mix all ingredients well and chill. Garlic, onion, parsley, dill or chives may be added to taste, if desired.
This is the real "French dressing."

Wine Dressing for Salad

3/4 cup white wine (Sauterne, Rhine, or Chablis)
1/4 Bermuda onion, finely minced
1/4 cup lemon juice
2 Tablespoons vinegar
2 Tablespoons sugar
1 teaspoon salt
1/4 teaspoon paprika
1/2 cup salad oil

Measure into jar and shake before serving. Makes approximately 2 cups. Use when wine is served with meals.

Mrs. J. T. Fouke
(Virginia Brown)

Cousin Nick's Salad Dressing
(Vinegar and Oil Type)

1 teaspoon salt
1 teaspoon basil seasoning powder (or basil leaves, pulverized)
1 teaspoon powdered ginger or dry mustard
1/2 teaspoon monosodium glutamate
6 drops garlic juice (or 1 bud, minced)
4 Tablespoons tarragon flavored white wine vinegar
1 1/4 cups Mazola oil (part may be olive oil for richer flavor)

Put ingredients into pint screw top jar and shake well. Makes nearly 2/3 of a pint.

Mrs. Robert W. Anthony, Jr.
(Nancy McGrath)

Dressing for Avocado and Grapefruit Salad

3/4 cup Wesson oil
1/2 cup chili sauce
1/2 cup catsup
1 hard boiled egg
1/2 cup pecans
1 Tablespoon vinegar
1 teaspoon salt
1 Tablespoon grated onion or juice

Mash egg. Mix all ingredients together. Keep in jar in refrigerator.

Mrs. W. W. Pate, Jr.
(Laura Peace Echols)

58

Green Goddess Salad Dressing

1 cup sour cream
1/2 cup mayonnaise
3 Tablespoons tarragon vinegar
1 Tablespoon lemon juice
1 teaspoon lemon rind
1 teaspoon salt
Dash pepper

2 cloves minced garlic
1/3 cup parsley, chopped
1/3 cup celery leaves, chopped
3 Tablespoons chopped onion
2 teaspoons chopped capers
3 Tablespoons chopped
 anchovy fillets

Mix all ingredients thoroughly in blender and chill.

Mrs. Harvey R. Plonsker
(Madeleine Pinsof)

Tomato Soup Dressing

1 1/2 cups Wesson oil
1/2 cup vinegar
1 can Campbell's tomato soup
1 clove garlic cut into
 quarters
2 teaspoons salt

2 teaspoons sugar
1 teaspoon dry mustard
1/2 teaspoon black pepper
Juice of 1 lemon
Paprika

Mix all ingredients and store in a jar. Add more lemon juice if dressing gets too thick. Use on tossed salad.

Mrs. Richard Quinn
(Kay Stribling)

White Dressing

3 eggs
1 large or 2 small garlic
 cloves
1/4 medium onion
1 teaspoon salt
1 teaspoon dry mustard

Dash Tabasco
1 teaspoon white pepper
2 ounces white vinegar
2 Tablespoons lemon juice
2 cups salad oil

Mix in blender as follows: Beat whole eggs well, add garlic, onion, mustard, salt, Tabasco and white pepper. Blend. Add vinegar and lemon juice. Pour salad oil in *slowly* as it is blending.

Good on baked potatoes, salad and fish.

Miss Brownie Piper

59

Roquefort Dressing

1 cup sour cream
1 cup mayonnaise
2 ounces Roquefort or blue
cheese

Juice of 1/2 lemon
1 clove garlic, minced (or 1/4
teaspoon garlic powder, not
salt)

Mix all ingredients until smooth in a blender or electric mixer. Let the dressing ripen in the refrigerator for several hours before using it. This is also a good dip for raw vegetables.

Mrs. Edward D. Sloan, Jr.
(Charlotte Ferguson)

Easy Blender Mayonnaise

1 cup Wesson oil
1 egg
1 teaspoon salt
1 teaspoon sugar
Dash Tabasco

1/2 teaspoon dry mustard
Several dashes paprika
2 Tablespoons lemon juice
or salad vinegar

Put 1/4 cup of oil and all other ingredients in blender and turn on at lowspeed. After about 1 minute (when it thickens), slowly add remaining oil (at first a few drops at a time and increasing). Yields 1 1/4 cups mayonnaise.

Mrs. F. T. Rice
(Claire Fontaine)

Mayonnaise

1 pint Wesson oil
2 egg yolks
1 teaspoon salt

1/2 teaspoon paprika
1/4 teaspoon sugar
3 Tablespoons lemon juice

Beat egg yolks until firm. Add oil a little bit at a time. After adding 3 tablespoons oil, add salt, paprika and sugar, blending each one separately. Continue to add oil slowly. As mayonnaise thickens, add a few drops of lemon juice. Continue process until all ingredients are used. It is preferable to use an electric mixer on speed No. 7 or medium speed.

Mrs. W. M. Wooten
(Elizabeth Adams)

Meats and Sauces

Barbecued Roast

3 to 4 pounds chuck or
 shoulder roast
1 bottle catsup
1 bottle water
1/4 to 1/2 cup Worcestershire
 sauce
Juice of 1 lemon
2 Tablespoons vinegar

1 large onion, chopped
1 green pepper, chopped
1 can tomatoes or tomato sauce
2 Tablespoons salad or olive
 oil
Salt
Pepper

Mix all ingredients, pour over roast in a heavy roaster, cover and cook in a 300 degree oven for 2 to 3 hours.

Mrs. Joe H. Piper
(Dodie Browning)

Chateaubriand

1 Chateaubriand (tenderloin or
 thick fillet)

1 small onion
1 small carrot, minced
2 Tablespoons oil
3/4 cup chopped mushrooms
2 Tablespoons flour
1 small bay leaf
1/2 teaspoon salt

Salt and pepper to taste
Butter
Sauce
1/4 cup red wine
1 1/2 cups beef stock
 or bouillon
1 Tablespoon tomato paste
Black pepper (ground to taste,
 if possible)

Salt and pepper meat to taste and brown in butter. When meat is done, cover with heated sauce or serve with sauce.

Sauce: Cook onion and carrot slowly in oil until golden. Add mushrooms and flour and cook until brown. Do not scorch. Add remaining ingredients and simmer for 30 minutes. The sauce should be well flavored and glossy. Taste for seasoning.

Mrs. Albert Taylor
(Katherine Ashmore)

Eye of Round Roast

4 or 5 pound eye of round
  roast
1/4 cup coarsely ground black
  pepper
1/2 Tablespoon ground cardamom

1 can tomato paste
1/2 teaspoon garlic powder
1 teaspoon paprika
1 cup soy sauce
3/4 cup vinegar

Mix pepper and ground cardamom together. Cover roast and press mixture in. In a shallow baking dish, mix tomato paste, garlic powder and paprika. Gradually add soy sauce and vinegar. Marinate beef for 24 hours. Remove beef. Wrap in foil with a little sauce. Bake in 350 degree oven for 2 hours.

This is a good main dish and even better sliced cold for sandwiches at cocktail parties!

Mrs. J. Maxwell Gregg
(Martha Norment)

Fillet of Beef

1 large whole fillet of beef,
  wrapped in fat
2 Tablespoons butter
  or margarine
1/4 cup soy sauce

1 garlic clove, crushed
1 Tablespoon powdered ginger
1 Tablespoon sugar
1 1/2 Tablespoons lemon juice

Melt butter in saucepan and add everything except fillet. Simmer 5 minutes to blend flavors. Place fillet on a broiler pan as far from heat as possible. Broil at the highest heat 15 minutes, turning and basting 3 times with the sauce. Remove fat from fillet. Broil another 10 to 15 minutes, basting and turning 3 more times. Slice and serve. This will be rare. Increase broiling time for medium and well done. Serves 4 to 6, depending on size of fillet. (Your butcher will wrap the fillet in fat.)

Mrs. Joe H. Piper
(Dodie Browning)

London Broil

Flank steak
Meat tenderizer
3/4 stick margarine, melted

2 Tablespoons Parmesan cheese
1 teaspoon dehydrated
  green onions

Tenderize meat. Broil 5 minutes each side 2 inches from flame or sear in iron skillet, 5 minutes on first side and 3 minutes on second side. This is for rare steak. Mix pan drippings and remaining ingredients to make a sauce. Pour sauce over steak and slice as thinly as possible at an angle across the grain.

Mrs. Zeke Bowen
(Anne Johnson)

Party Pot Roast

3 pound roast
3 cups claret wine
Garlic (optional)
Salt and pepper
Flour
2 Tablespoons fat
6 whole potatoes, peeled

6 whole carrots, scraped
6 whole onions, peeled
1 large green pepper, cut in
  strips
1/4 cup chopped onion
1 Tablespoon Worcestershire
  sauce

For Stock, If Needed

1 can consommé

1/2 cup claret wine

Marinate roast (sirloin tip or rump) in 3 cups claret wine for 1/2 day. Remove from marinade (save marinade) and wipe roast. Rub with garlic. Season with salt and pepper and dredge with flour. Heat an iron pot over a hot fire. Saute' onion lightly in 2 tablespoons fat. Remove onion. Sear meat on all sides until it is dark brown. Pour the marinade over it. (There should be 1/2 inch liquid in the pot.) Reduce the heat and cover tightly or put in closely covered pot and place in 350 degree oven for 2 hours. Place potatoes, carrots, onions and green pepper in marinade around roast. Cook for 1 hour more, adding more stock if needed. Remove roast and vegetables from pot. Thicken stock with flour and add 1 tablespoon Worcestershire sauce for gravy.

Serve pot roast with rice, dark cherry salad and hot buttered rolls.

Mrs. R. S. Campbell
(Betsy McDavid)

Hungarian Pot Roast

3-4 pound chuck roast
1/4 cup and 2 Tablespoons
  flour
1 Tablespoon salt
1/4 teaspoon ground pepper
3 Tablespoons bacon drippings,
  butter or vegetable oil
1 clove garlic, crushed

1 large onion, sliced
1/2 cup chopped celery
1/4 cup beef broth
1 8-ounce can tomato sauce
1/2 cup sour cream
3 Tablespoons chopped parsley
8 ounces wide noodles, cooked
  and drained

Dredge meat in flour mixed with salt and pepper. Brown meat on both sides in bacon drippings. Pour off excess drippings. Add the garlic, onion, celery, broth and tomato sauce. Cover tightly and simmer 3 to 3 1/2 hours or until tender. Remove roast to heated platter. Mix in the sour cream and parsley, never allowing mixture to boil. Surround roast with noodles and pour gravy over all. Serves 8.

Mrs. Harvey R. Plonsker
(Madeleine Pinsof)

Low Calorie Beef Main Dish

2 pounds boned lean beef,
  round or chuck
1 Tablespoon margarine
1 1/2 cups water
1 envelope Good Seasons Onion
  Dressing Mix
3/4 teaspoon salt

1/2 teaspoon marjoram leaves
1 1/2 cups carrot strips
1 cup celery strips
2 medium squash, cut in strips
1 small can early June peas,
  drained

Brown beef in margarine. Add water, dressing mix, salt, and marjoram leaves. Simmer 30 minutes. Add carrots and simmer 30 minutes. Add celery and squash. Cook until all vegetables are tender. Add peas. If desired, remove vegetables and meat and thicken with 1 tablespoon flour before serving. Serve with tossed green salad. Serves 6. 302 calories per 1 1/2 cups main dish.

Mrs. Junius H. Garrison, Jr.
(Sarah Cannon)

66

Buffet Beef à la Stroganoff

3 1/2 pounds lean beef steak
4 small cans whole button
   mushrooms
2 Tablespoons olive oil
6 Tablespoons butter
6 large onions, chopped
2 Tablespoons flour
2 small cans tomato paste

2 pints sour cream
4 cloves garlic, finely
   chopped
4 cups beef stock
   (or 2 10 1/2 ounce cans)
Salt and pepper to taste
4 Tablespoons Worcestershire
   sauce

Buy about four packages of pre-packaged round steak at grocery store and have butcher trim all fat off and cut the steak in about one inch cubes. This saves much work later. Fry steak in 4 tablespoons butter. When brown, add flour and cook until it thickens. Meantime in another heavy fry pan sauté onions and garlic in 2 tablespoons butter and all of the olive oil. Add mushrooms, stock and tomato paste. Stir well. Combine this with beef. Season. Simmer over low heat two hours (or until meat is very tender). Stir in sour cream. Serve over rice or noodles.

This is great for a party. It can be cooked early in the morning and reheated when ready to serve. One large box instant rice can be cooked at last minute. Serves 10 to 12.

Mrs. A. Welling LaGrone
(Martha Dunson)

Beef Stroganoff

1 medium onion
3 Tablespoons butter
Small can sliced mushrooms,
   drained

Cold left-over roast beef
1 jigger brandy
1/2 to 1 cup sour cream
Salt and pepper to taste

Sauté onion in butter, mix in mushrooms and warm. Add beef, cut in thin strips. Turn up heat, clear one side of frying pan and add brandy into cleared side of pan. Light brandy and stir flaming into other ingredients. Cut off heat and add sour cream. Serve plain or over rice or noodles. Servings depend on amount of beef.

Mrs. John P. Mann
(Wayne Smith)

Easy Beef Stroganoff

1 pound ground chuck
1/2 onion, minced
1 can cream of chicken soup
1 can mushrooms, sliced

1 1/2 teaspoons salt
1/4 teaspoon pepper
1 cup sour cream

Brown beef and onions in butter. Add other ingredients except sour cream and cook slowly, uncovered for 1 1/2 hours. Just before serving, stir in sour cream. Serve over rice, topped with chopped dill pickles if desired. Serves 4 to 6.

Mrs. Julian W. Dority
(Jean Eidson)

Burgundy Beef

1 1/2 pounds beef cubes
3 medium onions, quartered
2 Tablespoons flour
2 teaspoons salt
1 Tablespoon parsley
1 bay leaf
1 can Dawnfresh mushroom sauce

1 clove garlic
1/4 teaspoon black pepper
1 teaspoon dried thyme
1/2 pound mushrooms
Red wine and water (equal
    parts)
1 slice bacon

Cut 1 piece of bacon in small pieces, fry out a bit, add meat and onions and brown slightly. Sprinkle with flour, let brown, add garlic and enough wine and water (half and half) to almost cover meat. Add mushroom sauce, mushrooms, salt, pepper, parsley, thyme, and bay leaf. Cover and simmer slowly until meat is tender. Serves 4.

Mrs. John C. Dunson
(Dana Coleman)

Beef Paprika

1/3 cup butter or margarine
1 large onion, chopped
1 clove garlic, minced
2 pounds boneless stew meat
1 Tablespoon paprika

1 1/2 teaspoons salt
1/2 cup water
2 Tablespoons flour
1 cup sour cream

68

Cut meat into 1/2 inch cubes. Melt butter in Dutch oven. Add onion and garlic. Cook, but do not brown. Remove from pan; set aside. Brown meat over moderate heat. Return onion and add paprika, salt and water. Cover; simmer 1 1/2 to 2 hours. Add more water, if necessary. Combine flour and sour cream. Stir in; cook until smooth and thickened. Serve with buttered poppy seed noodles. Serves 6.

Mrs. J. A. Harris, Jr.
(Dolly Martin)

Savory Chuck Roast

4-6 pound roast
1 cup water
2 teaspoons soy sauce
2 Tablespoons Worcestershire
  sauce
2 Tablespoons parsley flakes
1/4 cup wine

1 teaspoon monosodium
  glutamate
1/2 teaspoon sage
1 teaspoon Fine Herbs
  (or favorite herb)
1/4 teaspoon seasoned salt
1/4 teaspoon pepper

Sear roast in roasting pan over high heat in little fat. Remove from heat, add rest of ingredients and bake covered for 2 1/2 hours at 350 degrees. Serves 6.

Mrs. Lewis Price, Jr.
(Joy Dee Hatchett)

Easy Beef Stew

2 pounds round steak, cut in
  pieces
1/4 cup flour
Salt and pepper to taste
1/4 cup salad oil

6 potatoes, cut
6 carrots
1 package Lipton onion soup
3 cups water

Flour, salt and pepper meat. Brown in oil and place in large casserole. Add carrots, potatoes, soup, and water. Cover and cook 2 hours at 325 degrees.

Mrs. Coy L. Huffman
(Lynn Speegle)

Chuck Wagon Stew

2 pounds cubed stew-beef
2 Tablespoons fat
1 teaspoon sugar
2 Tablespoons flour
1/2 teaspoon pepper
1 teaspoon chili powder
1/4 teaspoon thyme
1 bay leaf
2 tomatoes, quartered

1 green pepper, sliced
1 cup beef bouillon
6 small potatoes, halved
6 small carrots
6 small whole onions
6 stalks celery
1 small can peas
Flour or corn starch
   to thicken

Brown meat in fat. Add sugar and continue browning; add flour and brown more. Add pepper, chili powder, thyme, and bay leaf. On top, add tomatoes, green pepper, and beef bouillon. Cover and simmer until meat is tender, about 1 1/2 to 2 hours. Add potatoes, carrots, onions and celery, and cook 30 minutes. Add peas. Thicken with flour or corn starch, if desired. Serves 6.

Mrs. Ben C. Trammell
(Gene Nash)

Rock House Stew

1/3 cup cooking oil
8 pounds chuck (2-inch cubes)
2 minced garlic cloves
2 cups chopped onions
2 cups diced celery
4 large fresh tomatoes,
   peeled and chopped
2 to 3 Tablespoons salt
   (keep tasting)

1 Tablespoon Worcestershire
   sauce
Dash Tabasco sauce
2 Tablespoons bouquet garni
   (most important)
24 small white onions
12 medium potatoes
1 bunch carrots, chopped
   2-inch cubes

Heat oil and brown chuck. Add everything except onions, potatoes and carrots, and simmer until meat is tender. Then add carrots. Thirty minutes later, add onions and potatoes. Cook until done. Serves 12 very hungry people after a football game!

Mrs. Harry Haynsworth III
(Linda Mayes)

70

Ruth's Brunswick Stew

1 pound pork, coarsely ground
1 pound beef, coarsely ground
2 medium onions, chopped
2 cans shoe peg corn, drained
and rinsed
2 cans green lima beans,
drained and rinsed
2 cans tomatoes

1 Tablespoon vinegar
Dash of sugar and seasonings
to taste
1 cup or more, according to
taste, leftover beef
gravy, and/or tomato or V-8
juice, and/or bouillon

Brown onions and meat. Add other ingredients and cook slowly for about 30 minutes. Freezes well. With corn muffins and salad, this is a meal.

Mrs. George M. Grimball
(Dot Glover)

Breakfast Beef Steaks

1 1/2 pounds extra lean ground
beef
Lowry's seasoned salt
Pepper
1 Tablespoon corn oil
margarine

Fresh (or frozen) mushrooms
1 teaspoon corn oil margarine
1/4 cup claret, burgundy or
sherry
1/2 Tablespoon Worcestershire
sauce

Shape beef into patties and salt and pepper liberally. Melt one tablespoon margarine in pan. Add patties and sauté over medium heat until done. As near the same time as possible, sauté mushrooms in separate pan by flipping them a few times in one teaspoon margarine. Remove patties from pan. Put mushrooms and juices into the "pattie pan." Add wine and Worcestershire sauce. Bring to boil and pour over patties to serve. Serves 4.

This is a low cholesterol dish.

Mrs. R. S. Campbell
(Betsy McDavid)

Easy Meat Loaf

1 pound ground chuck
1 package dried onion soup mix

2/3 cup Pet evaporated milk

Mix well in bowl. Put mixture into an ungreased shallow baking pan. With wet hands, shape into a loaf. Bake at 350 degrees for 50 minutes. Serves 4.

Mrs. G. P. Apperson, Jr.
(Frances Towles)

Frosted Meat Loaf

2 pounds ground beef
1/2 cup dry bread crumbs
1/2 cup French dressing
  or catsup
1 small onion, chopped
2 eggs

1 teaspoon salt
Parsley
1/4 teaspoon pepper
2 cups prepared hot instant
  mashed potatoes
Mushrooms or pimento

Combine meat, French dressing, crumbs, onions, eggs, salt, parsley and pepper. Shape into oval loaf; place in baking dish. Bake at 350 degrees for 1 hour. Place on baking sheet or heat-proof platter. Frost loaf with mashed potatoes. Broil until lightly browned. Garnish with mushrooms or pimento. Serves 6.

Mrs. Wake H. Myers, Jr.
(Mary Jane Webster)

Meat Loaves in Sherry Sauce

1 1/2 pounds ground beef
1 cup dry bread crumbs
1/2 can tomato sauce

1 egg
2 Tablespoons onion, minced
1 teaspoon salt

Sauce

1 Tablespoon cornstarch
2 Tablespoons sugar
2 Tablespoons brown sugar
1/2 can tomato sauce
3/4 cup sherry

1 Tablespoon vinegar
1 teaspoon dry mustard
3/4 cup hot water
1 bouillon cube

72

Make mixture of meat, etc., and shape into 8 to 10 small loaves. Place in casserole. Dissolve bouillon cube in hot water. Mix sauce and pour over loaves. Cook at 350 degrees for 40 minutes.

Good as cocktail meatballs also.

Mrs. James R. Jacobs
(Beryl Martin)

Meat Balls

1 pound hamburger	1/2 cup onions, finely chopped
1/2 cup soft bread crumbs	1/2 cup bell pepper, diced
1 teaspoon salt	2 1/2 Tablespoons brown sugar
1 teaspoon pepper	4 Tablespoons vinegar
1/2 cup evaporated milk	1/2 cup water
1 small bottle catsup	

Combine hamburger, bread crumbs, salt, pepper and milk. Mix and roll into small balls. Put in long pyrex dish. Combine remaining ingredients and pour over meat balls. Bake in oven 45 minutes at 475 degrees. Serves 6-8.

Mrs. Donald Harrison
(Barbara Farr)

Meat Loaf Champignon

2 pounds ground chuck	2 cans mushroom soup
2 slices white bread, cut in	1 egg
1/2 inch cubes	1 envelope Good Seasons Onion
1 Tablespoon Worcestershire	Dressing mix
sauce	1 small can mushrooms
1 Tablespoon steak sauce	Milk
(A-1, etc.)	

Mix meat with bread, sauces, 1 can mushroom soup, egg and dressing mix and shape into 2 loaves. Place in a large shallow dish. Bake at 350 degrees for about 1 1/4 hours. Dip off grease while baking. When done, remove to a platter. To pan drippings, add 1 can mushroom soup and 1 can mushrooms and enough milk for right consistency. Serve over the meat loaves.

Mrs. W. Alfred Moore, Jr.
(Anne Griffin)

Beef Casserole for Ten

1 pound sharp cheese, grated
1 large onion, chopped
1 green pepper, chopped
1 pound ground beef
1 cup chopped stuffed olives
1 large can mushroom pieces

1/2 can chili powder
1 large package thin noodles
1 can white cream corn
1 large can tomatoes
Salt to taste
Pepper to taste

Brown onion and pepper in small amount oil. Add meat and brown. Cook noodles. Drain. Put noodles, onion, pepper and meat mixture in large pan or deep well. Add remaining ingredients, saving half of grated cheese for topping casserole. Cook this mixture on low heat for 5 minutes. Pour into two casseroles. Sprinkle with cheese when cool. Bake at 350 degrees for 45 minutes. Better made the day before. Freezes well.

Mrs. G. S. Tompkins, Jr.
(Caroline Arrington)

Johnny Mizetta

1 large package flat noodles,
  cooked and drained
1 1/2 pounds lean ground pork
1/2 pound lean ground round
2 whole green peppers, chopped
2 small onions, chopped

4 cans chopped mushrooms
1 pound sharp cheddar cheese,
  grated
3 cans tomato soup
1 medium can tomato juice

Put onions and green peppers in pan and brown. Sear meat in same pan. Salt and pepper to taste, add tomato soup, juice, mushrooms, and noodles last. Fold in cheese leaving enough for top of casserole. Place in 2 large casseroles and cook in 350 degree oven for 30 to 40 minutes. This may be frozen or stored in refrigerator until ready to cook. Serves 8.

Mrs. W. L. Carpenter
(Blanche Owen)

Barbecued Beef

1 pound hamburger
1 medium onion, chopped
2/3 cup cold water
1 Tablespoon flour

1 1/2 teaspoons prepared
  mustard
1/2 cup chili sauce
1/4 cup catsup

Brown beef and onion in skillet. Thicken with paste made with flour and water. Add remaining ingredients. Simmer.

Mrs. Thomas E. Harder
(Audrey McCulloch)

Saxapahash

1 pound ground beef
1 teaspoon salt
1 teaspoon sugar
Garlic salt
16-ounce can tomato sauce
1 cup sour cream

1 3-ounce package
  cream cheese
6 spring onions
Cheddar cheese
8-ounce package small noodles

Brown beef, add salt, sugar, garlic salt and tomato sauce. Simmer 20 minutes. Chop onions and mix with sour cream and cream cheese that are at room temperature. Cook noodles as directed. In buttered casserole, place a layer of noodles, layer of cream cheese mixture, and a layer of meat mixture. Repeat. Top with grated cheddar cheese. Bake at 350 degrees for 20 to 25 minutes. Serves 6.

Mrs. Russell Goodale
(Sissy Cannon)

Ground Beef Chop Suey

1 pound ground beef
1/2 cup chopped onion
1 Tablespoon margarine
1 cup chopped celery
  with leaves
1 can bean sprouts
1 can bamboo shoots (optional)

1/2 cup broth or bouillon (use
  1 beef bouillon cube in
  1/2 cup boiling water)
2 Tablespoons flour
3 Tablespoons soy sauce
1 can mushrooms
  (approximately 1/2 cup)

Sauté onion in margarine. Add meat and brown. Add celery, bean sprouts, bamboo shoots and 1/4 cup bouillon. Make paste of remaining broth and flour. Add to other ingredients. Stir and cook until it boils. Stir in soy sauce to taste and then add mushrooms. Serve on rice. Serves 4-6.

Mrs. Frank Shaw
(Ellen Gibson)

Italian Delight

3 pounds lean ground beef
1 garlic clove, mashed
2 medium onions, minced
1/2 bell pepper
1 4-ounce can mushrooms (and liquid)
2 15-ounce cans Hunt's tomato sauce
1 12-ounce can white shoepeg corn

1 Tablespoon brown sugar
1 Tablespoon Worcestershire sauce
Salt and pepper to taste
Chili powder to taste (optional)
1 small box elbow macaroni, cooked and drained
1/2 cup sherry
1 cup grated sharp cheese

Brown beef with garlic, bell pepper, and onion. Add mushrooms and liquid, tomato sauce, corn, brown sugar, Worcestershire, salt, pepper, and chili powder. Bring to a boil. Add macaroni. Cool. Add sherry and cheese. Place in casseroles and refrigerate overnight to mellow. Bake in 350 degree oven until bubbly. This freezes well.

Mrs. R. L. Cashwell
(Mary West)

Chili

1 pound ground meat, lean
1 bell pepper, chopped
1 onion, chopped
2 cups celery, chopped
1 can tomatoes

1 can tomato paste
2 Tablespoons chili powder
1 can red kidney beans
Salt to taste
Pepper to taste

Brown onion, bell pepper, and celery. Add meat and brown. Add tomatoes, tomato paste, chili powder, salt and pepper. Let cook about 1 hour. Add beans and cook about 15 minutes longer. Serve with saltine crackers and a salad.

Mrs. Neill M. Perrin
(Lena Glover)

Wild Rice Casserole

1 package Uncle Ben's Wild
  Rice
1 1/2 pounds ground beef

1 can mushrooms
1 can consommé
1 Tablespoon oil

Cook rice by directions on box, leaving it a little moist. Brown beef in oil. Add mushrooms. Combine beef, mushrooms, and rice in covered casserole dish. Add consommé and mix. Bake in moderate oven for 45 minutes to 1 hour.

Mrs. Robert S. Small, Jr.
(Elaine Barton)

Original Italian Spaghetti

3 Tablespoons olive
  or salad oil
2 to 3 large onions, chopped
3 to 4 cloves garlic, chopped
1 pound stew beef, chopped
  bite size
1 pound hamburger
1 bell pepper, chopped

1 large carrot, grated
2 cans tomatoes
1 Tablespoon Italian seasoning
1 large bay leaf
2 8-ounce cans tomato paste
Sharp cheddar cheese
Salt to taste

Put oil in large pot. When hot, add chopped onion and garlic. Brown. Add stew beef and hamburger, squeezing it in little balls as you drop in and brown well. Add chopped pepper and carrot. Mix. Add tomatoes, bay leaf and Italian seasoning. Stir well. After it has come to a boil, turn to simmer and simmer all day (6 hours), stirring occasionally. About a half hour before serving, add tomato paste and mix well. Heat thoroughly. Grate cheese on spaghetti before adding sauce. Serves 6.

Mrs. G. T. Buckland
(Kay Tolbert)

Spaghetti Sauce and Meatballs

Sauce

2 large cans Italian tomatoes
2 large or 4 small cans
  tomato paste
2 large or 4 small tomato
  paste cans of water
1/2 teaspoon pepper

3 teaspoons salt
3 Tablespoons sugar
1 cup olive oil
1 whole rosette garlic
1 large onion
1/2 cup grated Parmesan cheese

Meatballs

1 1/2 pounds ground
  round steak
1 medium onion, chopped
1 cup parsley, chopped
1 egg

1/2 cup grated Parmesan cheese
  (approximately)
2 Tablespoons bread crumbs
Salt and pepper to taste

Sauce: Put olive oil in heavy duty pot and warm. Then add the rest of the ingredients stirring after each one. Simmer almost all day, stirring occasionally. Strain sauce.

Meatballs: Combine ingredients. For liquid use strained spaghetti sauce. Add enough liquid so that meat mixture is moist, but not too wet. Form into small meatballs (about 1 inch to 1 1/2 inches diameter). Fry until just brown in not-too-deep olive oil. Then put meatballs into spaghetti sauce. I like to make this a day ahead of time and then re-heat the whole mixture before using. Each re-heating makes the flavor richer. Serves 8-10.

Mrs. Alex Mumford
(Fritzie Carroll)

Spaghetti Sauce

1 1/2 pounds ground beef
1 bell pepper
1 or 2 large onions
1 cup diced celery, if desired
3 Tablespoons bacon grease
  or olive oil
2 or more cloves garlic,
  crushed
1 can tomato paste

1 can tomato soup
1 can mushroom soup
1 can sliced mushrooms
  (optional)
2 cans tomatoes
2 bay leaves (optional)
Worcestershire sauce to taste
Salt and pepper to taste (not
  much salt because of soup)

78

In large pot cook diced onion, celery, and bell pepper in bacon grease for 20 to 30 minutes. Add ground beef and brown. Then add other ingredients. Cook 3 or more hours.

Mrs. William H. Wallace, Jr.
(Jane Brown)

Pizza

Crust

1 cup and 1 Tablespoon sweet
  milk
1 stick margarine or butter
1 teaspoon salt

3 Tablespoons yeast
  (3 packages dry yeast)
3 2/3 cups plain flour

Scald milk and butter. Let cool to little more than lukewarm. Add yeast. When yeast is dissolved, add flour and salt. Mix and let rise until doubled. Grease pans with *butter* (shortening will prevent browning). Sprinkle cornmeal over pan surface. Divide dough into needed number of crusts. Roll out very thin; put into pans. (4 = 11 x 17 oblong pans or 6 = 9 x 9 round pans.)

Filling

1 1/4 pounds ground beef
1 teaspoon garlic salt
1/2 teaspoon oregano
2 teaspoons light brown sugar

3/4 cup tomato paste
  (6 ounce can)
3/4 cup water
Mozzarella or New York State
  cheese, grated

Cook meat until red is out and add all other ingredients. Sprinkle meat mixture over pastry. Bake in 400 degree oven for 15-20 minutes. You may add pepperoni, onion, bacon, mushrooms, if desired. Remove pizza from oven and sprinkle with grated cheese.

Mrs. Roy J. Watkins
(Lucile Prevost)

79

Lasagne

1/2 pound ground beef
1/2 pound ground sausage
1 clove garlic, mashed
1/2 cup chopped onion
1/2 cup chopped celery
2 Tablespoons chopped parsley
2 6-ounce cans tomato paste
3 cups hot water
2 teaspoons sage
2 bay leaves

1 teaspoon salt
Pepper to taste
1 teaspoon oregano
1/2 pound lasagne noodles,
  cooked
1/2 pound Ricotta cheese (or
  small curd cottage cheese)
1/2 pound Mozzarella cheese
1/2 pound Parmesan cheese

Cook meat in a little oil until crumbly. Add garlic, onion, celery, and salt. Cook until tender. Stir in tomato paste, water and seasoning. Blend well. Cover and simmer 50 minutes. Drain off extra fat.

Arrange alternate layers of noodles, meat sauce, Ricotta, Mozzarella and Parmesan cheese in a greased 13 by 9 by 2-inch baking dish, beginning with very small amount of meat sauce in bottom of pan before beginning layers and ending with Parmesan on top.

Bake in moderate oven 350 degrees for 25 to 30 minutes. Let stand out of oven 5 minutes before cutting in squares. Makes 4 to 6 servings. Recipe may be doubled to make 10 servings.

Serve with a good green salad and French bread. This can be made up ahead, refrigerated and then cooked later. Allow a little more time, if cold.

Mrs. James F. Gallivan
(Joan Fisch)

Glazed Corned Beef

Corned beef brisket
1 box pickling spices

Potatoes
Cabbage

Glaze

5 Tablespoons catsup
1 Tablespoon mustard
3 Tablespoons white vinegar

1 Tablespoon brown sugar
2 Tablespoons butter

Put beef in boiling water and add the pickling spices. Pick out the red pepper if you do not wish very hot. Boil for 3 hours until a fork goes in easily. (Reserve liquid) Place beef on a broiling pan, top with glaze and cook in 350 degree oven for 30 to 45 minutes. Peel potatoes and cook in boiling water for 30 minutes and cook quartered cabbage for 20 minutes. (Strain out spices and use water from beef.)

Glaze: Put ingredients in saucepan, heat and mix.

Mrs. Lawrence Nachman
(Lynne Thalheimer)

Pete's Chipped Beef in Cornbread Ring

Bread

3/4 cup flour	3/4 cup sweet milk
3/4 cup meal	2 eggs
2 Tablespoons sugar	6 slices bacon, crumbled
3 teaspoons baking powder	1/4 cup bacon drippings
3/4 teaspoon salt	1 Tablespoon parsley

Cook bacon and save it and the drippings. Sift flour, meal, sugar, baking powder and salt together. Add milk, eggs, bacon, parsley and bacon drippings. Cook in 1 1/4 quart greased ring mold at 425 degrees for 15-20 minutes.

Beef

1/4 cup butter	1/4 pound dried beef
6 level Tablespoons flour	2 boiled eggs, sliced
3 cups milk	or chopped
3/4 teaspoon salt	Pimento
1/4 teaspoon pepper	Paprika

Make white sauce using butter, flour, milk, salt and pepper. (Use additional milk, if sauce is too thick) Add beef, eggs and pimento and mix well. Turn hot cornbread ring onto large round serving platter. Put beef in middle and sprinkle with paprika. Put English peas around outside of the ring.

Mrs. H. T. Williams
(Catherine Hudson)

Savory Corned Beef Brisket

4 or 5 pounds corned
  beef brisket
1 can undiluted consommé

3 Tablespoons soy sauce
1 lemon, thinly sliced

    Combine consommé, soy sauce, and lemon slices. Place brisket in this marinade for 24 hours in refrigerator. Turn several times if marinade does not cover brisket completely. Cook in a 300 degree oven for 6 hours. A covered earthenware container is best for roasting. Cool in marinade and refrigerate until well chilled. Slice thinly, and serve as cold cut. Do not attempt slicing until thoroughly chilled.

Mrs. Robert L. Chickey
(Gail Gonce)

Veal Cordon Bleu

Salt and pepper
4 veal fillets (1/8 inch
  thick)
Swiss cheese, very thinly
  sliced

Ham, very thinly sliced
Flour
Egg
Bread crumbs (Old London
  dry bread crumbs)

    Have veal pounded by butcher or beat very thin. Salt and pepper each fillet of veal on both sides. Put slice of ham and Swiss cheese in each fillet and fold over, pressing all sides together. Dip in flour, egg and bread crumbs, in that order. Refrigerate before frying. Fry in butter or margarine for about 4 to 5 minutes on each side. Serve with lemon wedges. Serves 4.

Mrs. Ben Geer Keys
(Martha Hardeman)

Veal Casserole for 12

4 pounds veal cutlet cut in 1
  inch cubes
1/2 cup butter
2 large onions, chopped
2 cloves garlic, crushed
2 1/2 cups chicken broth
1/2 cup tomato paste
1 bayleaf, crushed
2 teaspoons salt

Pepper to taste
1 Tablespoon fresh parsley,
  chopped
1 teaspoon oregano
4 Tablespoons flour
Cold water as needed
1/2 cup heavy cream
30 button mushrooms

Heat 2 tablespoons butter in skillet and sauté veal, little at a time, until brown. Add more butter as needed. Drain veal on paper towels and transfer to 3 1/2 quart casserole. In same skillet, sauté onions and garlic in 2 tablespoons butter until golden. Add chicken broth, tomato paste and seasonings. Make a paste with flour and cold water and add to skillet. Cook and stir until smooth and thickened. Pour over veal, cover tightly and bake at 350 degrees for 1 3/4 hours until fork tender. Uncover for last 1/2 hour. When tender add cream and stir gently, keeping warm. Sauté mushrooms in 4 tablespoons butter until golden. Add to casserole before serving. Serve with rice or noodles.

Mrs. H. William Carter, Jr.
(Margaret Kelley)

Ambrosia Veal Chops

4 veal chops
2 Tablespoons lard
Flour
Salt
Pepper

1 clove garlic (if desired)
1 lemon
1 bay leaf
1 teaspoon Worcestershire
  sauce

Rub frying pan with garlic. Melt lard and season flour with dry ingredients. Flour chops and brown. Put lemon slice on each chop. Add 1/2 cup hot water, Worcestershire and bay leaf. Cover and cook slowly for one hour.

Mrs. William H. Wallace, Jr.
(Jane Brown)

83

Baked Veal and Ham Birds

2 pounds veal round	1 cup corn flake crumbs
8 slices boiled ham	1 can mushroom soup
8 slices Swiss cheese	1/2 cup light cream
1 egg, beaten slightly	2 Tablespoons cooking sauterne

Cut veal in 8 slices 1/2 inch thick. Put each piece through tenderizer or have butcher tenderize. Top each with a slice of ham and cheese and loosely roll up. Secure with toothpicks. Brush rolls with mixture of egg and 2 tablespoons of milk and roll in crumbs to coat. Place seam side down in 13 x 9 x 1 1/2 inch baking dish. Combine soup, cream, and sauterne — heat to bubbling and pour around rolls. Cover dish with foil and bake at 350 degrees for 50 minutes. Uncover and bake 10 minutes more or until crumbs are crisp.

Mrs. Robert L. Chickey
(Gail Gonce)

Stuffed Pork Chops Baked in Apple Juice

6 double pork chops	3/4 cup water
1/2 cup chopped onion	2 cups apple juice
1/2 cup chopped celery	Salt and pepper
2 cups herb dressing mix	

Ask butcher to cut large pocket in chops, leaving a small opening for stuffing. Salt and pepper chops and brown in frying pan and set aside. Cook onions and celery in a little margarine until soft and then pour water into pan. Combine this mixture with dressing mix to get a dressing consistency. You may add more water if necessary. Stuff the dressing mixture into chops and place in a flat baking pan. Pour apple juice over all and cover pan. Bake in a slow oven, about 325 degrees, for two hours. If you use more chops just increase the ingredients a bit. Optional ingredients for dressing mix are green pepper and chopped mushrooms.

Mrs. James Earle Huffman
(Anne Pettit)

Baked Pork Chops

Thick loin pork chops
Salt (minimum)
Pepper
1 cup sour cream

1 can concentrated
  beef bouillon
Chopped parsley
Freshly ground pepper

Season chops and brown. Pour off fat. Mix sour cream and bouillon. Pour over chops and bake in 350 degree oven until tender. If more liquid is needed, dilute bouillon cube with water.

To serve, sprinkle with chopped parsley and freshly ground pepper.

Mrs. Harold E. Chittenden, Jr.
(Sue Woods)

Sweet and Sour Pork
Pork

1 pound lean pork
Salt to taste
Pepper to taste
1 teaspoon soy sauce
Mazola oil

Pancake flour
1/2 cup diced green peppers
1 cup chopped carrots
1 egg
1 1/2 cups milk

Sauce

1 cup sugar
3/4 cup white vinegar
1 teaspoon salt
1 teaspoon soy sauce

1 teaspoon lemon juice
1 teaspoon catsup
1 teaspoon chopped garlic
Dash of ginger

Pork: Cut pork into bite size pieces, removing all fat. Add salt, pepper and soy sauce. Using a deep fat fryer, cook pork in Mazola until done. Remove and dip into mixture of egg and milk. Then roll meat in pancake flour. Place meat in deep fryer for 5 additional minutes. Remove from heat. Fry peppers and carrots in deep fryer for 1 minute. Mix meat, peppers and carrots. Serve on rice with sauce.

Sauce: Bring ingredients to a boil and use as gravy for pork. (This may be thickened and used as gravy for fried pork chops.)

Mrs. L. L. Echols
(Billie Rainey)

Sweet and Sour Pork

1 1/2 pounds lean pork shoulder, cut in 2x2 1/2 inch strips
1 number 2 can pineapple chunks
1/4 cup brown sugar
2 Tablespoons cornstarch
1/4 cup vinegar
1/4 cup lemon juice
2 to 3 Tablespoons soy sauce
1/2 teaspoon salt
1 small green pepper, cut in strips
1/4 cup thinly sliced onion

Brown pork in small amount hot fat. Add 1/2 cup water and simmer, covered, until tender, about 1 hour. Drain pineapple, reserving syrup. Combine sugar and cornstarch. Add syrup, vinegar, lemon juice, soy sauce, and salt. Add to pork. Cook and stir until gravy thickens. Add pineapple, green pepper, and onions. Cook 2 to 3 minutes. Serve over hot fluffy rice. Serves 7.

Mrs. R. A. Mattson, Jr.
(Jane MacLean)

Virginia Country Ham

Virginia Country ham   5 cups cold water

Scrub ham with vegetable brush. Cover with cold water and let it soak 24 hours. Preheat oven to 350 degrees. Put ham in roaster. Add 5 cups cold water. Place cover on roaster. Put ham in preheated oven at 7:00 P.M. Turn temperature to 500 degrees and allow it to remain in oven for 15 minutes, then cut off heat. At 10 P.M. turn heat on to 500 degrees for 20 minutes, then cut off heat. Ham will be ready to remove from oven at 7 A.M.

Never open the oven door after ham is placed in it.

Mrs. Hugh Aiken, Jr.
(Clairene Harris)

Ham in Wine with Cream and Mushroom Sauce
Ham

8-12 pound dry cured ham (not water packed)
3 medium carrots, sliced
3 medium onions, sliced
1 Tablespoon rendered ham fat, sautéed
8 fresh parsley sprigs

1 bay leaf
8 peppercorns
1/2 teaspoon thyme leaves
3 whole cloves
3 cans beef bouillon
1 bottle Chablis (white) wine

Trim ham fat all over to 1/8 inch layer. Sauté vegetables in rendered ham fat in a roasting pan (large enough to hold the ham) until tender. Place ham, fatty side up, over vegetables. Add remaining ingredients and bring to bubbling simmer on top of stove. Cover and place in 325 degree oven until done, about 20 minutes per pound. Test with long-tined fork. Drain and place on pan. Cover with brown sugar. Return to 450 degree oven and brown without basting for 10-20 minutes.

Cream and Mushroom Sauce

4 boxes Birdseye frozen mushrooms
3 Tablespoons spring onions, finely chopped
Salt and pepper to taste

1/2 cup port wine
4 Tablespoons flour
4 Tablespoons softened butter
1 to 1 1/2 pints whipping cream

Cook mushrooms by directions on box until lightly browned. Stir in onion and sauté one minute longer. Season to taste. Decrease liquid in roaster to 3 cups by simmering on top of stove. Add wine and simmer for 2 minutes longer. Strain into saucepan. Make paste of flour and butter and whip into liquid. Stir in cream and mushrooms and simmer for 5 more minutes. Thin by adding more cream. Sauce should not be thick. This sauce is served as a gravy.

Mrs. E. Calhoun Haskell, Jr.
(Pat Corbin)

Snappy Supper Pie
(Quick casserole under a cheesy crust)

3 eggs, separated
1 cup sour cream
1/2 cup plain flour

1 can (10 1/2 ounce) cream
  of chicken soup
1/2 teaspoon instant minced
  onion
3 Tablespoons flour
Dash pepper

1/2 teaspoon salt
1 cup shredded cheddar cheese

Filling

1 cup cubed, cooked ham
1 can (8-ounce) green beans,
  drained
1/2 cup cubed cheddar cheese,
  if desired

Separate eggs, putting whites in small mixing bowl and yolks in large mixing bowl. Beat whites at high speed until soft mounds form. In large mixing bowl, combine egg yolks, sour cream, flour and salt. By hand, blend well. Fold egg whites gently but thoroughly into egg yolk mixture. Pour half of batter into a greased, 10-inch pie pan or 1 1/2 quart casserole. Sprinkle 1/2 cup shredded cheese. Bake 375 degrees for 10 minutes. Remove from oven; spoon filling into center. Pour remaining batter over filling. Sprinkle with cheese. Return to oven. Bake 20-25 minutes or until golden brown. Let stand 5 minutes before serving.

Filling: In large pan, combine undiluted soup, instant onion, pepper and flour. Simmer 4 minutes and stir in ham, beans and cheese.

Seafood Supper Pie: Substitute 1 can (6 1/2 ounce) tuna, drained or 1 can (4 1/2 ounce) large shrimp, drained (or 1 cup) for the ham. Gently stir tuna in with cubed cheese.

Mrs. H. Raiford Laney
(Mary McMahan)

Curried Ham Roll

6-8 center cut ham slices
1 cup regular long grain rice
Curry Sauce

1 Tablespoon minced onion
1 Tablespoon parsley

Curry Sauce

3 Tablespoons butter, melted
2 Tablespoons cornstarch
2 teaspoons curry powder
3 cups milk

1/2 teaspoon monosodium
glutamate
1 cup blonde seedless raisins

Curry Sauce: Add cornstarch and curry powder to melted butter to make a paste. Then slowly blend in milk, add monosodium glutamate and raisins and cook sauce slowly until thickened, stirring to avoid lumps.

Cook 1 cup of rice, then add one tablespoon minced onion, parsley and 1 cup of curry sauce to rice. Fill ham slices with rice mixture and roll. Place ham rolls in a shallow dish, seam down. Pour remainder of sauce over ham. Bake at 300 degrees for approximately 35-40 minutes. Serves 6-8. Fix ahead and pop into oven at last minute.

Mrs. James K. Cass, Jr.
(Barbara Ann Brannon)

Baked Canadian Bacon

1/2 cup brown sugar
2 Tablespoons prepared mustard
1 cup pineapple juice

1/4 cup sherry
1 stick Canadian bacon

Make paste of sugar and mustard and spread on bacon. Mix pineapple juice and sherry and pour around bacon. Bake 1 hour at 350 degrees. Baste often. If needed, add more pineapple juice.

Mrs. C. Douglas Wilson
(Lois Mundy)

Fried Rice with Beef or Ham

6 cups cold cooked rice
1 pound browned round steak
  or 1 1/2 cups ham
3 Tablespoons oil

1 onion, chopped
2 Tablespoons cold water
2 eggs, if ham is used

Condiments

3 Tablespoons soy sauce
1 Tablespoon sherry
1/3 teaspoon salt

1/8 teaspoon pepper
1 Tablespoon cornstarch

Chop meat either in blender or by hand. Add cold water to rice, separate the grains and heat. Marinate meat in sauce made of condiments 3-4 minutes. Heat frying pan to 375 degrees or more (hot), add oil and heat thoroughly. Fry onion until tender. Add meat with sauce and cook 2-3 minutes, stirring constantly. Add rice and mix well with ingredients in pan. (If using ham, add two beaten eggs with rice.) Serve hot. Can be main dish or side dish.

Mrs. Philip Wilmeth
(Harriet Perkins)

Sausage Casserole

2 cups uncooked rice
3 packages Lipton noodle soup,
  dry
2 chicken bouillon cubes
9 cups boiling water
2 pounds pork sausage
1 green pepper, chopped
2 cups chopped celery

2 cups chopped onions
1 package sliced almonds
1 Tablespoon soy sauce
1 large can mushrooms
Cornflakes
Parsley
1 can chicken soup
1/2 can water

Dissolve bouillon cubes in water and add rice and dry soup. Cook until moisture is gone, but rice is not dry. Fry and drain sausage. Sear pepper, celery and onions. In a large casserole, combine rice mixture with sausage, celery, pepper and onions. Add almonds, soy sauce and mushrooms. Sprinkle cornflakes and parsley over top. Mix chicken soup with 1/2 can of water and pour over mixture. Bake in a 325 degree oven for 1 hour. Serves 20.

Mrs. Fred Gilmer, Jr.
(Mary Ann Chamblee)

90

Savannah Quiche

1 bought 9-inch pie shell
2 fresh tomatoes
Salt
Pepper
Flour
2 Tablespoons oil

1 cup chopped onions
3 slices Provolone cheese
  (broken into bite size)
2 eggs, beaten
3/4 cup heavy cream
1 cup grated Swiss cheese

Brown pie shell in 350 degree oven for 5 minutes. Peel and slice tomatoes. Salt and pepper and dip in flour. Sauté in oil. Remove and drain. Place tomatoes and onions in bottom of pie crust. Then place Provolone cheese. Mix cream and eggs together. Pour into pie shell. Sprinkle Swiss cheese on top. Cook in 375 degree oven for 35 to 40 minutes.

Mrs. L. T. Runge
(Evelyn Thornton)

Lamb Stew

2 pounds lamb roast, cut
  into stewing pieces
1/2 cup onions, sliced
2 Tablespoons butter
3/4 cup water
2 cups carrots, sliced
1/2 teaspoon thyme

1/4 teaspoon marjoram
1/2 teaspoon Accent
1 package frozen peas
1 small can tomato purée.
  (optional)
Salt and pepper to taste

Sauté onions in butter. Add meat and brown on all sides. Salt to taste. Cover meat with water and cook covered on simmer for 3/4 hour. Add carrots, thyme, marjoram, Accent and tomato purée. Cook for 1/2 hour more. Add peas the last 10 minutes. Salt and pepper to taste.

Mrs. Harvey R. Plonsker
(Madeleine Pinsof)

Roasted Lamb

Leg of lamb   1/2 cup vinegar
2 medium onions   Salt and pepper
4-6 stalks celery

With a sharp knife, cut off most of skin and fat from lamb. Then salt and pepper meat generously. Put it in roast pan with onions, quartered, celery, cut in pieces, and vinegar. Cook, covered, 20 minutes to the pound at 325 degrees. Serve sauce (including onions and celery) with meat.

Mrs. R. D. Sellers, Jr.
(Ann Garrison)

Baked Eggs and Cheese

1/2 pound sharp cheese   1/2 cup sour cream
1/2 teaspoon dry mustard   1 pound cooked and crumbled
1/2 teaspoon paprika   sausage, well drained
1 teaspoon salt   10 eggs

Cover bottom of 10 x 6 x 2-inch baking dish with 1/2 the cheese sliced 1/2 inch thick. Mix seasonings with sour cream and pour half of this over cheese. Follow with the sausage. Break 10 eggs over this and cover with remaining sour cream mixture. Grate remaining cheese and sprinkle on top. Bake at 325 degrees for 20 minutes until cheese is melted and eggs are set.
  Good for brunch.

Mrs. Ben Geer Keys
(Martha Hardeman)

Ham and Cheese Pie

1 frozen 9-inch pie shell   2 eggs
Sliced Swiss cheese   1 carton (1 cup) sour cream
Ham, thinly sliced

92

Beginning with cheese, alternate layers of cheese and ham in pie shell. Beat the 2 eggs with the sour cream and pour over pie. Bake for 30 minutes at 425 degrees. Cool in oven 15 minutes before cutting.

Mrs. W. Allen Traver, Jr.
(Edith H. Jones)

Children's Delight — Gas House Egg

Slices of bread
Eggs

Butter
Salt and pepper

Place bread in buttered frying pan. Cut hole in bread with biscuit cutter and break egg into hole; replace center bread. Fry over slow heat; turn to fry other side. Butter browns quickly, and so avoid fast cooking. For hard center punch egg while cooking. Salt and pepper to taste. Crumbled bacon can be added to egg.

Mrs. Perry Earle, Jr.
(Louise Jordan)

Marinade for Roast Beef

1/3 cup apple cider vinegar
1/4 cup catsup
2 Tablespoons oil
2 Tablespoons soy sauce
1/4 teaspoon garlic powder

1 Tablespoon Worcestershire
sauce
1 teaspoon prepared mustard
1 teaspoon salt
1/4 teaspoon pepper

Mix well. Marinate in this mixture any good cut of beef roast for 24 hours. Cook over charcoal on a rotisserie until medium done. (Use a meat thermometer.)

Mrs. Ben Brockman
(Margaret Mardre)

93

Pork Roast Sauce

1 teaspoon salt
1 teaspoon chili powder
1 teaspoon celery seed
1/4 cup brown sugar
1/4 cup vinegar
1/4 cup Worcestershire sauce

1 cup catsup
2 cups water
Tabasco sauce
1 Tablespoon butter
1 medium onion, chopped

Mix all ingredients and bring to a boil.

Mrs. John E. Johnston
(Caroline Cannon)

Marinade for Flank Steak

2 cloves minced garlic
1 cup dry red wine
1 Tablespoon Worcestershire
  sauce
1 teaspoon dry mustard

1 teaspoon prepared mustard
1 teaspoon rosemary
3 Tablespoons chili sauce
Meat tenderizer

Sprinkle steak with meat tenderizer. Mix other ingredients and marinate steak 8 hours. Broil 12 minutes per side. To grill outdoors, grill 4 minutes per side.

Mrs. John E. Pettett, Jr.
(Margaret Ann Mitchell)

Steak Marinade

1 jigger soy sauce
1 jigger lemon juice

1 jigger honey
3 or 4 pepper corns, cracked

Marinate steak in sauce for 2 1/2 hours at room temperature.

Carter Poe

Poultry and Seafood

Chicken-Artichoke Casserole

3 pounds frying pieces
1 1/2 teaspoons salt
1/2 teaspoon paprika
1/4 teaspoon pepper
1/4 pound mushrooms, cut in
large pieces

12-15 ounce can artichoke
hearts
2 Tablespoons flour
2/3 cup chicken consommé or
bouillon
3 Tablespoons sherry

Salt, pepper and paprika chicken and brown in 4 tablespoons butter. Put in large casserole. Put other 2 tablespoons of butter into frying pan and sauté mushrooms for 5 minutes. Then sprinkle the flour over them and stir in the chicken consommé and the sherry. Cook 5 minutes. Arrange the artichokes between the chicken pieces. Pour mushroom-sherry sauce over, cover and bake at 375 degrees for 40 minutes. Serves 6.

Mrs. G. Barton Middleton
(Barbara Mann)

Chicken with Vegetables (Chi Ch'ao Ts'ai)

1 pound raw chicken, cut
into cubes (approximately)
1 Tablespoon cornstarch
2 Tablespoons sherry
1 teaspoon salt
1/4 cup water
1/2 cup finely chopped onion
2 Tablespoons chopped fresh
ginger or 1/4 teaspoon
ground ginger
1 cup bamboo shoots,
cut into cubes

8 Tablespoons oil
1 cup dried mushrooms, cut
into cubes (or 1/2 cup
drained canned mushrooms)
4 Tablespoons soy sauce
1 cup snow peas or
English peas, frozen
(Cook until barely tender)
1 cup drained, sliced
water chestnuts
Cooked rice

Dredge chicken in cornstarch, wine, salt, water, onion, and ginger, mixed. Sauté mushrooms, bamboo shoots in 4 tablespoons oil, remove from pan. Reheat pan, add 4 tablespoons oil and chicken. Sauté until tender. Add mushrooms, bamboo shoots and all remaining ingredients, except rice. Heat thoroughly and serve over rice. Serves 4.

Mrs. Robert J. Walker III
(Lucille Benson)

Country Captain

2 1/2 to 3 pound chicken, cut in pieces
1 Tablespoon butter or bacon grease
1 medium onion, sliced very thin
1 large bell pepper, diced fine
1 or 2 cloves garlic, minced
2 cans tomatoes
1 teaspoon salt
1/2 teaspoon pepper
1 teaspoon powdered thyme
1 teaspoon curry powder
1 teaspoon chopped parsley
1/4 pound almonds, blanched and browned, but unsalted
1 Tablespoon dry currants, thoroughly rinsed
Rice

Salt, pepper, flour and fry chicken. Save 2 tablespoons of the fat the chicken was cooked in. Make a sauce of the butter or bacon grease, onion, bell pepper and garlic. Brown about 10 minutes, or until golden brown. Add tomatoes and cook about 10 minutes. Then add herbs and seasonings. Cook 5 minutes longer. Place chicken in a covered pan, pour sauce over and add the two tablespoons grease saved after frying the chicken. Cover tightly and bake in moderate oven for 45 minutes. When ready to serve, mix the almonds and currants in the sauce. Border platter with hot, fluffy white rice.

Serve with green asparagus and a salad of grapefruit sections on lettuce topped with chutney and French dressing.

Mrs. James W. Knox
(Katherine Richards)

Onion Baked Chicken

6 chicken breasts (or desired number)
1 can onion soup or 1 envelope dry onion soup in 2 cups boiling water
1 can mushrooms
Butter or margarine
Salt and pepper

Arrange chicken breasts in baking pan. Salt and pepper. Place pats of butter on all pieces. Pour soup over chicken, add mushrooms, and bake for 1 hour in 325 degree oven.

Mrs. Charles Quinn
(Patricia Padgett)

98

Chicken Boudini

9 chicken breast halves
1 1/4 to 1 1/2 cups strong
  chicken stock
3 Tablespoons margarine
3 heaping Tablespoons flour
1 small can evaporated milk

3 ounces pale dry sherry
1 medium size can sliced
  mushrooms
1 small jar sliced pimentos
1/2 cup whole blanched almonds
1 cup grated sharp cheese

Simmer chicken until done, reserving strong stock. Cut boned, skinned chicken into large chunks. To this add mushrooms, pimentos and almonds, cut in half. Make cream sauce using margarine, flour, reserved stock and canned milk. Thin with sherry. Pour sauce over chicken mixture, combining well. Put all into a greased casserole with cheese on top. Heat until bubbling hot. Serve on toast. Serves 6 to 8.

Mrs. James L. Jameson, Jr.
(Ruth Wellmon)

Poulet Nouveau

Large fryer, quartered
Salt
Pepper
Dried chives
1/4 cup margarine
1 small can mushroom caps
1 small can artichoke hearts

1 small can hearts of palm
  (optional)
5 to 6 water chestnuts,
  quartered
1 can asparagus soup
1 cup sour cream
1/2 cup sauterne

Sprinkle chicken with seasonings. Brown in margarine. Arrange in shallow dish with mushrooms, artichokes, palm and chestnuts. Stir soup, sour cream and wine into drippings. Pour over chicken and vegetables. Bake 1 1/2 hours at 350 degrees, basting as needed. Garnish with paprika and sprigs of fresh parsley. Serve sauce over buttered noodles or fluffy rice.

Mrs. Philip G. Hill
(Marjorie Ellen Fyfe)

Southern Fried Chicken

2 young chickens weighing
  about 2 pounds each
2 cups self-rising flour
1 teaspoon salt

1 teaspoon pepper
Sweet milk
Crisco or liquid shortening

Get a deep frying pan ready with at least 2 inches of melted grease. Sift flour, salt and pepper. Have a small bowl of sweet milk next to flour bowl. Salt disjointed chicken lightly. First dip chicken, piece by piece, in flour, then in milk, then back in flour. Drop in hot grease. Brown on both sides. Cover for 5 to 10 minutes on low heat. Remove cover and let chicken re-crisp. Takes about 30 minutes in all. The secret of this chicken is self-rising flour. Try it.

Mrs. A. Welling LaGrone
(Martha Dunson)

Japanese Style Fried Chicken

1 whole chicken
1 Tablespoon salt
1/2 Tablespoon sugar
9 to 13 Tablespoons soy sauce

1/2 Tablespoon ginger
2 inches green onion, chopped
1 1/2 cups vegetable oil
7 Tablespoons cornstarch

Wash and clean chicken. Cut meat off bone into 2-inch serving pieces. Add salt, sugar, soy sauce, ginger, and chopped onion and mix. Add meat pieces and mix. Let stand 30 to 40 minutes. Then dip meat into cornstarch and deep fry in oil until brown.

Mrs. Kiyohro Tsuzuki
(Chigusa Kimura)

Sesame Oven Fried Chicken

1 cup flour
2 teaspoons salt
1 teaspoon baking powder
1/4 teaspoon pepper
2 teaspoons paprika
1 egg

1/2 cup milk
Chicken legs or pieces
1/2 cup melted butter
3/4 cup slivered almonds
1/2 cup sesame seeds

Mix flour, salt, baking powder, pepper, and paprika. Beat egg slightly and mix with milk. Dip chicken into this mixture, and then into flour mixture. Put in buttered casserole. Pour melted butter over chicken, then sprinkle almonds and sesame seeds over it. Bake in 375 degree oven for 1 hour.

Mrs. Gordon B. Sherard
(Eleanor Bronaugh)

Cheezy Chicken

2 broiler-fryers, cut into
 serving-size pieces
1/2 cup salad oil

1 6-ounce package Cheese Ritz
 crackers, crushed
2 teaspoons seasoned salt

Place cracker crumbs in pie plate. Stir in seasoned salt. Pour oil into second pie plate. Dip chicken into oil, and then into crumbs to coat well. Place in single layer in ungreased shallow pan. Bake at 350 degrees for 1 hour, or until tender and golden brown.

Mrs. Thomas G. Hawpe
(Kitty Faulconer)

Company Casserole

1 1/2 cups wild rice
1 4-ounce can cut mushrooms,
 undrained
2 cans cream of mushroom soup,
 undiluted
1 teaspoon Worcestershire
 sauce

1 pound bulk pork sausage
12 large slices turkey or
 chicken in bite size pieces
1 1/2 cups day-old bread
 crumbs
1/4 cup butter

Cook rice according to package directions. Meanwhile, in skillet cook sausage until brown, break in bits and pour off fat. Stir in mushroom soup, mushrooms, Worcestershire sauce and meat. Put all together in greased baking dish. Cover with buttered crumbs. Bake for 30 minutes at 375 degrees. Can be made a day ahead or frozen. Serves 8-10.

Mrs. Henry D. Prickett
(Erna Pritzlaff)

Chicken Casserole

Chicken breasts (medium)
Potatoes

1 can cream of mushroom soup
1 package dry onion soup mix

Place as many medium sized chicken breasts as desired in casserole dish. Slice potatoes over them and cover with one can cream of mushroom soup. Sprinkle with one package dry onion soup mix. Cover and bake at 375 degrees for 50 minutes.

Mrs. C. D. Bessinger, Jr.
(Jane Prevost)

Chicken Divan

The original Chicken Divan recipe, from an old New York restaurant by the same name, called for cheese sauce, Hollandaise sauce and whipped cream mixed together. This is a deceitfully easy and surprisingly superb substitute.

3 whole chicken breasts
2 packages frozen broccoli
2 cans cream of chicken soup
1 cup mayonnaise
1 carton sour cream
1 cup grated sharp cheese

1 Tablespoon lemon juice
1 teaspoon (or less to taste) curry
Salt and pepper to taste
Parmesan cheese
Paprika

Cook chicken breasts. (I simmer mine in water with onion, celery, carrot, bay leaf, pepper corns, salt, etc.) Cook broccoli. Mix soup, sour cream, mayonnaise, grated cheese and seasoning. Drain broccoli and arrange in bottom of flat greased casserole (3 quart). Sprinkle generously with Parmesan cheese. Remove skin from chicken and take chicken from bone, pulling apart into pieces, and spread over broccoli. Sprinkle again with Parmesan cheese. Pour sauce over all. Sprinkle with Parmesan and paprika. Dot with butter. Cook 30 to 40 minutes in 350 degree oven or until bubbly and hot through. Serves 6 to 8.

This can be made ahead and refrigerated or frozen and cooked later. Good with tomato aspic for luncheon or buffet supper or with baked stuffed tomatoes and green salad.

Mrs. James F. Gallivan
(Joan Fisch)

Hot Chicken Casserole

3 pounds cooked chicken,
  cut up
8 hard boiled eggs, cut up
1 can mushroom soup
2 cans cream chicken soup
2 cups diced celery

1 small onion, grated
1 cup Duke's mayonnaise
1 cup slivered almonds
3 teaspoons lemon juice
1 teaspoon salt
Potato chips

Put all ingredients (except potato chips) in mixing bowl and blend well. Pour into 2-quart casserole, top with crushed potato chips and bake in oven at 350 degrees for 30 minutes until bubbly. Casserole may be prepared the day ahead and refrigerated. Add potato chips before using. Serves 8-10.

Mrs. William H. Orders
(Carolyn Lee)

Boned Chicken Breasts and Rice Casserole

1 6-ounce package wild rice
  and long grain mix (2 boxes
  if more rice preferred)
4 large chicken breasts, boned
  and skinned (8 halves)
1 can cream of chicken soup

4 Tablespoons butter or
  margarine
3/4 cup sauterne
1/2 cup chopped celery
1 3-ounce can mushrooms
2 Tablespoons chopped pimento

Prepare rice according to directions on box. Brown chicken in butter. Arrange chicken breasts on top of cooked rice in 2-quart casserole. Put soup (undiluted) in pan used to brown chicken. Add sauterne and other ingredients. Heat to boiling and let thicken slightly. Pour mixture over chicken and rice and bake at 350 degrees for 25 minutes, covered, and 15 minutes more, uncovered.

Mrs. Walter Mayfield
(Luta Sullivan)

Chicken Cacciatore

1 fryer, cut up
1/3 cup salad or olive oil
1 large onion, chopped
1 medium can tomatoes
1 8-ounce can tomato sauce
1/2 cup dry wine — white or
   red

1/4 cup bell pepper, chopped
1 clove garlic, minced
1 teaspoon salt
1/4 teaspoon pepper
1/2 bay leaf
1/4 teaspoon marjoram
1/8 teaspoon thyme

Saute chicken in oil until brown. Add rest of ingredients. Simmer for 1 hour. Can be made ahead and reheated. Serve with spaghetti or rice. Serves 6.

Mrs. Ben K. Norwood, Jr.
("Sunshine" Connor)

Chicken Tetrazzini

3 2-pound chickens, cut up
1 1/2 cups celery tops,
   chopped
1/4 cup parsley, chopped
1 medium onion, sliced
8 ounces mushrooms, sliced
5 Tablespoons butter
4 Tablespoons flour
1 cup whipping cream

2 1/2 Tablespoons dry sherry
1 8-ounce box egg noodles,
   boiled and drained
3/4 cup dry bread crumbs
5 Tablespoons grated Parmesan
   cheese
2 1/2 teaspoons salt
1/4 teaspoon pepper
White almonds, sliced

Place chicken in saucepan with celery, parsley, onion, and 2 teaspoons salt. And 3 1/2 cups water. Bring to boil, cover, reduce heat and simmer until tender. Remove chicken and bone it. Strain broth and keep it. Saute mushrooms in butter. Stir in flour, 1/2 teaspoon salt and pepper. Add 2 cups broth and the cream, slowly, and cook, stirring constantly until thickened. Add chicken and sherry to sauce. Add almonds. Place noodles in greased shallow baking dish. Top with chicken mixture. Sprinkle with bread crumbs and cheese. Brown under broiler. Serves 6 to 8.

Mrs. William B. Ellis, III
(Judy Baarcke)

104

Chicken and Seafood Tetrazzini

3 chicken breasts
4 ounces spaghetti or macaroni
1 pound or 2 cans shrimp
1 large onion
1 garlic clove, chopped
1/2 green pepper, chopped
1 cup chopped celery

1 Tablespoon parsley
1/2 pint oysters
1 can mushroom soup
1 can cream of tomato soup
2 Tablespoons Worcestershire
  sauce
Sharp cheese

Cook chicken and cut into bite size pieces. Cook spaghetti. Cook and clean shrimp. Sauté onion, garlic, green pepper and celery in bacon drippings. Drain oysters and add oysters, parsley and Worcestershire to onion mixture. Remove from stove as soon as oysters curl. Mix with all other ingredients in casserole and cover with sharp cheese. Cook at 325 degrees for 45 minutes. Serves 6 to 8. Can be made ahead of time and frozen, but don't add cheese until ready to cook.

Mrs. G. T. Buckland
(Katherine Tolbert)

Chicken Creole

1 frying chicken, cut up
2 Tablespoons butter
1 small onion, chopped
1 small bell pepper, chopped
2 stalks celery, chopped

2 Tablespoons flour
1 No. 303 can tomatoes (2 cups)
1 teaspoon sugar
1 teaspoon salt

Rub chicken with salt and pepper. Melt butter in heavy skillet, add chicken and brown slowly (about 10 minutes). Remove chicken from skillet. Add onion, bell pepper and celery to butter remaining in skillet. Cook until tender. Add flour and brown, and then add sugar and salt. Return chicken to skillet and cover. Simmer slowly until tender (about 1 hour). Serve with rice. If more gravy is needed, add boiling water. Serves 4 to 6.

Mrs. Faust Nicholson, Jr.
(Frances Ravenel)

Broiled Chicken with Almonds

Chicken

1 medium-sized chicken
(about 2 1/2 pounds)
2 Tablespoons margarine
Flour

Salt and pepper
Almonds (slivered or whole,
depending on who's coming
for dinner!)

Gravy

2 Tablespoons margarine
1-2 Tablespoons soy sauce
(optional)
Water, if necessary

2 Tablespoons flour
Dash Worcestershire sauce
(optional)

Chicken: Split chicken down the back or into as many cut pieces as desired. Sprinkle salt and pepper on under side of chicken. In a covered roaster steam, skin side up, until tender; this may be done on top burner or in oven. On top burner you must add a little water to keep meat from sticking to bottom of pan. Place almonds in a slow oven (300 degrees) until lightly toasted. Remove. Increase oven heat to 450 degrees. Rub margarine over chicken, sprinkle with a light coating of flour and place uncovered in the hot oven until evenly browned on top. Using sharp, pointed knife make small slits in the meaty parts and insert almonds about halfway point side down.

Gravy: Melt margarine, add flour and stir. Slowly add stock, left in pan, stirring constantly until boiling. The soy sauce and Worcestershire sauce will add extra flavor. Add water, if necessary.

Mrs. Charles Weisel
(Kay Roberson)

Company Chicken

4 large chicken breasts, boned
and halved
2 center slices of ham
(country ham best)
8 strips of bacon

1 can mushroom soup
1 can mushrooms (or equivalent
of fresh mushrooms)
1/2 cup sherry
Paprika

Sear ham, cut into 8 pieces, and wrap one piece around each piece of chicken. Wrap a strip of bacon around each and skewer. Put into casserole or baking dish. Mix mushroom soup, mushrooms and sherry and pour over chicken. Bake in oven at 325 degrees for 1 1/2 hours. Sprinkle with paprika. Serves 8.

Mrs. Howard E. Newton, Jr.
(Jourdan Jones)

Chicken Elegante

6 whole chicken breasts, split
3/4 cup olive oil
1 onion
1 stick butter

2 cans chicken consommé or
   broth
15 ounces tomato juice
4 Tablespoons flour
1/2 cup cooking sherry

Split, skin, and salt chicken breasts, making 12 pieces. Brown in oil and butter, and baste both sides. Remove extra fat. Add onions and brown. Place chicken and onions in baking dish. Add consommé and juice thickened with flour. Simmer 10 minutes and add sherry. Cover and cook for 3 hours at 300 degrees. Serve with rice and salad. Serves 6 at dinner or 12 at luncheon. Freezes well.

Mrs. B. Allston Ellis
(Virginia Hutchinson)

Chicken in Red Wine

4 chicken breasts
4 chicken legs
1/2 stick butter or margarine
1 or 2 cloves garlic
  (chopped fine)

1 Tablespoon Kitchen Bouquet
2 cups dry red wine
Salt and pepper to taste
Several shakes Accent

Brown chicken which has been salted, peppered and accented, in butter. Sauté garlic while you brown chicken. Add Kitchen Bouquet and red wine, cover and simmer over low heat until chicken is tender, approximately 45 minutes. There will be a sauce with chicken. Good served with rice. Easily prepared in electric frying pan. May be made ahead and heated at mealtime. Serves 4.

Mrs. Gordon R. Vinson
(Carolyn Godwin)

107

Chicken Curry

1 4 1/2 to 6-pound hen
Salt and pepper to taste
2 bay leaves
2 celery tops
1/2 cup chicken fat
1/2 cup finely chopped onion
1 peeled and finely chopped
  apple

1/2 cup flour
3 cups chicken stock
3/4 cup evaporated milk
  or light cream
1 teaspoon salt
1 teaspoon curry powder
1/4 teaspoon ginger

Cook hen in 3 cups water, seasoned with salt, pepper, bay leaves, and celery tops until tender (2 to 3 hours). Strain broth and chill. Remove meat from bone and cut into pieces. When broth is chilled, the fat rises to the top. Put 1/2 cup of the fat into large saucepan. Add onion and apple and cook slowly until tender. Blend in flour. Combine chicken stock and evaporated milk, and add to saucepan. Cook, stirring constantly, until thickened. Stir in salt, curry powder, and ginger. Add chicken. Cook over very low heat for 15 minutes. Serve with rice and any of the following accompaniments: chutney, raisins, salted almonds, shredded coconut, grated orange rind, or crumbled bacon. Can be made ahead and heated before serving. Serves 8.

Mrs. W. A. L. Sibley, Jr.
(Nancy Holland)

Chicken with Rice and Mushrooms

1/2 fryer per person
1/3 cup Minute Rice
1/3 cup undiluted cream of
  mushroom soup

1 ounce chopped mushrooms
Pinch of rosemary
Pinch of thyme
1 ounce sherry

Salt and pepper 1/2 fryer, place skin side down on a piece of aluminum foil and fill cavity with Minute rice that has been dipped in boiling water for 1 minute. Spread mushroom soup over this, and chopped mushrooms on top. Sprinkle with rosemary and thyme. Pour 1 ounce of sherry over the top and seal foil tightly. Bake in oven at 350 degrees 1 to 1 1/2 hours.

Mrs. W. S. Adams
(Lucy Boyd)

Chicken Pie

4 Tablespoons flour
4 Tablespoons butter
1/4 teaspoon black pepper
Dash red pepper
2 cups hot milk

2 cups baked chicken, chopped
2 hard boiled eggs, chopped
1/4 cup slivered almonds
Toasted bread crumbs
1/2 teaspoon salt

Put flour and salt in blender. Add butter, black and red pepper, hot milk and blend. Pour into saucepan and cook over medium heat stirring constantly for 3 minutes. Add chicken, eggs and almonds and mix. Put in buttered baking dish and cover with crumbs (2 pieces of toast in blender). Will keep in refrigerator several days. Cook in 450 degree oven for 15 minutes or until crumbs are brown. Serves 6 to 8.

Miss Elizabeth Arnold

Hot Turkey Salad Souffle

6 slices white bread
2 cups diced cooked turkey
  or chicken
1/2 cup chopped onion
1/2 cup chopped green pepper
1/2 cup finely chopped celery
1/2 cup mayonnaise

3/4 teaspoon salt
Dash pepper
1 1/2 cups milk
2 beaten eggs
1 can mushroom soup
1/2 cup shredded sharp cheese

Cube 2 slices of bread, place in bottom of 8x8x2-inch greased baking dish. Combine turkey, vegetables, mayonnaise, and seasonings and spoon over bread cubes. Trim crusts from remaining bread, arrange slices on top of turkey or chicken mixture. Combine eggs and milk; pour over all. Cover and chill 1 hour or overnight. Spoon soup over top. Bake in a slow oven 350 degrees about 1 hour or until set. Sprinkle cheese over top during last few minutes of baking. Serves 6.

Mrs. Joe Coble
(Sally Hudson)

Chicken Mayonnaise

1 5-pound hen, cooked
2 cups chopped celery
5 boiled eggs, chopped
1/2 cup India relish
3/4 cup toasted almonds
  or pecans
1 cup tiny peas (optional)
Juice of 1/2 lemon

2 teaspoons Worcestershire
  sauce
1 cup mayonnaise
Salt and pepper to taste
2 envelopes plain gelatine
1/2 cup cold water
1 cup chicken broth

Chop chicken finely. Soak gelatine in cold water. Heat chicken broth and pour over soaked gelatine. Mix all ingredients together. Congeal in refrigerator in large pyrex dish or individual molds. Add a bit of mayonnaise on top, if desired. Serves 16.

Mrs. H. T. Williams
(Catherine Hudson)

Mighty Mousse

1 10-3/4 ounce can tomato
  soup
1/2 cup sour cream
1 Tablespoon lemon juice
2 envelopes unflavored
  gelatine
1 cup diced chicken

3/4 cup chopped cucumber or
  celery
1/4 cup sliced stuffed olives
2 Tablespoons minced onion
1/2 teaspoon salt
Dash of pepper

Blend soup with sour cream, add lemon juice, salt and pepper. Soften gelatine in 1 soup can of water, stir over low heat until gelatine dissolves. Remove from heat; blend with soup mixture. Chill until slightly thickened; fold in remaining ingredients. Pour into five-cup mold and chill in refrigerator for 4 hours. Makes 4 ample servings.

Mrs. W. H. Gowan
(Carol Mahon)

110

Rock Cornish Game Hens with Wild Rice Stuffing

10-12 Rock Cornish Game Hens
10-12 slices bacon
Melted butter
Salt
20-24 onions
1 cup wild rice
1/2 cup chopped onions
1/2 pound mushrooms, sliced

1 1/2 cups diced ham
6 Tablespoons butter
1/2 teaspoon salt
1/2 teaspoon marjoram
1/2 teaspoon thyme
1/2 cup toasted almonds,
   chopped

Wash and prepare hens for roasting. Sprinkle cavities lightly with salt. Stuff with the rice mixture. (Cook rice according to package directions. Drain. Sauté chopped onions, mushrooms and diced ham in 6 tablespoons butter. Mix with rice. Season with salt, marjoram, thyme and almonds.) Truss hens. Lay two half slices of bacon over each hen. Roast uncovered at 325 degrees for 1 to 1 1/2 hours or until thoroughly tender. Baste with drippings and melted butter. Cook par boiled onions around in pan. (The dressing can be steamed in a chafing dish until heated for use at a buffet.)

Mrs. T. J. Benston
(Lyda Gerrald)

Chicken and Avocado Salad

2 1/2 cups cooked chicken,
   diced
3/4 cup celery, diced
3/4 cup small raw
   cauliflower buds
1/3 cup toasted almonds,
   chopped

1/3 cup French dressing
1/2 cup sour cream
1/4 cup mayonnaise
Salt and pepper to taste
3 avocados, chilled
1 head lettuce

Mix chicken and vegetables. Marinate with French dressing; let stand in refrigerator several hours. Shortly before serving, add sour cream, mayonnaise, almonds, salt and pepper. Peel and halve avocados; arrange halves in lettuce cups and fill with chicken salad. Serves 6.

Mrs. David G. King
(Judy Compton)

Chicken Salad

4 to 5 cups cooked chicken,
   cut in large chunks
2 teaspoons grated onion
1 cup celery, cut on an angle
1 cup minced pickle
1/4 cup light cream

2/3 cup mayonnaise or cooked
   salad dressing
1 teaspoon salt
1/8 teaspoon pepper
2 Tablespoons vinegar

Combine chicken, onion, celery and pickle. Mix cream with mayonnaise, salt, pepper and vinegar — toss with chicken. Refrigerate until served.

Mrs. Hugh Aiken, Jr.
(Clairene Harris)

Chicken Livers Stroganoff

1 pound chicken livers
   (halved)
2 Tablespoons butter
1/2 teaspoon oregano
1/2 teaspoon Worcestershire
   sauce

1 medium onion, chopped
2 Tablespoons flour
1/2 teaspoon salt
Dash pepper
6-ounce can mushrooms
1/4 cup sour cream

Brown livers in butter with oregano and Worcestershire sauce. Remove from pan. Sauté onion. Blend in flour, salt and pepper. Add mushrooms and juice. Heat until boiling, then add livers. Cook until done (5 minutes). Mix in sour cream just before serving.

Mrs. Richard W. Riley
(Ann "Tunky" Yarborough)

Sautéed Chicken Livers

1 pound chicken livers
1/4 cup olive oil
1/4 cup sherry

1/4 cup soy sauce
Grated garlic
Dry mustard

112

Marinate chicken livers in oil, sherry and soy sauce, seasoned with grated garlic and dry mustard (a touch of curry powder can be added for variation). Let them marinate at least 3 or 4 hours. Pour everything into a large saucepan and cook until livers are done. Serve over rice, etc.

This is good with rice for dinner or with eggs for breakfast.

Mrs. Lawrence Nachman
(Lynn Thalheimer)

Wine Sauce for Chicken

1 medium onion
2 carrots
Parsley
2 1/2 cups water

3 Tablespoons butter
3 Tablespoons flour
1/2 pint sour cream
1/2 cup sherry

Cook onion, carrots and parsley in water until tender. Strain. Melt butter, stir in flour until smooth. Gradually add 1 1/2 cups vegetable stock, stirring until smooth and thickened. Add sour cream and sherry. Pour over chicken breasts. Bake covered at 350 degrees for 1 1/2 hours.

Mrs. Raymond Williams
(Elizabeth Martin)

Marinated Chicken Breasts
Charcoal-Broiled

4 boned chicken breasts
1 1/4 cups melted butter
1 cup soy sauce
1 1/4 cups white wine

4 teaspoons tarragon
4 teaspoons mustard
1 teaspoon Accent

Marinate chicken in marinade made of last 6 ingredients for 3-4 hours. Cook over low charcoal fire until tender but juicy, basting frequently with marinade.

E. Calhoun Haskell, Jr.

113

Barbecue Sauce

2 cups vinegar
4 cups water
15 Tablespoons sugar
8 Tablespoons prepared mustard
1 Tablespoon pepper
2 Tablespoons salt
1 teaspoon red pepper

3 lemons, sliced
6 onions, sliced
1 pound margarine
4 cups catsup
15 Tablespoons Worcestershire
  sauce

Mix first 10 ingredients — simmer, uncovered, 20 minutes. Add catsup and Worcestershire and bring to boil. Refrigerate. Leave onion and lemon in sauce. Keeps for several months. This recipe makes 14 cups. I make 1/4 recipe for family use.

Mrs. B. Allston Ellis
(Virginia Hutchinson)

Barbecue Sauce for Chicken

1/4 pound butter
1/2 pint vinegar
1 lemon, sliced thin
1 onion, sliced thin
1 Tablespoon dry mustard

2 Tablespoons Worcestershire
  sauce
2 pods red pepper or a dash or 2
  of Tabasco

Put all ingredients in a saucepan, bring to boil and simmer 30 minutes. Use to baste chickens (enough for 1 1/2 or 2 chickens) on grill or in 275 degree to 300 degree oven, basting every 15 to 30 minutes for 2 1/2 to 3 hours. Serves 6.

This was given to my mother years ago by a friend in New Orleans.

Mrs. James F. Gallivan
(Joan Fisch)

Salmon Cakes with Mushroom Soup Topping

2 cups canned salmon
1 egg, beaten
Salmon liquid plus enough milk
  to equal 3/4 cup
1 cup cracker crumbs

1 Tablespoon lemon juice
1/4 cup chopped onion,
  optional
Salt and pepper to taste
1 can cream of mushroom soup

114

Combine salmon and egg. Stir in remaining ingredients, except soup. Mix well. Spoon mixture into greased cup cake or muffin pans. Bake at 350 degrees for 30 minutes. Remove from pan. Spoon heated mushroom soup over each salmon cake. Garnish with parsley. Serves 6.

Mrs. Wake H. Myers, Jr.
(Mary Jane Webster)

Western Scalloped Salmon

2 cups canned salmon
4 Tablespoons butter
1/4 cup flour
1 1/2 cups milk
1/2 bay leaf
1/4 teaspoon salt
1/4 teaspoon black pepper

1 Tablespoon chopped parsley
1 Tablespoon grated onion
2 beef bouillon cubes
1/2 cup ripe olives (cut in
  large pieces)
1/2 cup dry bread crumbs
1/2 cup grated cheese

Melt butter in saucepan and blend in flour. Add milk, salt, pepper, bay leaf, grated onion, parsley and bouillon cubes. Cook and stir until thickened. Remove bay leaf. Place layer of salmon (which has been drained and flaked) in bottom of greased casserole (1 1/2 quart), sprinkle with olives, bread crumbs and cheese. Repeat until all is used, topping with crumbs and grated cheese. Bake at 350 degrees for 30 minutes. Serves 5 or 6.

Mrs. Juanita S. Groff
(Juanita Sikes)

Baked Flounder With Sauce

1 baked flounder
1 can frozen shrimp soup
1/4 cup grated cheesc

2 teaspoons A-1 sauce
2 Tablespoons grated onion
Bread crumbs

Cook fish first for a few minutes. Place onion on fish, then pour sauce over it. Sprinkle bread crumbs on top and brown.

Mrs. Dan Hair
(Elizabeth Harris)

115

Gratin of Fresh Fish

1 pound of flounder fillet
2 1/2 Tablespoons margarine
4 Tablespoons flour
1 cup milk

1/8 teaspoon nutmeg
1 teaspoon salt
3 eggs, separated

Cut fish into small pieces (about one-half inch square or less). Melt margarine, stir in flour and gradually add milk. Let thicken, add seasoning and cool. Add egg yolks, fish and finally fold in stiffly beaten egg whites. Turn into buttered casserole. Sprinkle Ritz cracker crumbs on top and bake 45 minutes to 1 hour in 350 degree oven. Serve with melted butter. Serves 4.

This is a Norwegian recipe.

Mrs. W. H. Arnold
(Lucy Furman)

Smoked Fish

Whole trout, salmon, bass,
    snapper or mackerel
Salt

Salad oil
Lemon juice (use 1/2
    lemon per fish)

Scald and dress fish, leaving head and fins intact. Salt fish inside and out. Place in glass dish. Pour salad oil over fish and squeeze 1/2 lemon over each fish. Store in refrigerator until fire is ready to smoke.

Build charcoal fire in one end of a smoker grill. When coals are ready add approximately 2 handfuls hickory chips, which have been soaked in water. Place fish at other end, not over coals. Open the draft under the fire and one over the fish. Close all other draft holes. For small fish, smoke about 45 minutes; for larger ones, 1 hour to 1 1/2 hours. Fish may be turned once but this is not essential. Serve hot as an entrée or cold with lemon and mayonnaise as an hors d'oeuvre with crackers.

Mrs. John McCutcheon
(Joanne Burn)

Barbecued Fish

Fish   Barbecue King Dry Seasoning

Use small bodied fish such as brook trout, rainbow trout, lake perch, blue gills and ocean fish boneless fillets. Lay fish to be cooked in pan evenly. Sprinkle well with Barbecue King Dry Seasoning. Cook at 300 degrees for approximately 45 minutes or until done.

Barbecue King

Crabmeat Cobbler

Cobbler

1/2 cup butter	1 cup shredded American cheese
1/2 cup chopped green peppers	1 pound crabmeat
1/2 cup chopped onions	(about 3 cups)
1/2 cup sifted plain flour	1 No. 2 can tomatoes
1 teaspoon dry mustard	2 teaspoons Worcestershire
1/2 teaspoon Accent	sauce
1 cup milk	1/2 teaspoon salt

Topping

1 cup plain flour	1/4 cup shredded American
2 teaspoons baking powder	cheese
1 teaspoon salt	2 Tablespoons shortening
1/2 cup milk	

Cobbler: In top of double boiler, melt butter. Add peppers and onions and cook over boiling water until tender — about 10 minutes. Blend in flour, mustard, Accent, milk and cheese. Stir constantly until cheese is melted and mixture is very thick. Add crabmeat, tomatoes, Worcestershire sauce and salt. Blend thoroughly. Pour into 2-quart casserole dish. Top with biscuits and bake at 450 degrees for 20-30 minutes.

Cheese Biscuit Topping: Sift together flour, baking powder and salt into mixing bowl. Add cheese. Cut in the shortening thoroughly, until the particles are fine. Add milk. Mix only until all the flour is moistened. Drop rounded teaspoons on top of hot crabmeat mixture. Bake at 450 degrees for 20-30 minutes.

Mrs. Wright Skinner, Jr.
(Virginia Bruorton)

117

Herb Crab

1 package herb dressing mix
1 1/4 cups chicken broth
1 cup onion, minced
1 cup celery, minced
3/4 cup green pepper, chopped
3 Tablespoons bacon drippings
1 pound crab meat
1/2 cup mayonnaise

1 teaspoon sugar
1 teaspoon prepared mustard
2 eggs
1/4 teaspoon Worcestershire
sauce
1 teaspoon parsley flakes
Juice of one lemon
Salt and pepper to taste

Sauté onions, celery and green pepper in bacon drippings. Prepare dressing mix with chicken broth and add onions, celery and green pepper. Add other ingredients and mix well. Cook in a preheated oven at 350 degrees for about 45 minutes or until top is brown.

Variations — This crab dish can be topped with grated cheese. To add a real gourmet touch, sprinkle with sherry just before serving.

Mrs. T. C. Adams
(Beulah Cunningham)
Mrs. Elliott A. Easterby
(Elliott Adams)

Crabmeat Casseroles

4 Tablespoons butter or
margarine
2 Tablespoons flour
1 cup milk
1 Tablespoon chili sauce
1 teaspoon lemon juice
1/2 teaspoon curry powder

1/2 teaspoon Worcestershire
sauce
1 7 1/2 ounce can king crab,
drained
3 slices bread, trimmed and
cut into tiny squares

Make a white sauce with 2 tablespoons of butter, flour and milk. Remove from heat. Stir in chili sauce, lemon juice, curry powder, and Worcestershire. Arrange crab in 3 individual glass pie plates or shells. Pour hot sauce over crab. Melt remaining 2 tablespoons butter and mix with bread. Sprinkle over sauce. Broil so that crab heats and crumbs brown in 7 to 10 minutes. Makes 3 servings.

Mrs. Joe H. Piper
(Dodie Browning)

Virginia Crab Meat in Shells

4 Tablespoons butter
2 Tablespoons flour
1 cup milk
1 1/2 cups bread crumbs
1/2 teaspoon mustard
1/2 teaspoon white pepper
1 teaspoon Worcestershire
  sauce
1 Tablespoon lemon juice
1 teaspoon salt
1 pound crab meat (fresh)
Cracker meal
1/2 green pepper, chopped
1 Tablespoon chopped pimento
1 Tablespoon chopped onion

Blend butter and flour in saucepan; add milk and stir until just boiling. Add bread crumbs (a frozen loaf of French bread is a quick and easy source for bread crumbs), seasonings, onion, pimento, and pepper (onion and green pepper can be sautéed in margarine while mixing first part of recipe) and crab meat (prefer lump back fin). Mix and remove from heat. Fill shells or ramekins (lightly grease) with mixture. Cover top with cracker meal and dot with butter. Bake in 450 degree oven until light brown. This makes 6 good servings.

Good with little peas and a green salad or fresh fruit salad.

Mrs. E. E. Stone IV
(Barbara McCready)

Shrimp Bisque

2 cans frozen shrimp soup
1 1/2 ounces garlic flavored
  processed cheese
1/2 cup coffee cream
1 can (4 ounces) mushrooms
1/2 teaspoon Accent
1/8 teaspoon pepper
1/2 teaspoon salt
10 ounces canned shrimp,
  drained
1 package frozen peas
Sherry (optional)
Hot, cooked parsley rice

Blend soup, cheese, cream and seasonings in heavy saucepan over low heat. Stir occasionally until hot. Cook peas and add mushrooms and shrimp to soup mix and heat to simmering. Add sherry (if used) and serve over hot rice. Serves 8.

Mrs. Harold Turner
(Anne Schade)

119

Beerded Shrimp and Sauce

Shrimp

3 pounds fresh shrimp
24 ounces beer
1 teaspoon thyme
1 Tablespoon dry mustard
2 bay leaves

1 Tablespoon chopped chives
1 Tablespoon salt
2 cloves garlic, chopped
2 Tablespoons chopped parsley
1/2 teaspoon pepper

Place all above ingredients except shrimp in large boiler and let come to a boil. Cut legs off shrimp but leave shells on. Add shrimp to above mixture. When shrimp mixture has returned to boil, let simmer for 5 minutes. Serve with sauce below.

Sauce

4 Tablespoons lemon juice
2 Tablespoons chives or onion
2 teaspoons salt

2 Tablespoons parsley
1 stick butter or margarine,
  melted

Serves 4. Serve shrimp hot with plenty of napkins and maybe a wet towel for sticky fingers.

Jim Harris, Jr.

Crayton's Shrimp Newburg

3 pounds cooked shrimp
1 1/2 sticks butter
7 Tablespoons flour
1 quart milk
6 ounces tomato catsup

2 Tablespoons Worcestershire
  sauce
1 Tablespoon salt
1/2 cup sherry

Melt butter and add flour slowly, stirring constantly to make a thick paste. Add milk, little by little, bringing mix to a boil each time milk is added. Add catsup, Worcestershire sauce and salt. When this is blended, add shrimp and bring to a boil. Remove from stove and stir in sherry just before serving on your choice of rice, toast points, pastry shells or Holland Rusk. Serves 10.

Mrs. Jenkins S. Crayton
(Betty Jane Goldsmith)

Shrimp and Red Rice Casserole

2 Tablespoons butter
1 teaspoon flour
1 medium onion, chopped
1 cup canned tomatoes
1/2 cup water
1 bell pepper, chopped fine
1 clove garlic, minced
1/2 teaspoon salt

1/4 teaspoon cayenne pepper
1/4 teaspoon thyme
1 Tablespoon Worcestershire
   sauce
3 cups cooked rice
2 cups cooked shrimp
1 cup tomato juice
1/2 cup grated cheese

Melt butter, blend in flour. Add onions and cook until tender. Add tomatoes, water, bell pepper, garlic, salt, thyme, Worcestershire sauce and cayenne. Cook until pepper is tender, stirring occasionally. Add rice, shrimp and tomato juice. Pour into a greased casserole dish. Sprinkle cheese over top. Bake at 350 degrees for 15-20 minutes. Serves 6.

Mrs. Ben K. Norwood, Jr.
("Sunshine" Connor)

French Shrimp in Shells

4 Tablespoons butter
1/2 teaspoon salt
3 Tablespoons all-purpose
   flour
3/4 cup milk
1/4 cup dry sherry
3/4 cup cream
1/2 cup chopped mushrooms

Dash of pepper, seasoning
   salt, lemon-pepper and
   paprika
1 pound small shelled shrimp,
   cooked (2 cups)
1 Tablespoon grated Parmesan
   cheese

Melt butter in saucepan and stir in flour. Add milk and cream. Cook and stir over low heat until thickened. Stir in salt, pepper and all seasonings. Add shrimp, sherry and mushrooms. Pour into five buttered baking sea shells (or ramekins). Sprinkle each with Parmesan cheese. Place under broiler about 3 to 4 inches from heat. Broil until cheese browns. Serves 5-6.

Mrs. Howard H. Lamar
(Betty Shepherd)

Shrimp and Cheese Pie

9-inch unbaked pie shell
4 ounces Swiss cheese, grated
4 ounces gouda or cheddar
  cheese, grated
1 Tablespoon flour
8 ounces cooked shrimp,
  coarsely chopped
1 medium onion, thinly sliced

1 small jar sliced mushrooms,
  drained
3 eggs
1 cup light cream
1/2 teaspoon salt
1/4 teaspoon pepper
2 Tablespoons Parmesan cheese

Toss cheese together with flour. Spread 3/4 cheese mixture in pie shell. Layer shrimp and mushrooms on top of cheese. Cover with remaining cheese mixture. Beat remaining ingredients together except Parmesan, and pour into pie shell. Sprinkle Parmesan over top. Bake in 400 degree oven for 15 minutes. Reduce heat to 325 degrees and continue baking about 40 minutes or until silver knife comes out clean. Makes 6 generous servings.

Mrs. Thomas W. Miller, Jr.
(Linda West)

Sweet and Sour Shrimp

2 pounds fresh shrimp
3 Tablespoons butter
2 1/2 cups (No. 2 can) pineapple
  chunks
1 green pepper in thin strips
1/2 cup vinegar

2 Tablespoons slivered
  crystallized ginger
1/2 cup sugar
Pinch salt
1 Tablespoon soy sauce
2 1/2 Tablespoons cornstarch

Clean and shell shrimp. Heat butter in saucepan, add shrimp and cook about 5 minutes, stirring occasionally. Add pineapple, pineapple juice, slivered ginger, pepper strips, vinegar, sugar, salt and soy sauce. Cook over low heat about 2 minutes. Spoon out a little liquid and mix with cornstarch until smooth paste. Pour back into shrimp mixture and cook slowly, stirring constantly until liquid is transparent and slightly thick. Serve with fluffy hot rice. Serves 6.

Mrs. Wright Skinner, Jr.
(Virginia Bruorton)

Curried Shrimp in Avocado Halves

1 or 2 avocados
Lime juice
1 Tablespoon butter
1 teaspoon curry powder
1 teaspoon salt
1/3 cup chopped onion

1 large tomato or 1 cup
chopped tomatoes
1 1/2 cups cooked shrimp
1 cup sour cream
2 cups rice, cooked

Brush avocado halves (or quarters) with lime juice. Place in shallow baking pan. Heat 10 minutes in 300 degree oven. In saucepan combine butter, curry powder, salt, tomato, and onion. Cook until onion is tender. Add shrimp and heat. Blend in sour cream. Place avocado on top of bed of rice (on *warm* plates!) and fill halves with curried shrimp. This recipe serves 4 modestly.

Mrs. T. L. Martin
(Eyleen Runge)

Congealed Shrimp Salad

1 package Knox gelatine
1/4 cup cold water
3 cups diced shrimp
3 boiled eggs, cut up
1/4 cup bell pepper, cut up
1 cup celery, cut up

Salt and pepper
1 small bottle stuffed olives,
sliced round
1 cup sweet pickle or 1/2 cup
capers
1 cup mayonnaise

Dissolve gelatine in cold water and add to mayonnaise. Pour over cut up shrimp and other ingredients. Mold into individual molds or one large one. Congeal in refrigerator. Serves 8-10.

Mrs. Wright Skinner, Jr.
(Virginia Bruorton)

Cocktail Sauce

3/4 cup chili sauce
1/4 cup lemon juice
3 Tablespoons horseradish (hot)
1/2 teaspoon minced onion

2 teaspoons Worcestershire
sauce
4 drops Tabasco sauce
Salt to taste

Combine ingredients. Makes 1 cup. Good served with boiled shrimp.

Mrs. Robert H. Yeargin
(Mary Ellen Sitton)

123

Shrimp Creole

2 pounds shrimp
1/4 cup chopped onion
1/4 cup chopped green pepper
1 clove garlic, chopped
1/4 cup melted butter

3 Tablespoons flour
1/2 teaspoon chili powder
1/2 teaspoon pepper
1 teaspoon salt
2 cups canned tomatoes

Cook shrimp and remove veins. Cook onion, green pepper and garlic in butter until tender; blend in flour and seasonings. Add shrimp and simmer for 20 minutes. Serve over rice. Serves 6.

Mrs. Fred Gilmer, Jr.
(Mary Ann Chamblee)

Remoulade Sauce for Shrimp

1 cup mayonnaise
1 teaspoon Coleman's dry
  mustard
1 teaspoon Worcestershire
  sauce
2 Tablespoons grated onion

1 teaspoon prepared
  horseradish
2 teaspoons tarragon vinegar
1/2 teaspoon salt
1/2 teaspoon white pepper
2 Tablespoons chopped parsley

Combine ingredients. If necessary, thin with 2 or 3 tablespoons milk.

Mrs. E. D. Sloan
(Caroline Young)

Tuna and Rice Casserole

1 to 1 1/2 cups rice
1 can tuna fish
1 can beef bouillon
1 can mushrooms

1 can peas
1 can onion rings
Salt
Pepper

Heat bouillon and pour into large casserole. Stir in uncooked rice and other ingredients except onion rings. Heat for about one hour (until rice absorbs liquid) in a 350 degree oven. Remove from oven and sprinkle onion rings on top. Return to oven and brown 5 to 10 minutes more. Serves 4 to 6 people.

Mrs. T. Frank Huguenin, Jr.
(Gaye Glover)

Tuna Casserole

1 can chunk tuna (7 ounces)
1 can chow mein noodles
1 can condensed cream of
  mushroom soup
1/4 cup water
1 cup sliced celery

1/4 cup chopped onion
1/2 teaspoon salt
Dash pepper
2 teaspoons soy sauce
1/4 cup chopped cashews

Put 3/4 chow mein noodles in a bowl and set rest aside for topping. Mix other ingredients with noodles. Put in buttered casserole dish and top with rest of noodles. You may add a few cashews on top, also. Bake at 350 degrees for 30 minutes. Serves 4.

Mrs. Walter G. King
(Mary Louise Bouchillon)

Lobster Casserole

4 to 8 frozen lobster tails,
  cooked
1/3 cup onion, chopped
1 clove garlic, minced
2 Tablespoons butter or
  margarine
1 can cheese soup

1 small jar sliced mushrooms,
  drained
1/3 cup "half and half" cream
1/4 cup dry sherry
2 Tablespoons chopped parsley
1 10-ounce package frozen
  peas, cooked and drained
Buttered soft bread crumbs

Remove lobster meat from shells and cut meat into large pieces. Melt butter in frying pan and cook onion and garlic until tender but not brown. Stir in soup and mushrooms. Slowly add cream, sherry and parsley. Add lobster and peas. Cook until heated through, stirring occasionally. Place in round casserole and sprinkle crumbs around the edge. Bake at 350 degrees for 25 minutes. Serves 4.

Mrs. C. D. Bessinger, Jr.
(Jane Prevost)

Lobster Cantonese

6 6-8 ounce frozen rock
  lobster tails, thawed
1/4 cup salad oil
1 clove garlic, finely chopped
  (use less if desired)
1/2 pound pork shoulder,
  ground
2 Tablespoons cornstarch

1/4 cup soy sauce
1 teaspoon sugar
1 teaspoon salt
1/2 teaspoon pepper
2 1/4 cups boiling water
2 eggs
1/2 cup slivered scallions
1/3 cup water

Shell lobster meat in one piece, if possible, and cut it crosswise in two sections. Heat oil in large skillet with cover. Add garlic and pork. Sauté, stirring until pork is no longer pink, about 10 minutes. Meanwhile, in a small bowl, make a smooth mixture of cornstarch and 1/3 cup water. Stir the soy sauce, sugar, salt, pepper, boiling water and cornstarch mixture into pork. Bring to a boil, reduce heat, simmer stirring until mixture is thickened and translucent, about 10 minutes. Add lobster pieces and cook, covered, and over low heat, until lobster is tender, about 8 to 10 minutes (do not over cook). In small bowl beat eggs slightly with fork. Blend in some of the hot lobster mixture; then stir, all at once, into lobster mixture (eggs will form shreds). Add scallions. Serve immediately. Serves 6.

Mrs. Ruth P. Caine
(Ruth Potts)

Oyster Pie

1 pint oysters
Saltine crackers
1 small can evaporated milk
1 can water

3 eggs, beaten
Salt and pepper
Butter

Place a layer of oysters in a casserole dish. Crumble over this a few saltines. Repeat for second layer. Pour milk, eggs and water, beaten together, over layers until milk mixture is standing on top. Season. Cook at 400 degrees until brown.

Mrs. James H. Austin
(Elizabeth Reid)

126

Scalloped Oysters

1 quart oysters
1 cup Carnation cream
1 teaspoon dry mustard
1 heaping Tablespoon flour
1 Tablespoon lemon juice

1 Tablespoon Worcestershire
  sauce
1 teaspoon Tabasco sauce
2 Tablespoons sherry
Buttered crumbs

Dry oysters with a towel and cut very fine. Dissolve dry mustard in cream. Dilute flour in enough cold water to make a thin paste free from lumps. Combine all ingredients except crumbs, and bake in casserole at 325 degrees for 20 to 30 minutes. Cover top with buttered crumbs.

Mrs. E. S. McKissick
(Jean Reamsbottom)

Colonial Oyster and Ham Pie

1 pint fresh oysters
1/2 cup butter
1/2 cup flour
1/2 cup oyster liquor
1/2 cup white wine
1/2 cup milk

1 1/2 cups cooked ham, diced
2 cups green peas, canned
  or frozen
1 medium onion, chopped
2 teaspoons butter

Drain fresh oysters and put aside liquor. Melt 1/2 cup butter and stir in flour. Add oyster liquor, white wine and milk. Cook until good and thick. Remove from heat and add oysters, ham, peas and onion which has been cooked soft in butter. Put into casserole and cook in pre-heated hot oven 15 minutes. Makes 4 generous servings.

Mrs. Richard W. Riley
(Ann "Tunky" Yarborough)

Oysters à la Poulette

1 pint shucked oysters
1 pint coarsely diced chicken
  or turkey
1 1/2 cups chicken or turkey
  broth

1/2 cup butter
1/2 cup flour
Salt to taste
Pepper to taste

Place oysters in casserole dish and put in 400 degree oven until oysters are reduced to approximately half size. Drain liquid from oysters and set them aside. Make roux of butter and flour. Mix broth and oyster liquid and bring to a rolling boil. Add roux to liquid until it becomes a thick sauce. Add chicken or turkey and oysters. Serves 6 to 8.

Serve on rissotto.

The Poinsett Club

Seafood Casserole

1 medium onion, chopped
1/2 cup green pepper, chopped
1/2 cup celery, chopped
1/4 pound sliced mushrooms
5 Tablespoons butter
1/3 cup plain flour
2 cups milk
1 teaspoon salt

1/8 teaspoon pepper
8 ounces shredded sharp
  cheddar cheese
1 pound cooked, shelled small
  shrimp
1/2 pound crabmeat
2 cups cooked rice
Paprika

Sauté onion, green pepper, celery, and mushrooms in butter. Stir in flour and cook until bubbly. Remove from heat, and gradually stir in milk. Cook over medium heat, stirring until thickened. Add salt and pepper. Stir in cheese until melted. Remove from heat, blend in shrimp and crabmeat. Spread rice in bottom of greased 9-inch square dish. Pour seafood mixture over rice; sprinkle paprika. Bake uncovered in 350 degree oven for about 25 minutes. Serves 8-10.

Mrs. James Austin Neal
(Leonette Dedmond)

Game

Tips on Cleaning Game

Mourning Doves:

The dove offers more gunning fun than food, especially early season young of the year. What they lack in size, they more than make up for in delicacy of taste. Dressing the "usual" way can take away the Pleasure of the Field and the Feast! Try it this way — the small amount of wasted bird is too insignificant for the time and trouble saved.

Use knife edge to break away wings as close to the breast as possible. Grasp craw and remove from junction of neck and breast. Push skin down until finger tip can be hooked under point or tip of breast. Pull breast away from carcass. Few remaining feathers and bits of skin are easily removed. This method results in fewer scattered feathers, too.

The less delay in dressing out game, the better the table fare and the prettier the meat. A strong brine soak (not over two hours — less if game is dressed relatively soon after the shoot) . . . removes undesirable blood for final "fine" cleaning without removing too much of the game flavor. After the salt water soak, game should be rinsed thoroughly in cold water and allowed to drain before packaging for freezing, if game is to be stored for future use. This works well with all small game.

Duck:

Duck is one of the toughest dressing jobs for the hunter ('s wife) because of the small feathers or down that defies removal with anything short of surgical tweezers and a magnifying glass! Singeing or burning away the down leaves a messy, smoked, darkened bird, not to mention .the odor (and some say, the taste) of burned feathers. This is better: Melt one or two blocks of paraffin in a large pot or pail of water. Plucked birds should be rather cold. Plunge bird into the water being sure that the entire bird is submerged. As the bird is withdrawn, a layer of wax will cover the carcass. The wax will set immediately. As the wax is then peeled away, the remaining short feathers, down and pin feathers are removed with the wax. A beautifully clean bird appears! (This will work with plucked quail, also.)

Duck, Quail, Grouse:

Duck, quail and grouse are drawn by opening from the vent along the backbone for removal of the "innards" and cleaning of the cavity.

Marsh Hen — Clapper Rail:

This makes delightful table fare — but, not when plucked. You "gotta skin 'em". Remove the head leaving as much neck as is desired. Insert the fore fingers between the neck and the skin. The rail's skin is rather fragile and is easily pulled apart. Open it up like a pair of long johns. The wings and legs will push out of the skin. Clip off the ends. After drawing, marsh hens need the salt water soak, mentioned above. Even after finishing the washing, your hands might have a better odor if a little vinegar rinse is applied. Most of the "hen's" fat is just under the skin. This and the crazy birds' appearance are the only unpleasant things about hunting the rail except the wind from the wrong direction, or the wind that blows too hard, or the tide that doesn't rise high enough or the boat that gets stranded in the marsh or the fact that you *can* miss the crazy bird with a load of 20 gauge No. 8's!

Jasper Culson Boles

Quail:

Dry plucking rather than skinning the birds conserves their flavor and moisture. They may be carried all day without cleaning but should be drawn as soon as possible even though the feathers should be left on until reaching home. After drawing the quail, wipe the body cavity dry. Hang them in a cool place to season. This will improve their flavor.

132

Tips on Preparation and Serving

Always thaw game in cold water — it helps retain moisture and flavor before cooking.

Mrs. Harold Goller
(Doris Baker)

Doves:

Freezing: Pack doves in 1/2 gallon paper milk cartons, fill with water, seal with masking tape and freeze. Will keep for at least a year.

Serving: 3 to 4 doves per person, if men; 2 doves per person, if women.

Mrs. D. B. Miller, Jr.
(Kitty Parker)

Ducks:

Freezing: Freeze in water in foil pans. If not enough room in freezer, wrap each duck in waxed paper and then in foil.
Defrosting: Defrost ducks in refrigerator.
Serving: 1 duck per person, if men; 1/2 duck per person, if women.

Mrs. C. Fred Manning
(Genie Weston)

Quail:

Rub the quail with a cut lemon before cooking. This tenderizes it and brings out the flavor.
Use currant jelly as a condiment with quail.
Serving: 3 quail per person, if men; 2 quail per person, if women.

Mrs. Harold Goller
(Doris Baker)

Venison:

To remove "gamey" taste from venison, marinate it overnight with cheap white wine. Pour off the wine the next day and proceed with recipe of choice.

Mrs. Robert C. Sykes
(Betsy Cloyd)

The one thing to remember about venison is that it has little or no fat of its own so that if it is not helped a bit, one can end up with a pretty dried up piece of meat! One should also be aware of what kind of deer the piece of meat came from — a champion size buck will invariably be tough, whereas a yearling, etc. can be the most succulent meat ever encountered.

Any venison can be marinated before cooking which certainly can do nothing but help.

Mrs. Nicholson Unger Tucker
(Elizabeth A. Smith)

Bass:

Freeze bass fillets in water — it seems to keep them from drying out.

Mrs. D. B. Miller, Jr.
(Kitty Parker)

Doves

Doves	Salt and pepper
Margarine	Sherry

Place doves in black iron frying pan. Salt and pepper. Dot generously with margarine. Pour enough sherry over doves to allow 1/4 inch sherry in bottom of pan. Cook in 350 degree oven 60 minutes. Baste frequently. Serve piping hot with wild rice. The whole dove or just the breast may be fixed.

Mrs. W. L. Brigham, Jr.
(Nancy Hopkins)

Doves

6-12 doves	Salt
Olive oil	Pepper
Dry mustard	3 teaspoons Worcestershire
Curry powder	sauce
Celery salt	Juice of 2 oranges
Garlic salt	Juice of 1 lemon

Grease doves well in olive oil. Sprinkle doves with curry powder, dry mustard, celery salt, garlic salt and pepper. Place in Dutch oven, add a little water and cover. Cook in preheated oven for 2 1/2 to 3 hours at 250 degrees. Add Worcestershire sauce, orange juice and lemon juice. Cook for 15 minutes or longer until they are tender.

Mrs. L. Jerome Alexandre
(Margot Edwards)

Doves

Doves	Pepper
Salt	Butter

Dress doves. Season with salt and pepper. Brown on both sides in butter. Add water so that the frying pan will be about 1/4 filled with liquid. Turn heat to simmer. Cover and let steam until tender. (This takes about an hour.) Any birds are better if the pan is rather crowded with birds while cooking.

Mrs. George Edwards
(Martha Scoville)

Doves

12 to 14 doves and giblets	Paprika
1/4 cup flour	1 stick butter or margarine
Salt	1/2 cup dry sherry
Pepper	Mushrooms (optional)

Mix salt, pepper, paprika and flour and dust the doves. Melt butter in heavy pan. Brown doves — back side, then breast side. Turn heat to low (simmer). Add giblets (They are trouble to clean, but you will be surprised at the flavor they add to the gravy.) Cover pan. You may have to add water or a little more butter or margarine. Cook on low 2 or 3 hours. (One nice thing is that they can stay on warm without harming them while you wait to get your guests to the dinner table!) Five minutes before serving, add sherry. Mushrooms added to the gravy are very good.

Mrs. D. B. Miller, Jr.
(Kitty Parker)

Dove Pie

12 doves	2 Tablespoons butter
1 cup potatoes, diced small	1 small onion
2 Tablespoons flour	1 cup milk
Salt to taste	1 cup broth
Pepper to taste	

Crust

2 cups plain flour, White Lily	3/4 cup Crisco

Parboil doves until tender. Also potatoes. Line baking dish with crust, and then arrange birds. Chop onion on top of bird very finely. Sprinkle flour on top. Pour in drained potatoes. Salt and pepper to taste. Add broth and milk. Dot with butter. Add top crust and bake one hour until golden brown.

Crust: Cut in shortening until fine. Add ice water until it is mixed well enough to be rolled out.

Mrs. Jasper C. Boles
(Betty Cousins)

Doves à la Bailey

Doves

Salt

Pepper

Flour

Butter or bacon drippings

1 onion

Celery

Water

Salt, pepper and very lightly flour doves (with sifter). Brown in butter or bacon grease in large, heavy frying pan. Pour off excess grease. Add one onion, finely chopped, and an equal amount of chopped celery. Add water so that doves are about half covered. Cover pan and simmer for at least 2 hours or until tender, adding water if needed. To make gravy, remove doves from pan and add one heaping teaspoon flour and brown on high heat. Add water, stirring constantly.

This recipe is excellent for all small game birds. Wild ducks should be quartered or halved and cooked slightly longer.

Ralph Bailey

Breast of Dove on Rice

12 dove breasts

1 1/4 teaspoons salt

Dash of pepper

Almonds, blanched, slivered
  (optional)

1/2 stick butter

3/4 cup New York State sherry

1 cup long grain white rice

2 cups water

Place dove breasts in pot and cover with water. Cover pot and slowly boil for 1/2 hour. Remove doves and place in 2-quart casserole. Add 1/4 teaspoon salt and dash of pepper. Dot with butter, and add sherry. Cover and cook in 350 degree oven for 30 minutes, basting often. Use liquid for gravy.

While doves are cooking, cook rice by bringing 2 cups of water to boil in top of double boiler over direct heat, add rice and 1 teaspoon salt. Cover and cook over boiling water for 40 minutes. Do not lift lid or stir while cooking. Yields 3 cups.

Serve doves on bed of rice. Almonds may be added to gravy and poured over all. Serve with asparagus with pimento slice on top and fresh fruit salad with lemon sauce.

Mrs. Wake H. Myers, Jr.
(Mary Jane Webster)

Charlie's Doves

4 large doves
1/4 cup butter
1 ounce dried Italian or
  canned mushrooms, chopped
1/2 onion, minced
1 Tablespoon flour

Several sprigs parsley and
  thyme, chopped
1/2 cup dry sherry
2 cups game bird stock (or
  Swanson's Chicken Broth)
1/2 cup sliced, stuffed olives
Salt and pepper to taste

Brown birds on all sides in skillet in butter. Season lightly and remove to a casserole. In the same butter brown onion, herbs and mushrooms for 5 minutes. Add flour and stir until it is slightly brown and bubbly. Lower heat, add stock and stir until sauce is smooth. Add sherry and olives, simmer an additional minute or so and check seasoning. Pour sauce into casserole, cover and bake at 350 degrees until tender — about 1 1/2 hours.

Charles P. Ballenger

Salsbury Doves

12 doves
3 slices bacon
1 stick butter
Salt to taste
Pepper to taste

1/2 cup red wine
1/2 can chicken broth or
  consommé
Flour

Cover doves with water. Let come to a boil, and then pour off the water. Cover again with water and parboil, simmering about 30 minutes. Place in casserole with all liquid. Lay bacon over birds and add the butter, salt, pepper, wine and broth. Sprinkle lightly with flour. Cover lightly. Bake in oven about 1 hour at 325 degrees, turning once. When turning, lift bacon off and then put it back on top.

Mrs. Sherrod Salsbury
(Margaret Bundy)

Doves in Wine and Mushrooms

12 doves
Salt and pepper
Crisco
3/4 cup white wine

1 small onion
1/3 cup water
1 can Franco-American
  Mushroom Gravy

138

Salt and pepper doves. Sear in Crisco. Remove and place in baking dish. Slice onion around on top. Add water, and then pour wine over doves. Cover baking dish and bake in 300 degree oven for 3 hours. After 2 1/2 hours add the gravy then continue in oven 30 minutes before serving. Serve over rice.

Marsh hen or clapper rail can also be prepared this way.

Mrs. Jasper C. Boles
(Betty Cousins)

Potted Doves

6 doves	2 Tablespoons Worcestershire
6 slices bacon	sauce
1 cup catsup	1 Tablespoon butter
1 small onion, sliced	Red pepper and hot sauce
Salt and pepper	

Steam birds for 20 minutes on top of stove with a little water. Add seasonings and catsup and place bacon on top of the birds. Cook covered for about 1 1/2 hours or until very tender. Remove cover and brown in oven.

Mrs. Clement F. Haynsworth, Jr.
(Dorothy Merry)

Ducks

Ducks	Bacon
Apples, cut in large pieces	1/4 cup orange juice per duck
Onions, cut in large pieces	1/4 cup red wine per duck

Wash ducks thoroughly after cleaning. Stuff the cavity with pieces of onion and apple. Place each duck in a piece of heavy duty foil. Place a piece of raw bacon on top of each duck. Do not wrap foil now. Brown duck in preheated oven at 425 degrees for 25 minutes. Turn oven to 325 degrees. Add 1/4 cup orange juice and 1/4 cup red wine to each duck. Wrap each duck separately in its foil very tightly and cook 3 1/2 hours. (If very large duck, may need to cook longer.) Ducks do not need to be basted!

Mrs. Fred C. Manning
(Genie Weston)

Duck

2 wild ducks (mallards, red
  heads, pintails or black)
3 cups water
1/2 small can frozen orange
  juice concentrate
1 cup cooking sherry

1 can consomme'
1 medium onion

Lowry's seasoning salt
  to taste
4 thin orange slices
2 kumquats or cherries
Grated orange peel
Sugar

Sauce

1 small green pepper
1 cup duck stock (see above)

Duck: Wash ducks thoroughly in cold water. Place in container and cover with water, orange juice and sherry. Soak overnight in refrigerator. (In a hurry, overnight soaking is not necessary.) Simmer in above stock until tender. Test with fork as some ducks are tougher than others, but 45 minutes is average cooking time. Do not cook until they fall apart. Save 2 cups of stock. Remove ducks and place on broiling pan, breast up. Sprinkle with seasoning salt. Cut 4 thin orange slices and place 2 on breast of each duck. Place kumquat or cherry in between. Sprinkle with grated orange peel and lightly with sugar. Moisten sugar with stock so duck will glaze. Broil in oven 400 degrees until oranges glaze. (If ducks are cold, bake 15 minutes before broiling.)

Sauce: Simmer 3 hours. Put in blender with large tablespoon of flour and whip. Add stock. Pour over duck. Serve with wild rice, watercress salad, and asparagus.

Robert Simms Campbell

Duck with Rice

2 ducks
4 cups water

1 package dried onion soup mix
1 cup raw rice

Place ducks in a large pot and add water and soup mix. When it comes to a boil, turn to low heat and simmer for 2 hours, covered. Remove ducks and add rice to liquid. Cook for 1/2 hour or until rice is soft. It may be necessary to add a little more water to finish cooking rice. Add ducks to rice when done to reheat for a few minutes. Serves 4.

Walter Griffin King

Ducks in Orange Sauce

4 ducks
1 onion
2 stalks celery
2 oranges
1/2 teaspoon salt per duck
1/8 teaspoon pepper per duck
1 cup flour
6 cups bacon grease

1 apple, peeled and chopped
1 teaspoon salt
1/4 teaspoon pepper
2 Tablespoons bacon grease
1 6-ounce can frozen orange
  juice, thawed
1/4 cup water

The day before, wash ducks in cold water, dry and refrigerate. Chop onion and celery coarsely. Add peeled and sliced oranges. Refrigerate. Three hours before serving, sprinkle outside of each duck with salt and pepper. Shake in bag with flour. Brown in bacon grease. Drain and cool. Stuff with onion, celery and orange combined with apple, salt and pepper. Heat oven to 275 degrees. Place 2 tablespoons bacon grease in roaster. Arrange ducks in roaster. Combine orange juice with water. Pour over ducks. Cover and bake 3 hours or until done. Remove ducks whole with stuffing still inside and pour gravy over them.

Mrs. I. L. Donkle, Jr.
(Jean McSween)

Basted Duck with Oyster Dressing

Duck
1 teaspoon salt
1/4 teaspoon pepper
1 quart bread stuffing
1 cup oysters

1/4 cup butter
1/4 cup lemon juice
1/4 teaspoon paprika
1/8 teaspoon thyme

Season duck cavity with salt and pepper. Add oysters, drained and chopped, to bread stuffing. Use oyster liquid as part of liquid to moisten. Lightly stuff duck. Place remainder in separate pan to bake with duck. Mix butter, lemon juice, paprika and thyme. Bake duck on rack in covered roaster in 325 degree oven for about 2 1/2 hours. Baste often with lemon mixture. Baste dressing with duck drippings. Remove cover at the last to brown duck.

Mrs. W. W. Pate, Jr.
(Laura Peace Echols)

141

Wild Duck Louisiane

For *each* duck to be cooked, you will need:

1 onion	1 1/2 strips bacon
1 piece celery	1 Tablespoon olive oil
1/2 green pepper	Salt

Sauce

For *each* duck you will need:

2 1/2 ounces tomato catsup	2 1/2 ounces sherry
1 1/2 ounces Worcestershire sauce	1 teaspoon olive oil
	1 small piece garlic, crushed
1 teaspoon hot pepper sauce	10 drops Tabasco sauce

Wild Rice Dressing

1/2 cup raw wild rice	Thyme
1 4-ounce can mushrooms	Marjoram
1/4 stick margarine	Sage
1/2 pound sausage, crumbled and fried	Salt
	Pepper

Duck: Salt inside and outside of each duck to taste. Put onion, celery, green pepper, and one bacon strip inside each duck. Place 1/2 strip bacon over the breast and pour olive oil over each duck. Cook, uncovered, at 300 degrees to brown. Then cover baking pan with tight cover and cook at same temperature for 2 hours until tender. Do not baste or lift cover during this time.

Sauce: Mix ingredients thoroughly, baste the ducks with the sauce and allow surplus sauce to run into bottom of pan. Cover pan and baste ducks occasionally for 1 hour. Serve with Wild Rice Dressing.

Wild Rice Dressing: Cook rice according to directions on package. Combine the ingredients, seasoning to taste. Place in casserole, heat and serve with the ducks.

Mrs. John Roberts
(Celeste Hamrick)

Roast Wild Duck

Ducks	Oranges
Salt and pepper	1 cup sherry wine

142

Preheat oven to 400 degrees. Season inside each duck with salt, pepper and 1/2 peeled orange. Place ducks in roaster, with sherry. Cook in oven for 2 hours at 375 degrees, basting frequently.

Fred Palmer

Duck Gumbo

2 Mallard or 3 Wood Duck	3 medium onions, chopped
5 large Irish potatoes, diced	8 celery stalks, chopped
or long-cooking white rice	Salt and pepper to taste

Clean birds. Boil them in covered pot until meat comes off bones freely. Remove ducks (save stock) and cut meat into small chunks. Cool stock. Dip the fats and oil from the stock. Add potatoes or rice, onions and celery to the stock. Add salt and pepper. Add enough water to cook the potatoes or rice. Cover pot and cook over medium heat to a firm done. Add meat at last minute to heat. Serve in a semi-liquid state. Serves 6.

W. Herschel Gowan

Ducks Roasted

Frozen ducks	1 onion for each duck
Unseasoned tenderizer	Pepper
Dry sherry, inexpensive	Bacon strips for each bird

Remove ducks from freezer, place in shallow roasting pan and sprinkle heavily with unseasoned tenderizer. Cover bottom of pan with 3/4 inch of inexpensive dry sherry and let ducks thaw overnight. Half way through, turn them over so both sides have a chance to sit a couple of hours in the wine. Place onion in each cavity. Pepper and sprinkle more tenderizer over them. Do not add salt because tenderizer is so salty. Criss-cross with strips of bacon. Pour more sherry over ducks, adding to the juices already accumulated from thawing. Cover with foil, place in slow oven 250 to 275 degrees, and baste every 30 minutes. A mallard or large duck can cook this way in 3 to 4 hours. Teal or smaller duck will be done in 2 hours. More wine can be added during cooking until the last 20 minutes. During last 20 minutes, remove the foil so ducks can brown. For gravy, just thicken the pan juices as desired and season well to serve over wild rice.

Mrs. Nicholson Unger Tucker
(Elizabeth A. Smith)

143

Wild Duck à la Charleston

Wild duck
Onions
Mashed potatoes
Seasonings

1 cup water
Bay leaf
Fat bacon

Cook ducks for about one hour in open roaster. (Start off in 450 degree oven, and then reduce heat to 350 degrees.) Stuff with mashed potatoes, onions, and seasonings. Pour 1 cup water over duck. Add bay leaf and cover breast with fat bacon. Remove from pan when making gravy.

Mrs. Clement F. Haynsworth, Jr.
(Dorothy Merry)

Rare Wild Duck

Duck
Salt

Thoroughly clean duck and remove all pin feathers. Rub duck well with salt. Put in preheated oven 500 degrees in open baking pan and sear 18 minutes only. Watch the clock! Remove and serve immediately.

Men particularly like this recipe and certain gourmets believe rare is the only true method of cooking ducks. Serve wild rice, currant jelly, a tossed green salad and red wine (full bodied). This will delight the true sportsman.

Mrs. L. Jerome Alexandre
(Margot Edwards)

Duck Breasts with Brandy Sauce

4 duck breasts
1/4 pound butter
1/3 cup brandy
 or 1/3 cup bourbon

1/3 cup sherry
1 Tablespoon currant jelly
1 Tablespoon Worcestershire
 sauce

Combine sauce ingredients in a skillet and bring to a boil. Add duck breasts and cover skillet. Reduce heat. Cook 20 minutes or until tender, turning once. Place breasts on serving dish, cover with sauce, and serve immediately.

Mrs. L. Jerome Alexandre
(Margot Edwards)

Wild Duck

2 ducks
1 slice bacon
1 can Campbell's beef broth

1/2 cup dry red wine
Currant jelly
Apricot Dressing, page 147

Wash ducks and salt and pepper them. Stuff with Apricot Dressing. (If ducks are very large, cut them in half and cook dressing in a separate pan. If you do this, add a little extra broth to the dressing.) Place 1/2 slice bacon on each duck. Put ducks in roaster. Mix the broth and wine and pour into roaster to cover bottom about 1/2 inch. For more ducks, use the same proportion of broth and wine. Cook, covered, in 325 degree oven for about 2 hours or until very tender. During the last 1/2 hour brush ducks several times with currant jelly to glaze.

Gravy: Mix enough cornstarch to thicken the gravy with a little cold water. Stir into juices in the roaster, adding more beef broth if necessary to make enough gravy. If the ducks are greasy, let the grease settle and remove from roaster before adding cornstarch.

Mrs. James W. Knox
(Katherine Richards)

Duck Over Charcoal

4 ducks
Salt
Pepper
3 cups wine vinegar
Juice of 4 lemons
1 cup olive oil

2 garlic cloves, pressed
2 chopped onions
1 can chopped pimento
3 Tablespoons soy sauce
1/2 teaspoon oregano
12 strips breakfast bacon

Wash ducks thoroughly in cold water and dry. Season to taste with salt and pepper. Combine vinegar, lemon juice, olive oil, garlic, onions, pimento, soy sauce, oregano, salt and pepper. Marinate ducks in this mixture at least 8 hours. Cook over charcoal fire that has burned down low. Close the top of grill. Cook about 1 1/2 hours. Place 3 strips of breakfast bacon on each bird and cook for 30 minutes more.

Fred Palmer

145

Wild Duck in Soy Marinade

2 wild ducks, quartered
1 13 1/2-ounce can
  pineapple tidbits
1/2 cup soy sauce
1 teaspoon ground ginger

1/4 cup shortening or
  bacon drippings
1 3-ounce can mushrooms,
  drained

Marinate ducks overnight in mixture of pineapple, ginger and soy sauce. Wipe meat; brown in fat. Place in shallow casserole. Pour on marinade and mushrooms. Bake, covered in moderate oven (350 degrees) for 1 1/2 hours, or until tender (add water, if necessary).

Mrs. W. W. Pate, Jr.
(Laura Peace Echols)

Orange Stuffing for Ducks

3 cups toasted bread cubes
1 1/2 cups warm orange juice
8 teaspoons sugar
Salt and pepper
2/3 cup orange sections,
  finely cut

1 egg
1/4 cup melted butter
2 cups diced celery
1/2 cup chopped pecans or
  almonds

Soak toast cubes in orange juice for 15 minutes. Add salt, pepper and sugar. Mix in finely cut orange sections, beaten egg, butter, celery, and nuts. Mix well and stuff into ducks.

Fred Palmer

Currant Jelly Sauce

1 part catsup
1 part currant jelly

1 part sherry

Heat jelly and catsup. Add sherry when ready to serve.
This is good with ducks or lamb.

Mrs. W. W. Pate, Jr.
(Laura Peace Echols)

146

Apricot Stuffing For Game

2 Tablespoons butter
2 Tablespoons chopped onion
1 1/2 cups soft bread crumbs
Salt and pepper

1/2 cup chopped tart apple,
  peeled
1/2 cup chopped dried apricots

Melt butter. Add onion and cook until tender. Stir in other ingredients, and stuff ducks or goose. The blender is good for making bread crumbs. If you cook the dressing separately, add a little Swanson's chicken broth so that it won't be too dry.

Mrs. James W. Knox
(Katherine Richards)

Wild Turkey

Wild turkey
Lemon juice
Salt and pepper
Tenderizer
Herb dressing
Onion
Celery

Eggs
Butter
Fresh oysters
Chestnuts
Bacon strips
Butter, melted

Wash turkey and wipe dry. Generously salt, pepper and tenderize. Stuff with herb dressing embellished with extra onion, celery, eggs, butter, oysters and chestnuts. Dressing should be moist. Pour melted butter over all. Criss-cross with bacon strips, cover and cook in 325 degree oven probably 2 hours, depending on size. Uncover last 20 minutes to brown. Drippings should make excellent gravy, with perhaps a little wine added.

Mrs. Nicholson Unger Tucker
(Elizabeth A. Smith)

147

Braised Wild Goose with Stuffing

1 6-pound wild goose	1 cup or more dry white wine
Salt	1 Tablespoon butter
2 slices bacon	Paprika
1 onion, chopped	Ground pepper

Stuffing

1 pound bulk pork sausage	1 rib celery, finely chopped
1/2 cup long-grain rice, cooked	Few twists of the peppermill
	1 clove garlic, minced
1/4 cup fine bread crumbs	1 teaspoon minced parsley
2 Tablespoons butter, melted	1 scant teaspoon thyme
2 eggs, well beaten	1/4 cup chopped pecans

Rub the cavity of the cleaned goose with salt. Stuff the cavity and secure with skewers, and then stuff the neck, pulling the neck skin under the bird and secure with a skewer. Place two slices of bacon in the bottom of a heavy casserole. Add onion, wine and butter. Place the goose on top, sprinkle with salt, paprika, and a few twists of the peppermill. Cover and place in a preheated 375 degree oven for 1 1/2 to 2 hours. Remove the cover, turn the heat up to 400 degrees and continue cooking until the goose has browned nicely or until the juices run clear when the goose is pierced with a fork, and the legs feel soft when squeezed. (Approximately 20 minutes longer.) A six pound goose will serve six.

Stuffing: Break up sausage, place in a heavy skillet and cook until it has lost its pink color. Pour off all fat. Stir in the rice and all remaining ingredients except pecans. Cook over a moderate heat for 30 minutes. Take off the heat and stir in nuts.

Mrs. W. W. Pate, Jr.
(Laura Peace Echols)

Baked Grouse

Grouse	Corn meal
8 oysters per grouse	Flour
Melted butter	Butter
Salt and pepper to taste	1 bacon strip per grouse

Wipe birds inside and out with damp cloth. Dip oysters in melted butter, and then in corn meal and place inside bird. Make flour and butter into a paste and rub breasts well with paste. Put birds in baking dish with a strip of bacon across each bird. Bake 45 minutes in 350 degree oven, basting well with butter. Serve on toast.

Fred Palmer

Marsh Hens

4 marsh hens
1/2 cup vinegar
4 Tablespoons shortening or
   bacon drippings
Salt and pepper

2 onions, sliced
Flour
3/4 cup water
2 Tablespoons Worcestershire
   sauce

Soak birds in enough water to cover, with vinegar, for 1 hour. Drain and wipe off excess moisture. Salt and pepper to taste and roll generously in flour. Brown onions and remove from pan. Then brown hens in shortening. Place in casserole. Place browned onions over hens and add 3/4 cup water with Worcestershire sauce. Cover and cook 45 minutes to 1 hour at 375 degrees.

Mrs. T. W. Satterfield
(Leoma Neal)

Quail or Doves in Bouillon

Quail or doves
Salt
Pepper
Flour

Water
1 bouillon cube per 6 birds
5-6 Tablespoons bacon grease
1 or 2 onions, chopped

Salt, pepper and flour birds. Dissolve bouillon cube in 1 cup water. Melt bacon grease in an iron skillet. Brown birds, add chopped onions and brown also. Pour off excess grease. Add a little bouillon and cook very slowly, covered, on top of stove until tender, about 2 hours. Add additional bouillon or water when necessary.

Mrs. G. Raymond McElveen, Jr.
(Harriet Felder)

Quail

6 quail
Salt
Pepper
1 stick butter
Flour

1 can mushrooms, chopped
1 cup red wine
Lemon slices
Parsley, chopped

Clean quail, split down back, and salt and pepper lightly. In heavy iron skillet, melt butter. Lightly flour birds on both sides. Golden brown birds (flat down) in skillet and add mushrooms and wine. Simmer a few minutes. Pour everything into long baking dish and cover quail, breast side up, with lemon and parsley. Cover dish tightly with foil and bake at 350 degrees for 1 hour or until tender. Serve over buttered toast.

Robert Freeman

Marinated Quail in Wine Sauce

18 birds, cleaned
1 1/4 cups red wine vinegar
1 1/4 cups red wine (optional)
2 Tablespoons grated orange
  rind

1/4 cup olive or other oil
2 cups chicken broth
1 cup cognac
Salt and pepper
Toothpicks (wooden)

Place birds in roasting pan. Pour vinegar, wine and oil over birds for 12 hours. Turn birds in the mixture so that they are all marinated well. Take birds out of marinator (save). Sprinkle with salt and pepper; secure the legs to the body with toothpicks. Place birds in roasting pan (without marinator sauce). Roast birds in hot oven (450 degrees) for about 10 minutes. Make sauce from drippings, chicken broth, part of marinator, one cup cognac and the orange rind. (Be careful to use only the skin of oranges.) Salt and pepper to taste. Cover the birds with sauce, cover pan and bake until done (30 to 45 minutes) at 350 degrees.

John A. DeJong

150

Quail with Sherry Sauce

6 quail	1 1/2 Tablespoons cornstarch
1/2 cup butter	3 Tablespoons dry sherry
1/2 cup chopped onion	1 cup chicken bouillon
1/2 cup chopped celery	3 Tablespoons chopped parsley

Sauté quail in butter for 10 minutes. Remove from pan. Sauté onion and celery in butter. Stir in cornstarch and add sherry, bouillon and parsley. Pour over quail and cook in 350 degree oven for one hour. Cover with foil until last few minutes of cooking. Serve quail and sauce over rice. (Sauce may be made ahead of time.)

Mrs. John Roberts
(Celeste Hamrick)

Par-Boiled Quail

Quail	Flour
Salt and pepper	Butter

Cover quail with cold water and add salt and pepper to water. Bring to a boil on high heat, lower flame and boil slowly for 1/2 hour. Remove quail from water when tender. Sprinkle a little salt on quail and dredge with flour. Put quail in flat oven-proof dish or pan. Dot with butter. Put in 350 degree oven and brown on both sides, 10-15 minutes on each side. Can also be browned under broiler.

Mrs. H. P. Goller
(Doris Baker)

Roasted Quail with Mushrooms

4 quail	1/2 cup hot water
4 slices thin bacon	1/2 cup mushrooms (if large,
1 Tablespoon butter	cut into pieces)
1/4 cup lemon juice	

Prepare quail. Wrap in bacon and fasten with picks. Place in shallow, buttered pan and cover. Bake at 350 degrees 45-60 minutes, basting often with lemon juice and hot water mixture. When tender, remove from oven, add mushrooms and serve over brown rice.

Mrs. Clement F. Haynsworth, Jr.
(Dorothy Merry)

Salsbury Quail

12 quail
3 slices bacon
1 stick butter
1/2 cup white wine

1/2 cup chicken broth
Salt and pepper
Flour

Cover birds with water and parboil about 30 minutes. Place in a casserole with all the liquid. Add bacon, butter, cut into chips, wine, chicken broth, and salt and pepper to taste. Sprinkle lightly with flour. Cover tightly. Bake about 1 hour in 325 degree oven, turning once.

Mrs. Sherrod Salsbury
(Margaret Bundy)

Broiled Quail

1 dozen quail
1 lemon
Salt
Crushed potato chips

1/2 stick margarine
Paprika
Slivered almonds

Dress the quail and slit them down the back. Simmer them in salted water for about 1 to 1 1/2 hours until tender. Use only enough water to cover them, and do use a Dutch oven or heavy pan with a tight lid. Then remove quail from the liquid and drain well. Rub each quail with a thin slice of lemon. Roll each quail in melted margarine and then in crushed potato chips and place in a large glass casserole. The quail should be spread out with the breast side up. Sprinkle slivered almonds and a slight bit of paprika over each bird. Place the casserole on the center rack of the oven and leave it until the quail are heated through and the nuts are slightly browned. A 400 degree oven is fine to start. Approximate time will be from 20 to 25 minutes, but watch it closely and turn the heat down if necessary to keep birds from browning too fast. Serve casserole right away, directly from the oven.

Good with a brown rice casserole and a tossed green salad.

Mrs. Harold P. Goller
(Doris Baker)

152

Southern Style Quail

12 quail
2 sticks butter
6 Tablespoons flour

4 cups chicken broth
1 cup sherry
Salt and pepper

Clean and wash quail. Salt, pepper and flour the birds. Brown the quail in a heavy skillet or Dutch oven in the hot butter. Remove quail from pan and add 6 tablespoons of flour to the butter in the pan and stir well. Add chicken broth and sherry to the hot flour and butter mixture in the pan. Add more salt and pepper if necessary. Pour this over the cooked quail in a baking dish. Cover baking dish and put in 350 degree oven (preheated) about 1 hour. Serves 12.

Mrs. William M. Webster, III
(Langhorne Tuller)

Quail Riverview

6 quail
Salt and pepper
Flour
1 stick margarine
Water

1 teaspoon Worcestershire
   sauce (approximately)
Dash garlic salt
2 slices lemon

Salt and pepper birds and then flour lightly. Brown birds in margarine on top of stove. Add small amount of water, Worcestershire sauce, garlic salt and lemon. Cover roaster and cook in 350 degree oven for 1 to 1 1/4 hours. Baste birds often. Water may be added if necessary while cooking to have desired amount of gravy.

Mrs. C. B. Cox
(Peggy Cochran)
Riverview Plantation
Camilla, Georgia

Roast Pheasant

2 pheasants
1 medium apple, peeled and
  quartered
1 medium orange, peeled and
  sectioned
1 medium onion, chopped fine
1 stalk celery, cut into small
  pieces
1 stick butter
1 cup sauterne wine
Salt, pepper and paprika

Rub salt, pepper and paprika on inside and outside of bird (about 1/4 teaspoon of each sifted together is sufficient). Mix apple, orange, onion and celery and put into cavity. Close cavity. Melt butter in heavy skillet and brown birds. When browned, transfer them to a covered pan for roasting. Cover birds with leftover butter from browning pan and add enough water to cover the bottom of the pan. Cover and cook for 1 1/2 hours in 300 degree oven. After the birds have cooked for one hour, pour the sauterne over them. In the last half-hour, the birds should be basted about 3 times. Serves 4.

Mrs. Walter H. Swayze
(Ena Cadman)

Pheasant

Pheasant
Salt
1 chicken liver
1 small onion

1/2 package stuffing mix
1/4 stick butter
3 Tablespoons tomato juice
Salt pork

Sauce

1 1/2 cups tomato juice
1 cup dry white or red wine
1 teaspoon Kitchen Bouquet
1 teaspoon Worcestershire
  sauce

Wash bird and salt cavity. Mix cooked chopped chicken liver, chopped sautéed onion, stuffing mix, melted butter and tomato juice. Stuff bird. Lace with narrow strips of salt pork and tie cavity together with string. Mix tomato juice, wine, Worcestershire sauce, and Kitchen Bouquet for basting sauce. Heat oven to 400 degrees. Reduce to 350 degrees when bird is placed in oven. Cook 25 minutes to the pound. Baste often. Use drippings as gravy.

Mrs. William B. Ellis, Jr.
(Caroline Burnett)

154

Pheasant Normandy

2 phcasants
Salt
Pepper

Lemon pepper
2 cups dry sherry
Sour cream

Thoroughly clean and dry pheasants. Season with salt, pepper, and lemon pepper. Place in roaster and add sherry. Cover and bake in 350 degree oven for 1 hour. Baste frequently. Add more sherry, if needed. Remove lid and fill each bird with sour cream. Return to oven. Bake at 400 degrees for 30 minutes or until browned. Serve with wild rice and mushrooms. Serves 4 or 5.

Wild Rice and Mushrooms

1 6-ounce package long grain
  and wild rice

1 6-ounce can mushrooms
2 Tablespoons butter

Cook rice 5 minutes less than directed. Add mushrooms and butter. Pour around pheasant and the drippings and let simmer 10 minutes.

Fred Palmer

Potted Pheasant

1 pheasant, about
  2 1/2 pounds
1 medium onion, thinly sliced
1 Tablespoon butter

1 6-ounce can sliced
  mushrooms, drained
1 pint light cream

Rub inside and outside of pheasant with salt and pepper. Lightly brown onion in butter or margarine. Fill cavity of pheasant with mushrooms and onions. Do not truss. Place pheasant in a deep casserole dish and pour the cream over it. Cover. Bake at 350 degrees for 1 1/2 hours. Uncover. Baste with cream and bake 10 minutes more.

Mrs. James W. Knox
(Katherine Richards)

155

Pheasant à la Lynn

1 pheasant (can substitute
    broiler)
1 1/2 cups sweet white wine
1/2 cup orange marmalade
1/4 teaspoon cinnamon
1/4 teaspoon nutmeg

1 stick butter
1/2 cup almonds
1/2 cup currants
1/4 cup chopped pecans
1 can small button mushrooms

Wash pheasant well. Salt and pepper. Line Dutch oven with tin foil and place bird in center. In a bowl mix wine, marmalade, cinnamon and nutmeg. Pour over bird. Cut butter into squares and put on and around bird. Then sprinkle over all remaining ingredients. Close tin foil tightly over and around bird. Cover and bake in 350 degree oven for 1 1/2 hours, checking and basting about every 20 minutes and being sure to seal tightly after basting.

Mrs. Thomas Mitchell
(Lynn Carroll)

Roast Partridge Bedingfield

Partridges
Salt
Pepper

1 part bread crumbs
1 part chopped walnuts

Butter, softened
1 Tablespoon dry sherry per
    bird

Stuffing
Salt to taste
Pepper to taste

Stuffing: Combine crumbs, walnuts, salt and pepper.

Stuff partridges. Salt and pepper them lightly and spread each with butter. Place in a covered roaster with about 1 cup of water and cook in 325 degree oven 2 hours or until tender. When half done, pour sherry over each bird.

Mrs. James W. Knox
(Katherine Richards)

156

Fried Squirrel

1 small tender squirrel
  per person
1 to 1 1/2 cups cooking oil

1/4 cup salt
Salt and pepper
Flour

Day before cooking: Clean squirrels, allow to soak overnight in water containing 1/4 cup salt.

When ready to prepare meal: Cut squirrels in half, crosswise. Legs may be left on the body or cooked as separate pieces. Sprinkle each piece lightly with salt and pepper and coat with flour. Place squirrels into hot oil in frying pan. When brown (about 10 to 15 minutes) turn pieces on other side and fry another 5 to 10 minutes, until brown. Take squirrels out of grease. Pour off part of grease and make gravy by adding flour while stirring to absorb remaining grease. When flour turns brown, add 3 or 4 cups of water, stirring rapidly. Simmer until thickened. Add salt and pepper to taste.

Mrs. Douglas Kennemore
(Barbara Holloway)

Venison Hors D'Oeuvres

Venison
Dry red wine
Wish Bone Italian Dressing
Salt

Pepper
Garlic, if desired
Flour
Cooking oil

Cut venison into little finger size strips. Pour wine over meat and let marinate 1 hour. Drain and then cover with Italian dressing. Let soak at least 2 hours or overnight in refrigerator. Drain. Season with salt, pepper and garlic. Put flour in brown paper bag. Drop in strips and shake to coat. Fry strips in hot oil until brown and crisp. Drain on paper towels and serve hot.

This deer is dear!

Fred Palmer

157

Venison Roast

1 5-6 pound venison roast	1 Tablespoon salt
1 onion, chopped	2 Tablespoons vinegar
1/4 cup barbecue sauce	Pepper

Barbecue Sauce
"Old Carolina Receipt"

1 Tablespoon black pepper	1 1/4 cups vinegar
1 Tablespoon salt	1/4 cup water
1 small box dry mustard	1 stick margarine or butter
1/4 cup sugar	

Sauce: Mix dry ingredients. Add vinegar, water and mix. Bring to full boil and add stick of butter or margarine and continue to cook until butter or margarine melts. Makes 1 pint sauce. (Good brushed on duck or dove.)

Soak venison in water, 2 tablespoons vinegar and 1 tablespoon salt for 4-5 hours. Remove and wipe dry. Sprinkle lightly with pepper and brush with sauce. Add onion and enough water to cover bottom of covered roaster. Bake in 325 degree oven the first hour; lower heat to 275 degrees for an additional 3 hours. Baste often with sauce and juices from roast.

Variation: Marinate roast in red wine, onion, salt and pepper. Remove, dry and brush with sauce and water and roast in covered roaster for 4 hours.

Mrs. Howard H. Lamar, Jr.
(Betty Hall Shepherd)

Roast Venison

1 haunch venison	Coarse ground black pepper
1 bottle port wine	Salt to taste
1 large jar crabapple jelly	

Hang haunch for 6 to 7 days or refrigerate for 10 days. Cook venison as for rare roast beef. Season with salt and pepper. Baste venison while cooking with sauce made of wine and melted jelly. Serve with wine sauce over venison.

Fred Palmer

158

Roast Loin of Venison

1 loin roast venison
1/2 pound salt pork, cut into
  larding strips
1 small onion, chopped
1 garlic clove, minced
1 Tablespoon parsley, chopped

1/2 bay leaf, crushed
1/2 teaspoon celery seeds
1/2 teaspoon dry thyme
Pepper to taste
4 whole cloves
1 teaspoon beef extract

Fold 2 large sheets of aluminum foil together with a double fold. There should be enough to enclose the roast. Place roast on foil. Lard with pork strips. Stick cloves into loin and sprinkle other ingredients over top. Enclose roast tightly in foil, and cook in 300 degree oven for approximately 45 minutes per pound. Serve hot or cold.

Mrs. William N. Poe
(Katherine "Katie" Little)

Pan Cooked Deer Steaks (Venison)

Venison steaks
Meat tenderizer (unflavored)
Onion salt
Salt and pepper
Flour

Cooking oil
1/4 cup water
1 Tablespoon cooking sherry
  per steak

Sprinkle an ample amount of tenderizer on each side of steak. Season each with onion salt, salt and pepper. Flour steaks and brown very quickly on both sides in 1/4 inch cooking oil. When browned, pour oil off, cut heat to low, and add water. Cover pan and simmer for 1 hour, adding water as needed to keep steam. Pour sherry on each steak for last 5 minutes of cooking. Steak drippings make excellent gravy when thickened.

W. Herschel Gowan

Venison Roast

Leg or saddle of venison
Bacon
2 cups dry white wine
2 cups vinegar
2 cups water
3 pieces lemon
6 cloves

1 small cinnamon stick
3 carrots
1/4 bunch parsley
1/2 teaspoon pepper
Pinch rosemary
1 onion, cut up

Gravy

1/2 cup cream
1 Tablespoon flour
1/2 cup (scant) lemon juice

1/2 cup (scant) orange juice
Sugar
Salt

Remove surplus skin and fibers from venison. Using a larding needle, lard venison heavily with bacon. Bring other ingredients to a boil and pour over meat. Let it stand 1 day in a roasting pan. If meat is not covered by marinade, turn occasionally. Remove meat and brown on all sides. Heat marinade in pan. Add meat, cover and bake at 400 degrees about 3 hours, basting often. If marinade is plentiful, use only part for roasting, adding the remainder during cooking and to the gravy. Remove meat and keep warm.

Gravy: Mix cream with flour. Stir into pan juices until thick. Add lemon and orange juice, sugar and salt. Strain. Slice meat and serve with potato balls, red cabbage and cranberry sauce. Makes 6 generous servings.

Mrs. T. W. Satterfield
(Leoma Neal)

Baked Trout

Trout
Lemon juice
Cracked pepper
Salt
Lemon slices

Butter
Onion slices
Parsley flakes
Fresh parsley

Clean fish thoroughly. (May leave on head and tail.) Squeeze lemon juice over fish. Place the salt, pepper, lemon slices and pats of butter on fish. (Raw onion slices may be used too.) Sprinkle with parsley flakes. Bake a small (1 to 1 1/2 pound) fish at 325 degrees for 30 to 40 minutes. A larger (2 1/2 pounds and over) fish takes 1 hour to 1 hour and 15 minutes. Serve with more lemon and fresh parsley. Serve with chilled Chablis. (A natural brook trout is far preferable to a stocked fish. Bass or salmon may also be used.)

Mrs. L. Jerome Alexandre
(Margot Edwards)

Fried Bass Fillets

10 fillets (from 2 to 3 pound bass)	Salt and pepper
	Paprika
3 cups yellow corn meal	Skim milk
1 cup flour, unsifted	Vegetable oil

Soak fillets in skim milk for 1/2 hour. Shake fillets in meal, flour and seasoning. Preheat oil in frying pan until water jumps 6 inches or more when dropped in oil. Place bass in hot oil. Cut stove down to medium and cook until brown and crispy. Serve with ample lemon wedges and tartar sauce if desired. Serves 6 to 8.

D. Byrd Miller, Jr.

Brook Trout

Trout	Pepper
Corn bread dressing	Butter
Salt	Birch bark

Stuff each trout with the dressing. Season with salt and pepper and dot with butter. Wrap each fish in birch bark and cook about 25 minutes, or until done, over live coals. (This is an old Indian guide method from the Canadian Northwoods.) Foil may be substituted for the birch bark, if necessary.

Mrs. Francis Edgar Haag, Jr.
(Anne Meyer)

161

Old Southern Country Dinner

Dove Pie
Corn Pudding
Field Peas
Tossed Salad
Hot Biscuits — Strawberry Preserves
Coffee or Tea

Duck Dinner

Consommé Solera
Homemade Melba Toast
Wild Duck with Apricot Dressing
Wild Rice and Gravy
Fresh Broccoli with Hollandaise Sauce
Orange and Onion Salad
Refrigerator Rolls
Czarina Cream
Pinot Noir Wine — Coffee

Quail Dinner for 12

Relish Tray of Raw Vegetables
Shrimp Dip
Marinated Quail in Wine Sauce (Double recipe)
Southern Style Quail (Double recipe)
Rice and Livers
Hot Asparagus
Pickled Peach Salad
Hot Rolls
Fresh Apple Cake
Dry Red Wine — Coffee

Dove Supper

Shrimp Delight
Doves à la Bailey
Garlic-Cheese Grits
Artichoke and Hearts of Palm Salad Vinaigrette
Potato Biscuits
Apple Pie
Dry Red Wine — Coffee

Quail Dinner

Quail in Bouillon
Wild Rice
Spinach Soufflé
Tomato Aspic
Pickled Peaches
Onion Crescents
Apple Strudel
Coffee

Trout Dinner

Liver Paté
Tomato Soup Supreme
Baked Trout
Petits Pois
Scalloped Oysters (optional)
Cucumber and Onion Salad
Ice Box Rolls
Coffee Ice Cream with Cointreau
Chilled Chablis or Dry Rhine Wine

Fruits and Vegetables

Baked Mincemeat Apples

Apples	Brandy
Mincemeat	Butter

Use a hard baking apple. Being careful not to cut through bottom and to leave thick sides, cut off tops and scoop out apples. Moisten mincemeat with brandy (preferably apple brandy) and stuff into apples. Put small pat of butter on each apple and bake until done, about 1 hour at 350 degrees. Baste occasionally.

Apples can be used as dessert or as side dish with meat.

Mrs. Robert J. Walker
(Lucille Benson)

Broiled Grapefruit

Grapefruit	Nutmeg
Brown sugar	Sherry
Butter	Maraschino cherry

Cut fruit in half and remove center and seeds. Cut around each section and sprinkle with brown sugar. Add dot of butter and a little nutmeg. Place under broiler for approximately 10-15 minutes. Serve hot with a tablespoon of sherry and a maraschino cherry added before serving.

Mrs. H. B. McBee
(Ava Ferguson)

Fruit Casserole

1 can pears	1 can spiced apples
1 can peaches	1 stick butter
1 can cherries (white)	2 Tablespoons flour
1 can pineapple	1 cup sherry wine
1 can apricots	

Drain juices from 6 cans of fruit and empty fruit into a casserole. Melt butter, add flour and sherry. Pour over fruit and put in icebox overnight. Heat casserole in oven for about 30 minutes and serve.

Mrs. Owen Willis Pittman, Jr.
(Susan Stovall)

Hot Curried Fruit

2 large jars mixed fruit for salads
2 teaspoons curry powder or
  to taste

1/2 stick butter
3/4 cup dark brown sugar or
  to taste

Drain fruit and put into 8-inch square pyrex dish. Melt butter and add curry powder and sugar. Pour over fruit and bake in oven at 350 degrees for about 1 hour.

Good with ham or chicken.

Mrs. W. S. Adams
(Lucy Boyd)

Hot Spiced Peaches

1 large can peach halves (free
  stone variety)
1/2 cup brown sugar

3 Tablespoons margarine
1 teaspoon cinnamon

Pour juice from peaches in large saucepan. Add brown sugar, margarine, and cinnamon and stir to mix. Add peach halves and simmer for 15 minutes. Take out of syrup with slotted spoon and serve as accompaniment with doves or ham. Serves 4.

Mrs. W. A. L. Sibley, Jr.
(Nancy Holland)

Asparagus and Egg Au Gratin

1 cup bread crumbs, buttered
4 hard boiled eggs
3 cups asparagus spears
Salt and pepper

1 cup cheese, grated
1 1/2 cups medium cream sauce
  may be made with juice
  from asparagus

Sprinkle crumbs in bottom of buttered casserole. Mix cheese in hot cream sauce. Place alternate layers of sliced egg, asparagus and sauce in casserole. Sprinkle salt and pepper on each layer. Cover top with crumbs. Bake in moderate oven 30 minutes. Serves 8.

Mrs. Thorne Clark
(Mabel Gossett)

168

Artichokes

Artichokes
Cooking oil
Salt
White pepper
M S G
Garlic powder

Hollandaise sauce for hot
  artichokes
Or —
Mayonnaise
Pinch dry mustard
Worcestershire sauce for
  cold artichokes

Select good fresh artichokes, checking them carefully for dried leaves and worm holes. Cut off the stem level with the base and trim the top off each leaf with scissors. Rinse the artichokes carefully, one at a time, under running cold water. Set them in about 3/4 inch of water in a pot big enough to hold them upright without undue crowding. Dribble about a teaspoonful of cooking oil over each artichoke; sprinkle them well with salt, white pepper, MSG,and garlic powder. Cover the pot, bring to a boil, reduce to a gentle simmer, and cook from 30 minutes for small ones to 45 minutes for large ones. When the artichokes are done, drain them upside down for a few minutes. Serve the artichokes hot with Hollandaise Sauce or chilled or at room temperature with the following sauce:

Mix into mayonnaise a pinch of dry mustard and enough Worcestershire sauce to make the mixture a rich caramel color. Stir until smooth.

Mrs. Edward D. Sloan, Jr.
(Charlotte Ferguson)

Asparagus Casserole

1/4 stick butter
1/2 green pepper
1 can cream of mushroom soup
1 small can pitted ripe olives

1 10-ounce can mushrooms,
  drained
2 hard boiled eggs, sliced
2 cans cut green asparagus,
  drained

Chop and sauté green pepper in butter for 5 minutes. Drain and slice the olives. Arrange in 1 quart casserole in layers and pour soup over all. Heat in 350 degree oven until bubbly. Serves 4 to 6.

Mrs. Kirby Quinn, Jr.
(Louise Albright)

169

Asparagus Casserole

2 cans asparagus
  (reserve liquid)
3 hard boiled eggs

1/2 cup chopped blanched
  almonds

Sauce

3 Tablespoons butter
3 Tablespoons flour
1/2 cup milk

1/2 cup asparagus juice
1/2 cup mayonnaise
1/2 cup cracker crumbs

Sauce: Make sauce with butter, flour, milk and asparagus juice. When thick, add mayonnaise, blend away from heat.

In casserole place layer of asparagus, eggs and almonds. Repeat. Pour sauce over. Put crumbs on top. Heat 30 minutes at 300 degrees. Mayonnaise is the secret.

Mrs. T. J. Benston
(Lyda Gerrald)

Company Asparagus

Canned green asparagus
Butter

Parmesan cheese
Paprika

Get the best canned green asparagus you can find. Drain it well and arrange it in a shallow, well buttered casserole. Dot the asparagus generously with butter and heat it for about 10 minutes in a moderate oven. Remove the casserole from the oven, dot it generously with butter again, sprinkle it heavily with grated Parmesan cheese, and dust with paprika. Put it under the broiler until the cheese is melted and the top is brown.

Mrs. Edward D. Sloan, Jr.
(Charlotte Ferguson)

Broccoli Puff

1 10-ounce package frozen
  broccoli cuts
1 can condensed cream of
  mushroom soup
2 ounces sharp American cheese
  grated (1/2 cup)
1/4 cup milk

1/4 cup mayonnaise or salad
  dressing
1 beaten egg
1/4 cup fine dry bread crumbs
1 Tablespoon butter or
  margarine, melted

Cook frozen broccoli as directed on package, omitting salt; drain thoroughly. Place broccoli cuts in 10 x 6 x 1 1/2 inch baking dish. Stir together soup and grated cheese. Gradually add milk, mayonnaise and beaten egg to soup mixture; stir until blended. Pour over broccoli in baking dish. Combine bread crumbs and melted butter or margarine. Sprinkle evenly over soup mixture. Bake in moderate oven, 350 degrees for 45 minutes, until crumbs are lightly browned. Serves 6.

Mrs. Warren J. Hughes, Jr.
(Jo Carr)

Broccoli Casserole

1 package broccoli, chopped
1 small onion, chopped fine
1/2 cup mushroom soup,
  undiluted
1/2 cup cheese, grated

1/2 cup mayonnaise
1 egg
Salt and pepper to taste
Bread crumbs

Cook broccoli by directions on package and drain. Combine all ingredients. Put in greased casserole, cover with bread crumbs and bake in 350 degree oven 25 to 30 minutes. Cream of chicken or cream of celery soup may be substituted for mushroom soup.

Mrs. Lloyd H. Smith
(Phyllis Page)

Shrimp Sauce For Broccoli Or Cauliflower

1/4 cup chive cream cheese
  (2 ounces)
1/4 cup milk
2 teaspoons lemon juice

1 can frozen condensed cream
  of shrimp soup
2 Tablespoons toasted slivered
  almonds

Blend in saucepan the cheese and milk, then add the soup. Heat and stir until hot. Add the lemon juice and pour over hot, drained broccoli or cauliflower. Sprinkle with the toasted almonds. Makes 1 1/2 cups of sauce. It takes 10 to 15 minutes to make.

Mrs. William Y. Quarles, Jr.
(Patricia Gibson)

171

Corn and Broccoli Casserole

1 8-ounce can cream style
corn (best brand)
1 package frozen chopped
broccoli
2 Tablespoons melted butter

1 cup well buttered crumbs
1 egg, beaten
1 teaspoon thyme
Salt, pepper and garlic salt,
sparingly

Prepare a buttered casserole. Pour boiling water over broccoli, let stand 5 minutes or until separated. Drain, mix all ingredients together except buttered crumbs which is the topping. Put in casserole. Bake 30 minutes at 350 degrees and 15 minutes at 450 degrees to brown. Serves 4 or 5.

Mrs. A. E. Bellune
(Marion Odom)

Broccoli Casserole

1 package frozen broccoli
Grated cheese

1 package frozen creamed
onions

Cook as directed on the package. Place in casserole. Cover with grated cheese. Bake at 350 degrees for 30 minutes.

Mrs. Robert W. Hunter, Jr.
(Nancy Welborn)

Broccoli Souffle

1/4 cup butter
1/4 cup sifted flour
1 1/4 cups milk
1/2 cup grated American cheese
5 eggs, separated

1 1/2 teaspoons salt
1/8 teaspoon minced garlic
1 1/2 cups chopped cooked
broccoli
2 Tablespoons lemon juice

Make a cream sauce with butter, flour, and milk. Add cheese. Remove from heat. Add egg yolks, well beaten with 1/2 teaspoon salt. Add garlic, broccoli, and lemon juice. Sprinkle egg whites with 1 teaspoon salt and beat until stiff. Fold in cheese mixture and mix until blended. Bake for 1 hour at 350 degrees in well greased 1 1/2 quart casserole which has been placed in 1 inch hot water. Serves 6.

Mrs. Ellison McKissick, Jr.
(Noel Parker)

172

Carrot Ring

2 Tablespoons butter
4 Tablespoons flour
3/4 cup milk
2 cups hot carrots, mashed
4 eggs, separated

1 cup soft bread crumbs
1 teaspoon salt
Pepper to taste
3 teaspoons baking powder
1 teaspoon onion

Melt butter in top of double boiler, add flour and blend. Add milk and slightly beaten egg yolks and cook until thickened. Cook carrots very well done, put through sieve and drain. Mix carrots, crumbs, salt and pepper to taste. Fold egg whites, beaten stiff, into carrot mixture and add baking powder. Then add sauce. Pour into a greased and lightly floured ring mold pan. Set this pan in a small amount of hot water in the oven and cook 45 minutes at 400 degrees.

For a vegetable platter, turn out carrot ring on plate, fill center with butter beans and place pickled beets around the outside. This makes a very pretty and different vegetable platter idea for a buffet supper.

Mrs. J. Bruce Harper
(Billie Bowie)

Cauliflower Casserole

1 large cauliflower
1 cup green pepper

1 cup onions

Sauce

3 Tablespoons butter
3 Tablespoons flour
1 1/2 cups milk

1/2 cup cheese
1/2 cup salted peanuts

Separate cauliflower, chop peppers and onions. Cook in salted water until tender.

Sauce: Make cream sauce using butter, flour and milk. Cook until thick. Add cheese and pour over cauliflower in casserole. Top with 1/2 cup salted peanuts, chopped. Cook 30 minutes at 350 degrees. The last 10 minutes an additional 1/2 cup cheese may be sprinkled on top.

Mrs. Ralph McPherson
(Julia Russell)

Coral Cauliflower

1 cauliflower, medium-size
1 cup boiling water
1 teaspoon salt
1 4-ounce jar pimento
1 cup milk

2 Tablespoons butter
2 Tablespoons flour
1 Tablespoon Worcestershire
   sauce
Parmesan cheese

Separate cauliflower into small flowerets; wash in cold water. Boil, covered, in boiling water and 1/2 of the salt until tender-crisp — about 8 minutes. Drain but keep warm. In blender, blend the undrained pimento and milk until combined. In 1 quart saucepan over low heat, melt butter; stir in flour, then pimento mixture; cook and stir constantly until thickened and bubbly. Stir in remaining salt. Pour sauce over cauliflower so that some of the flowerets show. Sprinkle with Parmesan. Serves 6.

Mrs. Lewis Price, Jr.
(Joy Dee Hatchett)

Cauliflower and Mushrooms

2 medium cauliflower
1 pound mushrooms, fresh or
   canned
Butter

2 cups rich cream sauce
1/3 pound Swiss cheese
1 Tablespoon onion juice
Buttered bread crumbs

Cook cauliflower; drain; break into flowerets. Broil mushrooms in butter. Add onion juice and combine all ingredients except bread crumbs. Put into large casserole and top with buttered bread crumbs. Bake until very hot at 350 degrees. Serves 10. (Sharp cheese may be substituted for Swiss cheese.)

Mrs. Otis Garrison
(Ann Massey)

Eggplant Casserole

2 cups cooked eggplant
1 Tablespoon chopped onion
6 Tablespoons butter
1 teaspoon salt
1/4 teaspoon pepper
1/4 teaspoon sage

1 cup saltine cracker crumbs
1 cup cubed cheese
2 eggs, beaten
1 cup milk
Pinch of nutmeg

174

While eggplant is hot, drain and add butter, mix until melted. Add other ingredients and mix well. Put in greased casserole. Bake at 325 degrees until center of mix rises and is set.

Mrs. T. J. Benston
(Lyda Gerrald)

Eggplant Casserole

4 small eggplant
1 large onion, chopped
1 cup bread crumbs
1 stick butter
1 pound sharp cheese

1 cup minced ham
2 eggs
4 slices crisp bacon
Salt and pepper

Peel and boil eggplant in salted water until soft; strain off water and mash. Sauté chopped onion in a little butter. Beat eggs. Grate cheese. Add 1/2 stick butter and 1/2 cup bread crumbs to all other ingredients except bacon. Salt and pepper to taste. Place in greased casserole. Cover with remaining bread crumbs and crumbled bacon. Dot with butter. Bake in 350 degree oven for 45 minutes. Serves 6.

Mrs. Thomas S. James
(Hessie Graham)

Eggplant Casserole

1 large eggplant
1 large onion, diced
1 can mushrooms
1 jar A & P Spaghetti Sauce

1/2 to 1 pound ground beef
Parmesan cheese
Mozzarella cheese

Peel and parboil eggplant in salted water. Slice eggplant. Brown onion and meat (optional). In a 1 1/2 quart casserole, using 1/2 of above ingredients, make layer of eggplant covered with onion, mushrooms, spaghetti sauce, ground beef and Parmesan cheese. Repeat with another layer. Cover top with Mozzarella cheese. Bake at 350 degrees about 30 minutes.

Mrs. Raymond McLees
(Martha Prince)

Creole Eggplant

1 medium eggplant	5 Tablespoons margarine
1 onion	Salt and pepper
1 green pepper	1 1/2 cups ground steak
Flour	2 1/2 cups tomatoes

Cut peeled eggplant into one inch squares. Cut onions into rings and pepper into small pieces. Flour lightly and sauté in melted fat. Add salt and pepper. Put in seasoned meat and tomatoes. Cook without top until done, about 30 minutes. May cook longer if more convenient for the cook.

This is a good dish cooked outdoors rather like a hobo stew.

Mrs. James Griffin, Jr.
(Elsa Rose)

Eggplant

6 slices bacon, crisped and drained	4 tomatoes, chopped
1/4 cup bacon fat in skillet	1 onion, chopped
1 clove minced garlic	2 teaspoons salt
1 green pepper, chopped	Pepper
1 medium eggplant, cubed	2 Tablespoons Parmesan cheese

Cook ingredients except bacon and cheese in covered skillet until tender and thick. Top with cheese and crumbled bacon. Brown under broiler. Serves 4.

Waffled Eggplant
Dip thin slice of eggplant into waffle batter and grill in waffle iron. Serve topped with creamed chicken or ham.

Mrs. Harold Edward Chittenden, Jr.
(Sue Woods)

176

Baked Onions

Large Bermuda onions   Salt
Bacon

Wash and peel onions. Wrap each one in a slice of raw bacon and sprinkle with salt. Enclose each onion in a piece of aluminum foil and bake for 45 minutes at 375 degrees.

This is an easy-to-prepare side dish for steak.

Mrs. Edmund A. Ramsaur
(Dorothy Peace)

Ginger Glazed Onions

16 peeled onions, medium size   1 teaspoon paprika
4 Tablespoons honey   1/2 teaspoon salt
2 Tablespoons butter or   1/4 teaspoon ginger
   margarine

Cook onions in boiling salted water for 20 minutes or just until tender and drain and place in baking dish. Combine remaining ingredients in saucepan and boil 5 minutes. Pour over onions and bake in slow oven at 325 degrees about 10 minutes or until glazed. Baste occasionally. Serves 4-5.

Mrs. Robert J. Walker III
(Lucille Benson)

Onion Pie

1 unbaked pie crust   2 Tablespoons flour
1 pound onions, chopped   2 eggs
2 Tablespoons butter   1 cup half and half or cream
Salt

Sauté onions in butter and take out of pan. Sprinkle salt and flour over them. Beat eggs, mix with cream. Mix onions with cream mixture and pour into pie shell. Bake in 375 degree oven for 30-45 minutes. Serve hot.

Mrs. Roger Varin
(Annemarie Louis)

Green Bean Supreme

1 cup finely chopped onions
2 Tablespoons minced parsley
4 Tablespoons butter
4 Tablespoons flour
2 teaspoons salt
1/2 teaspoon pepper
1 cup sour cream

2 packages frozen French style
  green beans, cooked
1 package sharp cheese
1 can onion rings
2 Tablespoons grated lemon
  rind
Juice of 1 lemon

Cook onions and parsley in butter until tender, but not brown. Add flour, salt, pepper, and lemon rind and juice. Take off heat, add sour cream, and mix well. Add beans, heat and stir. Put in baking dish and top with cheese and then onions. This can be broiled slowly until bubbly and a little brown or refrigerated and heated later. Serves 12-16.

Broccoli spears may be used instead of green beans.

Mrs. William B. Long, Jr.
(Ann Shields King)

Gladys Brinckerhoff's Beans

2 packages frozen Fordhook
  lima beans
2 small cans water chestnuts,
  drained and halved
1 can bean sprouts, drained

2 cans mushroom soup
Ritz crackers, crushed
Lowry's seasoning salt,
  to taste

Cook limas in salted water until not quite done. Drain and add bean sprouts, water chestnuts and mushroom soup. Season to taste. Place in oblong pyrex and top with Ritz crackers. Cook 325 degrees until it has bubbled for 15 minutes.

Mrs. E. Calhoun Haskell, Jr.
(Pat Corbin)

Baked Beans

1 large onion, chopped
1 green pepper, chopped
3 strips bacon
1 Tablespoon Worcestershire
  sauce

1 8-ounce can tomato sauce
3 Tablespoons Karo syrup
Salt and pepper
1 large can pork and beans

178

Cook bacon and remove from pan. Cook onion and pepper in bacon fat until limp. Add tomato sauce, Worcestershire sauce, syrup, salt, pepper and pork and beans. Put in greased casserole and bake in 300 degree oven for 2 to 3 hours. Crumble bacon in last. Serves 8.

Mrs. Joe H. Piper
(Dodie Browning)

Mushroom Casserole

100 fresh mushroom caps	4 scant Tablespoons flour
Butter	100 thin toast rounds
Garlic salt	Paprika
1 quart whipping cream	1/2 cup bourbon
4 egg yolks	Salt and pepper

Lightly sauté mushrooms in butter. Salt lightly with garlic salt. Make cream sauce of cream, egg yolks and flour. In a buttered casserole dish place a layer of mushrooms, toast and cream sauce. Use salt, pepper and garlic salt on each layer. Top layer should be toast. Sprinkle with paprika. Bake at 350 degrees until bubbly. Pour bourbon over top. Serves 25 to 30.

Mrs. L. Jerome Alexandre
(Margot Edwards)

Savory Onions

4 onions (3 inches in diameter)	1/2 teaspoon salad mustard
2 Tablespoons brown sugar	2 Tablespoons melted butter
1 cup chili sauce	Buttered bread crumbs

Cut onions in halves. Cook slowly in frying pan in salted water until almost done. Be careful to keep intact. Keep cut side up. Place in baking dish and top with mixture of brown sugar, chili sauce, mustard and butter. Garnish with buttered bread crumbs. Bake at 350 degrees until topping melts down into onion and bread crumbs brown. Serve with roast beef or steak. Serves 8.

Mrs. B. Allston Ellis
(Virginia Hutchinson)

Vey Casserole

1 onion, chopped
1/2 stick margarine
1 can sliced mushrooms
1 can cream of chicken soup
2 to 4 hard boiled eggs

1 large can small peas
1/2 cup slivered almonds
Worcestershire sauce
Salt and pepper to taste
Potato chips

Sauté onion in margarine. Add mushrooms and soup and heat thoroughly. Add eggs, cut in bite sized pieces, peas and almonds. Season to taste with Worcestershire sauce, salt and pepper. Mix well. Pour into casserole. Let stand in refrigerator overnight. Just before serving, top with crumbled potato chips. Heat in 350 degree oven until bubbly. Serves 8 as vegetable or 4 to 6 as luncheon or supper main dish.

Mrs. David Quattlebaum
(Mary Jane Galloway)

Fried Peppers

4 large green peppers
3 Tablespoons olive or salad
  oil

1 clove garlic
1 1/2 teaspoon salt
1/2 teaspoon oregano

Cut peppers, remove seeds, wash, and cut each into 8-12 pieces.
Heat oil, toss in crushed garlic and cook 1 to 2 minutes. Add rest and cook over brisk heat, stirring. Reduce heat, cover. Cook slowly 15 to 20 minutes. Serves 4.

Mrs. Henry D. Prickett
(Erna Pritzlaff)

Simple Spinach Casserole

2 packages frozen spinach
1 pint sour cream

1 package Lipton's dry onion
  soup

Cook spinach and drain. Combine all ingredients, using onion soup to taste. Put in casserole in 350 degree oven to heat through. Serves 6.
This is simple and tastes fancy.

Mrs. John W. Norwood III
(Jackie Torkington)

180

Corn Pudding

2 eggs
1/4 cup flour
1 teaspoon salt
1/2 teaspoon pepper
2 cans cream style corn

2 Tablespoons melted butter
1 14-ounce or 13-ounce can
evaporated milk
Chopped pecans, if desired

Beat eggs and combine with remaining ingredients. Pour into 1 1/2 quart baking dish. Bake in a pan of water for 1 1/4 hours to 1 1/2 hours in a slow oven at 300 degrees.

Mrs. Gerry Prevost
(Grace Steele)

Spanish Corn

1 can creamed corn
1 cup cooked rice
1 small onion, chopped
1 small green pepper, chopped
2 Tablespoons butter

1 Tablespoon sugar
Salt and pepper
1/4 cup cream
1 egg
Bacon strips

Mix all ingredients except bacon. Place in a casserole and top with bacon strips. Bake in 350 degree oven for 1 hour. Serves 6.

Mrs. R. A. Mattson, Jr.
(Jane MacLean)

Corn and Smoked Oyster Casserole

2 cups cream-style corn
3 eggs slightly beaten
2 cups milk
1 Tablespoon soy sauce
1 Tablespoon sugar
2 Tablespoons flour
1 Tablespoon minced onion

1 3 1/2 ounce tin smoked
oysters
6 butter wafers or soda
crackers
2 Tablespoons chopped parsley
for garnish

Combine corn, eggs, milk, soy sauce, sugar, flour, onion and oysters in large casserole. Sprinkle with crumbs and bake 325 degrees for 1 hour or until mixture sets. Remove from oven and sprinkle with parsley.

Mrs. Hugh Z. Graham
(Hessie Morrah)

Vegetable Casserole

Casserole

1 can peas, drained
1 can cut green asparagus, drained
1 can mushroom soup
1 bell pepper, chopped
1 cup finely cut celery
1 large can mushrooms and juice

1/2 cup chili sauce
1 Tablespoon Worcestershire sauce
1 1/2 cups medium or thick cheese sauce
6 hard boiled eggs, chopped
Ritz crackers
Butter

Sauce

3 Tablespoons butter
3 Tablespoons flour
1 cup milk

1 cup grated sharp cheddar cheese

Sauce: Mix flour into melted butter. When thoroughly mixed add milk and cheese. Heat slowly.

Casserole: Cook pepper and celery in mushroom soup until tender. Mix all ingredients including cheese sauce and put into 2-quart casserole. Cover with cracker crumbs and dot with butter. Bake in 325 degree preheated oven for about 25 minutes until brown. Serves 10-12.

Mrs. Byrd Miller
(Estelle Houston)

Peas and Corn In Sour Cream

2 boxes frozen English peas
2 boxes frozen or canned whole kernel corn
1 cup chopped celery
1 cup chopped green onions
1/2 stick butter

1/4 to 1/2 teaspoon thyme
1/4 to 1/2 teaspoon summer savory (optional)
Salt
Cracked black pepper
1 pint sour cream

Steam vegetables until done. Drain thoroughly. Meanwhile, sauté celery and onions in butter and add seasonings. Combine vegetables and butter mixture in a pan. Add sour cream and heat but do not boil. Serves eight.

Mrs. K. D. Adcock
(Judy Liggett)

Spinach Rockefeller

2 packages (10 ounces) frozen chopped spinach	1/2 Tablespoon garlic salt
1 cup bread crumbs	1/4 Tablespoon thyme
1 small onion, finely chopped	1/2 teaspoon pepper
3 eggs, slightly beaten	1/8 teaspoon red pepper
1/2 cup grated sharp cheese	Salt to taste
1/2 Tablespoon MSG or Accent	Parmesan cheese
	8 medium tomatoes

Cook spinach, drain and set aside. Mix together all other ingredients, except tomatoes, with spinach and put into tomatoes that have been scooped out. Sprinkle Parmesan cheese on top. Place in buttered casserole. Bake in oven 350 degrees for approximately 15 minutes.

Mrs. Heyward Sullivan
(Kay Williamson)

Spinach Soufflé

2 packages frozen chopped spinach, cooked	1 egg, beaten
1 1/2 cups thin cream sauce	1/2 teaspoon salt
	Parmesan cheese

Mix all ingredients together and put in a baking dish. Sprinkle with Parmesan cheese and bake at 350 degrees until set and barely browned on top (approximately 30 minutes).

Mrs. Edmund A. Ramsaur
(Dorothy Peace)

Stuffed Acorn Squash Elegante

2 medium acorn squash
2 cups coarsely chopped onion
3 Tablespoons butter
1 can mushrooms, drained
2 Tablespoons parsley, chopped

Salt
Pepper
1 cup shredded cheese
1 Tablespoon buttered fine
   crumbs

Cut squash in half (from stem) and scoop out seeds. Bake squash, cut side down, in shallow pan 35 to 40 minutes at 350 degrees. Cook onion in butter until almost tender. Add mushrooms and parsley. Season squash with salt and pepper and fill with onion mixture. Top with cheese and crumbs; return to oven and bake 15 to 20 minutes.

Mrs. R. A. Mattson, Jr.
(Jane MacLean)

Aretha Fuller's Squash Casserole

1 pint cooked squash, mashed
1 small onion
3 Tablespoons butter
2 eggs, beaten
1/2 cup cheese, grated

Lowry's salt to taste
Pepper to taste
1/2 cup biscuit crumbs, sautéed
   in more butter

Combine ingredients, season, and cover with sautéed crumbs in 1-quart casserole. Cook, uncovered, at 325 degrees for 30 minutes or until bubbly. Serves 4.

Mrs. Frank Halter
(Shirley Caine)

Squash Casserole

1 1/2 pounds yellow squash
1 can cream of chicken soup
1 cup sour cream
2 small onions, chopped
1 small can pimento

1/4 pound butter
4 carrots, grated
1 package Pepperidge Farm Herb
   stuffing

184

Cook squash in salted water, drain and mash. Add remainder of ingredients, except for 1/2 the stuffing and the butter. Mix well. Line shallow casserole dish with stuffing which has been mixed with butter, reserving small amount for topping. Fill dish with squash mixture, top with stuffing mixture and bake at 350 degrees for 35 minutes.

Mrs. W. H. League
(Elizabeth Flack)

Squash Casserole

2 pounds yellow summer squash,
  sliced
Salt and pepper to taste
1 teaspoon sugar

1/4 stick butter
1/2 package dry onion soup mix
1 cup sour cream

Boil squash just until tender and drain well. Add the other ingredients and blend. Turn into buttered casserole and bake for about 20 minutes in 375 degree oven until mixture begins to bubble. Serves 6.

Mrs. K. D. Adcock
(Judy Liggett)

Zucchini Origanum

1 1/2 pounds zucchini
3/4 cup grated sharp
  cheddar cheese
1 small onion, finely chopped
1 teaspoon crushed oregano (or
  3 teaspoons chopped, fresh)

Salt to taste (preferably
  seasoned salt)
Pepper to taste
Bread crumbs
2 large tomatoes,
  peeled and chopped

Do not peel zucchini; wash and slice rather thin, steam approximately 2 minutes and drain well. Mix zucchini, tomatoes, onion, oregano, 1/2 cup cheese, salt and pepper and place in casserole dish. Sprinkle remaining cheese on top and cover with bread crumbs. Place lid on dish and bake on middle shelf of oven for 30 minutes at 350 degrees. Makes 6 generous servings.

Miss Elizabeth Wicker Mahon

Garlic Tomatoes

4 large firm tomatoes
4 Tablespoons olive oil (more
  or less)
1 onion chopped
2 Tablespoons chopped parsley
  (may use dried)

Salt, pepper and garlic powder
  to taste
Bread crumbs (2 or 3 slices of
  bread)

Peel tomatoes and quarter. Sauté onions and tomatoes in olive oil about 5 minutes. Add part of parsley, salt, pepper and garlic to taste. Remove tomatoes and onions to a baking dish. Top with bread crumbs, rest of parsley and sprinkle on a little more salt, pepper and garlic. Drizzle oil left from sautéing over bread crumbs and bake in 350 degree oven for 20 to 30 minutes. Serves 4.

Mrs. Harry A. Dawes
(Zermah Smith)

Ritzi Tomatoes

Toast rounds
Tomato slices
Cheese slices
Sugar
Salt
Pepper

Minced onion
Minced green pepper
Butter
Parsley
Grated cheese

Butter rounds of toast and arrange in shallow pan. On each round place a slice of cheese and a slice of tomato. Sprinkle with sugar, salt, pepper, and a little minced onion and minced green pepper. Top with a piece of butter and add grated cheese. Cook in 350 degree oven until the tomatoes are cooked and the cheese is brown. Top with a sprig of parsley.

Mrs. John C. Dunson
(Dana Coleman)

Stuffed Tomatoes

6 tomatoes (medium)
2 4-ounce cans of mushrooms,
  chopped
1/2 cup sour cream
2 Tablespoons butter

2 beaten egg yolks
3/4 cup dry bread crumbs
1 teaspoon salt
Dash pepper
Dash thyme

186

Topping

1/4 cup bread crumbs
2 Tablespoons butter

1 1/2 teaspoons garlic salt

Cut out stem and scoop out pulp. Chop pulp fine and measure 1 cup and set aside. Drain shells. Cook mushrooms in butter. Combine sour cream and egg yolks and add to mushrooms with the cup of tomato pulp. Mix well and add bread crumbs, salt, pepper, and thyme. Cook and stir until the mixture thickens. Place tomato shells in baking dish and spoon in mixture.

For topping melt butter with garlic salt and stir in bread crumbs. Then sprinkle over the tomatoes and bake in 375 degree oven for 25 minutes. Remember to put about a tablespoon of water for each tomato in bottom of baking dish so tomatoes will not scorch.

Mrs. Thomas Mitchell
(Lynn Carroll)

Broccoli Stuffed Tomatoes

8 medium tomatoes
1 package frozen chopped
  broccoli
2 Tablespoons minced onion
1/4 cup butter
1/2 cup flour

1/2 teaspoon sweet basil
1/4 teaspoon nutmeg
1/2 cup chicken broth
1/2 cup sherry
1/2 teaspoon salt
1/3 teaspoon pepper

Scald tomatoes, peel and scoop out pulp. Drain tomatoes thoroughly. Place in 6-ounce custard cups. Cook broccoli and drain. Cook onion until transparent in 1/4 cup butter. Remove from heat. Stir in flour, basil, nutmeg. Cook paste, stirring constantly for 3 minutes. Gradually add chicken broth and sherry. Stir until smooth. Cool 3 minutes. Add salt, pepper, broccoli. Stuff tomatoes with broccoli mixture. Place custard cups in pan of hot water. Cook at 350 degrees in oven for 25 minutes.

Mrs. Joe Coble
(Sally Hudson)

Home-Stuffed Potatoes

6 large baking potatoes
   (3 1/4 pounds)
1/4 pound butter or margarine
1/2 pint commercial sour cream

1 teaspoon salt
1/4 teaspoon white pepper
Paprika

Bake potatoes in 400 degree oven until tender — 1 hour. Cut in half lengthwise. Scoop out pulp, reserving shells. Mix potatoes and butter. Then add sour cream, salt and pepper. Spoon back into shells and sprinkle with paprika. Cover and refrigerate until 30 to 45 minutes before serving. Then put into 400 degree oven until piping hot and browned, about 30 to 45 minutes.

Mrs. C. C. Withington, Jr.
(Hamlin McBee)

Whipped Potatoes With Almonds

4 cups cooked mashed potatoes
   (6 medium)
3 cups cream-style cottage
   cheese
3/4 cup sour cream
   (commercial)

2 teaspoons salt
1 1/2 Tablespoon finely grated
   onion
1 teaspoon pepper
1/2 cup toasted almonds
   sautéed in melted butter

Mash potatoes thoroughly. Mix cottage cheese in blender. Mix together warm mashed potatoes and cheese. Add sour cream, onion, salt and pepper. Mix well. Spoon into shallow, buttered 2 quart casserole dish. Brush top with melted butter. Bake in moderate oven (350) for 1/2 hour. Place under broiler for a few minutes to brown. Sprinkle with almonds. Serves 8.

Mrs. William B. Ellis III
(Judy Baarcke)

Quicker Potatoes

Potatoes
Shortening

Butter
Paprika

188

Scrub potatoes (white or sweet). Halve lengthwise and score with paring knife (1/2 inch deep, 1/4 inch apart, crisscross pattern, on cut sides). Brush or rub cut sides with shortening. Bake 425 degrees (on cookie sheet, cut sides still up) for approximately 40 minutes or until tops are brown and crisp. Add butter and paprika after about 30 minutes cooking time.

Mrs. John C. Dunson
(Dana Coleman)

Rice Casserole

1/2 stick margarine	1 rib celery, diced
3/4 cup long grain rice	1/2 cup almonds, slivered
4-ounce can mushrooms with	1 can beef bouillon
juice	1 medium onion, chopped

Melt butter and sauté celery and onion 3 minutes. Add mushrooms and almonds and cook 1 minute. Add other ingredients; put in casserole and bake 40 to 45 minutes at 300 degrees. If using 1/2 can mushrooms, add 1/4 cup water instead of juice. Serves 6.

Mrs. Stanley Ryan
(Elizabeth Shaw)

Green Rice

2 cups uncooked rice	1 pound grated New York State
1 1/2 cups milk	sharp cheese
1/2 cup salad oil	1 cup chopped spring onions
1 cup chopped parsley	plus tops
1 cup chopped green pepper	Salt and pepper to taste
2 garlic cloves, chopped	

Cook rice as usual. When done add milk and other ingredients. Mix well. Pour into greased casserole and bake at 350 degrees 1 hour, covered. Serves 10 to 12.

Good with chicken.

Mrs. T. R. Easterby
(Margaret West)

189

Oriental Rice Casserole

1/2 cup uncooked wild rice*
1/2 cup uncooked long grain
  rice*
1 cup chopped onions
1 cup chopped celery
3 Tablespoons butter
1/4 cup soy sauce

1 3-ounce can sliced
  mushrooms, drained
1 5-ounce can water chestnuts,
  drained and sliced
1/3 cup slivered almonds,
  toasted

Add washed wild rice to 2 1/4 cups boiling water, simmer covered, 20 minutes. Add white rice, bring to boil, reduce heat, cover, and cook 20 minutes longer. Cook onions and celery in butter until tender. Mix all ingredients. Bake in 1 1/2 quart casserole in 350 degree oven for 20 minutes. Serves 8.

* Can use 6-ounce package of long grain and wild rice mix instead and cook according to directions. Reduce soy sauce to 2 tablespoons.

Mrs. Julian Wade, Jr.
(Maggie Echols)

Red Rice

1 cup chopped onions
1/2 cup chopped bell pepper
1 can tomatoes (2 cups)
6 Tablespoons bacon drippings
1 Tablespoon salt

1 teaspoon sugar
3 Tablespoons chili sauce
A dash cayenne pepper
1 cup rice (Uncle Ben's)

Saute' onions and bell pepper in bacon drippings, about 10 minutes. Mix all remaining ingredients and let stand about 20 minutes. Then add to onions and peppers and simmer covered for 30 minutes. If it isn't dry enough, cover and continue cooking, checking about every 5 minutes.

Mrs. Thomas Mitchell
(Lynn Carroll)

Rissotto

1/2 medium onion
2 cloves garlic
1/2 cup butter

1 1/2 cups rice
2 1/2 cups chicken broth
Salt and pepper to taste

190

Chop onion and garlic very fine and sauté in butter. Add rice and stir until rice starts popping. Add broth, salt and pepper and mix well. Put on cover and cook in 325 degree oven for 1 hour. Serves 6 to 8.

The Poinsett Club

Spanish Rice Puff

3 Tablespoons butter	3 hard-cooked eggs, chopped
1/3 cup chopped onion	1/2 teaspoon salt
1 1/2 cups cooked rice	1/2 teaspoon celery salt
1/2 cup grated Parmesan cheese	1 egg white
1/2 cup cooked chopped spinach	1/3 cup mayonnaise

Melt butter in a large saucepan. Add onion and sauté until tender. Add rice, cheese, spinach, eggs, salt, and celery salt. Cook over low heat, stirring frequently until cheese is melted and mixture is hot. Spoon rice mixture into a colorful baking dish. Beat egg white until stiff, but not dry. Fold in mayonnaise. Spread over rice mixture. Broil until topping is lightly browned. Serve as a side dish to shish kabob. Serves 4 to 6.

Mrs. Harvey R. Plonsker
(Madeline Pinsof)

Rice Gumbo

1 cup rice	French fried onions (canned)
1 pound okra	1/2 teaspoon salt
6-8 fresh tomatoes, stewed	Pepper
Bacon, crumbled	1/2 teaspoon sugar

Cook rice. Cut up and cook okra in salted water until tender. Combine 2 vegetables, season and cook until thickened. Taste and adjust seasonings. Serve on cooked rice. Sprinkle with crumbled bacon and crumbled French fried onions.

Mrs. Perry Earle, Jr.
(Louise Jordan)

191

Rice and Livers

4 cups cooked white rice
4 cups cooked wild rice
1 pound chicken livers
3 Tablespoons chicken fat,
  butter or margarine
1 large onion, chopped fine
1 cup chicken broth, homemade
  or canned

Tabasco sauce
2 cups grated cheese
7 teaspoons butter or
  margarine
Paprika
Salt and pepper
14 tomatoes, not too ripe

Mix white and wild rice. Bring chicken livers to a boil in salted water and let simmer 5 minutes. Remove livers from water and cool. Cut them very fine. Put 3 tablespoons chicken fat (butter or margarine) in a frying pan and brown the chopped onions in this until crisp. Add onions (fat, too) and livers to the rice mixture. Add salt, pepper and Tabasco to taste. Add chicken broth to the rice, livers and onions so that it will not be dry. Mixture may be wrapped in individual servings and frozen at this point. If frozen, thaw 2 hours at room temperature or overnight in the refrigerator. Cut large holes in the tomatoes, fill them with the rice mixture. On the top of each tomato filling put: grated cheese, 1/2 teaspoon melted butter and sprinkle paprika (to cover top). Bake at 350 degrees preheated oven for 15 minutes. Be careful not to overcook tomatoes. Serve hot. (Makes 2 extra parts of rice for the ones who want seconds or to be used as stuffing for game birds.) Serves 14.

John A. DeJong

Macaroni Pie

1 8-ounce package vermicelli,
  broken
2 Tablespoons butter
2 cups sharp cheese, grated
1 teaspoon salt

Dash pepper
1 1/2 teaspoons dry mustard
3 eggs
2 cups milk

192

Cook vermicelli in rapidly boiling water for as long as package directs. Drain. Stir in butter and cheese, saving about 1/2 cup cheese for top of pie. Add salt, pepper and mustard. Beat in eggs, then add milk, mixing well. Put in greased baking dish. Sprinkle cheese over top and dot with butter. Bake in 350 degree oven until cheese browns lightly — about 40 minutes.

Mrs. Ralph Bailey
(Pappy Godbey)

Garlic - Cheese Grits Casserole

1 cup grits, cooked
1 1/2 Tablespoons
  Worcestershire sauce
3/4 pound or more grated
  American cheese

1 stick butter
1 clove garlic, grated
Dash of Tabasco
2 egg whites

Cook grits to a thick, but not stiff, consistency. When still hot, add butter, Worcestershire, cheese, garlic and Tabasco. Let cool. Beat egg whites until stiff. Fold into grits. Pour into 2 quart casserole. Just before serving, bake in 400 degree oven for 20 minutes or until slightly brown on top.

This can be put in refrigerator in the morning and served at night. Serves 12.

Mrs. Andrew J. White
(Elizabeth Haynsworth)

Hollandaise Sauce

2 Tablespoons lemon juice
2 egg yolks

1 stick margarine

Put lemon juice and eggs in crockery bowl and set in pan of water over low heat. Divide margarine into three parts. Add 1/3 stick at a time and stir until melted. Sauce will thicken with addition of margarine. Make at the last minutes because continued cooking may cause separation.

Mrs. Lewis W. Thomas
(Lib Leatherwood)

193

Mis' Sallie's Candied Yams

4 or 5 large potatoes
3/4 cup water
1/2 teaspoon nutmeg

1 cup granulated sugar
1/2 teaspoon salt
1/2 cup butter

Select yellow yams. Wash and peel. Cut them lengthwise in 1/4 inch slices. Place in baking pan. Cover with water and boil until tender but not soft. Sprinkle with sugar, salt and nutmeg. Dot with butter and bake until syrup is formed — about 15-20 minutes at 325 degrees. Serves 4 to 6.

Nu-Wray Inn
Burnsville, N. C.

Old South Sweet Potato Pone

3 eggs
1 cup sugar
3 cups grated raw sweet
potatoes

2 cups milk, scalded
1/4 cup butter
Salt and flavoring (nutmeg)
to taste

Beat eggs and add sugar, scalded milk, butter and potatoes and seasoning. Pour in greased dish. Bake in 350 degrees oven for 1 1/4 hours.

Mrs. Sidney B. Paine
(Elaine Brooks)

Baked Macedonia

3 Tablespoons butter
3 Tablespoons flour
2 Tablespoons chopped onion
1 can tomatoes
1 cup cooked rice
1 small can corn

2 hard boiled eggs, sliced or
chopped
2 Tablespoons lemon juice
1 teaspoon Worcestershire
sauce
Grated cheese
Salt and pepper

Cook onion in flour and butter for three minutes, add drained tomatoes and cook. Then add rice, corn, eggs, lemon juice, Worcestershire sauce and salt and pepper to taste. Place in baking dish. Cover with grated cheese and bake at 350 degrees for 30 minutes. Serves 6 to 8.

Mrs. Dan Hair
(Elizabeth Harris)

194

Breads, Stuffings and Soufflés

Cream Cheese Biscuits

1 3-ounce package cream
  cheese

1 stick margarine
1 cup flour

Soften cream cheese and margarine at room temperature and cream together. Blend in flour and shape into rolls in waxed paper. Chill several hours or overnight in refrigerator, slice and bake at 400 degrees on ungreased cookie sheet.

These are good for a buffet since they don't need to be buttered.

Mrs. John Kulze
(Betty Earp)

Drop Cheese Biscuits

2 cups sifted, all-purpose
  flour
2 teaspoons baking powder
1/2 teaspoon salt

1 cup (1/4 pound) grated
  American cheese
4 Tablespoons butter
1 cup milk

Sift flour, baking powder and salt. Add cheese. Cut in butter, fine. Add milk gradually to form soft dough, but do not beat. Drop by teaspoons on greased baking sheet. Bake 450 degrees for 10 minutes. Makes 2 dozen small biscuits.

Mrs. Lewis Price, Jr.
(Joy Dee Hatchett)

Sour Cream Biscuits

3 cups all-purpose flour
1/2 pint sour cream
1 teaspoon salt

1/2 pound margarine
2 egg yolks

Put all ingredients in mixer and beat. Turn out on lightly floured board and roll out three times. Cut into desired size. Bake in 400 degree oven for 10-15 minutes. Freeze, if desired, before cooking. Yields 4 dozen.

Mrs. Newton Stall, Jr.
(Kitty Williams)

Angel Biscuits

5 cups flour
3 teaspoons baking powder
1 teaspoon soda
1/4 cup sugar
1 Tablespoon salt

1 cup shortening
1 package yeast
2 cups buttermilk
2 to 3 Tablespoons warm water

Sift dry ingredients together into large bowl. Add shortening and blend until consistency of meal. Dissolve yeast in warm water and add to above with buttermilk. Mix until smooth. Put into greased bowl, cover and refrigerate. When ready to use, pinch off amount of dough needed and knead. Roll and cut as biscuits 30 minutes before baking time. Bake in preheated oven at 450 degrees for 10 minutes. Dough will keep in the refrigerator for a week or ten days.

Miss Jessie Hunter

Potato Biscuits

1 cup shortening
3/4 cup sweet potatoes, cooked
    and mashed
5 cups sifted self-rising
    flour
1 teaspoon baking powder

1/3 cup sugar
1 egg
1/2 package yeast dissolved
    in a little warm milk
1 cup buttermilk

Cream shortening. Add potatoes. Cream together well. Add flour, baking powder and sugar. Mix. Add egg and yeast in the milk. Add buttermilk. Work together enough to hold together. Roll to 1/2 inch thickness. Cut with biscuit cutter. Place on greased pan. Brush with melted butter. Let rise overnight or from morning to night (the secret). Bake in 400 degree oven until golden brown.

Mrs. Kirby Quinn, Jr.
(Louise Albright)

Refrigerator Rolls

1/2 cup butter or shortening	1 egg (2 yolks for yellow
1/3 cup sugar	rolls)
1/2 cup mashed, cooked	2 packages yeast
potatoes	1/3 cup lukewarm water
1/2 cup scalded milk	3 to 4 cups self-rising flour

Cream butter or shortening and sugar. Add potatoes, eggs, and milk. Mix well. Soften yeast in water and add to mixture. Add 2 cups flour and beat 3 minutes. Add remaining flour to make an easy-to-handle soft dough. Turn out on floured board and knead until dough is elastic, smooth, and satiny. Place in buttered bowl. Grease top of dough. Cover and store in refrigerator. Knead again before shaping. Let rolls rise 2 hours or until doubled in size. Bake at 450 degrees for 10 minutes or until brown.

Mrs. Robert L. Chickey
(Gail Gonce)

Bran Rolls

1 cup shortening	2 eggs, beaten
1 cup boiling water	2 yeast cakes
3/4 cup sugar	1 cup *lukewarm* water
1 1/2 teaspoon salt	6 cups flour
1 cup All Bran	

Mix shortening, boiling water, sugar, All Bran, and salt, stirring until shortening has melted. Let cool until lukewarm. Add yeast cakes which have been dissolved in lukewarm water. Add eggs. Add 2 to 3 cups flour first — then the rest. Mix and blend well. Cover and put in refrigerator until ready to use. This dough is very soft when first made up and so needs to be refrigerated. Make out on floured board, either by rolling out as biscuit dough and making into pocketbook style rolls or by placing in greased muffin pan to let rise. Allow to rise 2 hours in warm place. Bake in hot oven 450 degrees for 10 to 15 minutes or until brown. Yields about 6 dozen rolls.

Mrs. J. E. Arnold
(Lillian Mitchell)

Ice Box Rolls

1/2 cup shortening	2 yeast cakes
2 cups water or milk	2 eggs
1/2 cup sugar	8 cups flour
1/4 cup lukewarm water	1 teaspoon salt

Melt shortening in boiling water or hot milk. Add sugar. Dissolve yeast in lukewarm water and add to mixture. Beat eggs and add, then flour and salt, and beat until smooth. Brush top with melted shortening and place in refrigerator. About 1 1/2 hours before dinner, pinch off amount of dough needed, roll out on lightly floured board and cut or form into desired shape. Place on lightly greased baking pan and let rise about 1 1/2 hours. Bake in a 425 degree oven until lightly brown, about 15 minutes.

Mrs. W. R. Steele
(Lena Edwards)

Onion Crescents

1/2 stick butter or margarine, softened	1 teaspoon dry onion soup mix
	1 can crescent rolls

Stir onion soup mix into softened butter. Spread generously over opened crescent roll triangles. Roll up according to directions on package. Bake as directed.

Mrs. Philip G. Hill
(Marjorie Ellen Fyfe)

Red Horse Bread

3 medium onions, chopped fine	1 Tablespoon baking powder
2 eggs	3 cups corn meal
1/2 to 3/4 teaspoon salt	1 cup flour
1/2 teaspoon pepper	Canned milk
1 Tablespoon sugar	Beer

200

Mix all ingredients, using enough beer and canned milk in equal parts to make a stiff mixture. These are cooked like hush puppies in deep boiling fish fat. Dip teaspoon into cold water each time before dipping into dough to make balls to fry. Large yield.

Mrs. James Griffin, Jr.
(Elsa Rose)

All Bran Muffins

2 cups Nabisco bran
2 cups boiling water
2 sticks plus 2 Tablespoons
   margarine
2 1/4 cups sugar
4 eggs

1 quart buttermilk
5 cups self-rising flour
5 teaspoons soda
1 teaspoon salt
4 cups Kellogg's All Bran
   and Nabisco bran

Place 2 cups Nabisco bran in the boiling water and set aside. Cream margarine and sugar and beat in eggs one at a time. Add buttermilk and stir in the dry ingredients. Add remaining bran plus the bran mixture. Bake at 400 degrees 15-25 minutes. Dough will keep in refrigerator for 6 weeks. You will need a gallon container if you make the full recipe.

Miss Jessie Hunter

Old Fashion Corn Meal Muffins

2 cups un-bolted meal
1/2 cup flour
1 teaspoon salt
1 teaspoon soda
3 Tablespoons sugar

3 teaspoons baking powder
1 cup buttermilk
1/2 stick margarine
Water

Sift meal, flour, salt, soda, baking powder and sugar together; then add buttermilk. Start mixing with spoon, adding water until mixture is of pouring consistency. Heat muffin pans with margarine divided into each section. When melted, pour in batter and stir thoroughly. This recipe makes 2 dozen muffins. Bake at 425 degrees for about 15 minutes or until golden brown.

Mrs. P. O. Hendricks
(Nannie Mae Jones)

Muffins

1 cup self-rising flour
1/2 cup milk
1 egg

2 heaping Tablespoons
  mayonnaise

Drop in greased muffin tins. Fill about 1/2 full. Bake at 450 degrees until done. Makes 12 muffins.

Mrs. Donald Harrison
(Barbara Farr)

Cornbread or Corn Muffin

2 cups cornmeal
3 Tablespoons plain flour
1 teaspoon baking soda
1 teaspoon baking powder
2 Tablespoons sugar
1 teaspoon salt

2 heaping Tablespoons Crisco
  or 1/4 cup oil
1 cup buttermilk
2 eggs
Cold water

Sift dry ingredients together into mixing bowl. Cut in Crisco. Mix in milk and eggs alternately, with mixer. Add amount of cold water to make consistency of cake batter. (If you substitute oil, add after milk and eggs.) Bake at 450 degrees for 20 to 25 minutes. Yields 1 dozen large muffins or good size pan of cornbread.

Mrs. Azelee Beeks

Homemade Melba Toast

Bee Slim Diet Bread (or any
  other thinly sliced bread)

Butter

Spread bread slices on both sides with softened butter. Remove crusts. Cut each slice lengthwise into three pieces. Bake in preheated 250 degree oven about 45 to 60 minutes, or until golden and crisp. We think this is the best bread to serve with caviar. For croutons, simply cut the bread into small squares before baking.

Mrs. James W. Knox
(Katherine Richards)

202

Homemade Loaf Bread

1 Tablespoon shortening
  or margarine
1/3 cup sugar
1 cup water

1 package yeast
1 egg
1 teaspoon salt
3 cups plain flour

Work shortening and sugar together. Add 1/2 cup boiling water. Cool. Dissolve yeast in 1/2 cup lukewarm water. Add salt, egg and yeast to shortening and sugar. Sift flour and mix thoroughly. Beat while adding flour. Dough will be almost runny. Cover dough with thin cloth and refrigerate overnight. Next day place dough on floured board and knead well. Use a good deal of flour to take up slack. Grease square loaf pan with unsalted shortening. Place dough in it and let rise to top of pan. Bake at 350 degrees for 30 minutes.

Mrs. A. Welling LaGrone
(Martha Dunson)

Apricot Bread

1 package apricots
1 cup sugar
2 Tablespoons butter
1 egg
1/4 cup water
1/2 cup orange juice

2 cups sifted flour
2 teaspoons baking powder
1/4 teaspoon baking soda
1 teaspoon salt
1 or 2 boxes raisins (small)

Soak apricots in warm water to cover for 30 minutes. Drain and cut into strips. Cream sugar and shortening. Add egg, water and orange juice to creamed mixture. Sift together flour, baking powder, soda and salt. Add gradually. Stir in apricots and raisins and allow to stand 30 minutes. Pour into well greased loaf pan. Bake in oven at 350 degrees for 1 1/4 hours.

Mrs. J. Cranston Gray
(Nell Johnson)

Banana Bread

3/4 stick butter
1 cup sugar
2 eggs, separated
1/2 teaspoon salt
2 cups plain flour

3 large or 4 small very ripe
  bananas, mashed
1/2 teaspoon soda
1 cup chopped pecans

Cream butter and sugar and add egg yolks and salt. Add flour. Add soda to mashed bananas and combine. Fold in stiffly beaten egg whites. Add nuts. Bake in oven in 2 small or 1 large teflon loaf pans at 350 degrees for 30 to 40 minutes.

Mrs. J. Henry Silton
(Nancy Morris)

Cinnamon Bread

Bread

1 package yeast
1/4 cup very warm water
1/2 cup sugar
2 cups flour

1 Tablespoon salt
2 cups warm milk
1/2 cup Wesson oil
Cinnamon sugar

2 Tablespoons butter
1 cup confectioners sugar

Icing

1 or 2 teaspoons canned milk
1 teaspoon vanilla

Bread: Dissolve yeast in warm water. Sift in flour, sugar, and salt. Add milk and Wesson oil to make a thin batter. Let rise 2-4 hours (until bubbly). Then add enough flour to knead well. Divide dough into thirds. Pat out on floured board. Sprinkle generously with cinnamon sugar. Roll up and place in 3 greased 7 1/2 x 3 1/2 x 2 1/4 loaf pans. Turn in pans to grease tops. Let rise approximately 1 hour. Bake at 325 degrees until brown, about 45 minutes. Remove from pans and ice immediately.

Icing: Brown butter. Mix with sugar and canned milk. Add vanilla. Add a little more sugar if necessary to make a thin icing.

Mrs. G. Lee Daniel
(Virginia Kay)

Mrs. Sloan Banister's Dill Bread

1/4 cup warm water
1 yeast cake (dissolved in
  warm water)
1 Tablespoon butter
1 cup cottage cheese
1 egg
2 Tablespoons sugar

3/4 teaspoon salt
1/4 teaspoon soda
2 teaspoons dill seed
1 Tablespoon minced onion
2 1/4 to 2 1/2 cups plain
  flour, sifted

Melt, but do not boil, butter and cottage cheese and mix in egg, dry ingredients and yeast; add flour and knead until satiny smooth. Let rise until doubled (1 hour) in warm place in greased casserole. Punch down and form into 2 balls. Cover and let rise 10 minutes. Shape into 2 loaves and place in greased loaf pans. Let rise until double (about 45 minutes). Bake in moderate oven (325 degrees) for 50 to 60 minutes, covering with foil the last 20 minutes to prevent over-browning.

Mrs. Harold Stuckey
(Leila Barr Sullivan)

New England Brown Bread

3/4 cup sifted flour
1 1/4 teaspoon soda
1 teaspoon salt
1 cup finely crushed graham
  crackers

3 Tablespoons shortening
1 cup buttermilk
1 egg, well beaten
1/2 cup molasses
1 cup seedless raisins

Sift flour, soda, and salt together. Mix in cracker crumbs. Cut in shortening with pastry blender until mixture resembles fine meal. Mix rest of ingredients and stir in until well blended. Pour into 2 well greased No. 303 cans, filling each a little over half full. Bake 45 to 50 minutes at 375 degrees. Let cool 10 minutes, then open other end of can and push through.

Mrs. Henry Truslow
(Gretchen Smith)

Cranberry Bread

2 cups flour
1 cup sugar
1/2 teaspoon salt
1/2 teaspoon soda
1 1/2 teaspoons baking powder
1 beaten egg
Grated rind of one orange

2 Tablespoons melted
  shortening
1/2 cup orange juice
2 Tablespoons hot water
1/2 cup chopped nuts
1 cup sliced fresh cranberries

Sift dry ingredients together and add other ingredients. Mix well. Bake in a greased and floured loaf pan at 325 degrees for one hour and ten minutes. Place in refrigerator for 24 hours. Slice when cold.

Mrs. Henry E. Barton
(Sarah Guess)

Loaf Bread with Prunes

2/3 cups chopped prunes
Orange rind
1 package yeast
3/4 cup lukewarm water
Salt to taste
1 egg, beaten

1/3 cup crushed bran flakes
1 full Tablespoon melted
  butter
1 full Tablespoon Grandma's
  Molasses
3 cups flour

Soak prunes in water to cover and simmer with a piece of orange rind until tender. Cool. Dissolve yeast in lukewarm water in large bowl. Add egg, salt and about 1 1/2 cups flour. Beat until smooth. Add prunes, molasses, bran flakes and butter. Add enough flour to make a soft dough — about 1 1/2 cups. Put in air-tight bowl and let it begin to rise well. Grease top of dough before placing in refrigerator overnight. Next day, knead well and place in a greased bread pan. Spread top with melted butter. Cover with a cloth and let rise to top of pan. Bake at 325 degrees about 30-35 minutes. Rub the entire loaf well with butter while hot. Makes good toast.

Mrs. F. W. Poe, Jr.
(Dit White)

Whole Wheat Bread

1 packet active dry yeast
1/2 cup packed brown sugar
3 Tablespoons shortening
3 Tablespoons honey

1 Tablespoon sugar
1 teaspoon salt
3 cups whole wheat flour
3 cups all-purpose flour

Soften yeast in 1/4 cup warm water. Combine next 5 ingredients in 1 cup boiling water in large bowl. Add 3/4 cup cold water. Cool to lukewarm. Stir in softened yeast. Add flour gradually to form a stiff dough. Knead on lightly floured surface about 7 to 10 minutes, until dough is smooth. Place in greased bowl and cover. Place in warm place (85-90 degrees) until light and doubled in size about 2 hours. Punch down and let rise 30 minutes. Divide in half. Shape into loaves and place in two 9X5X3-inch loaf pans. Cover. Let rise in warm place until doubled in size 1 hour to 1 1/2 hours. Bake in oven at 350 degrees for 50 to 60 minutes. Remove from pans at once.

Mrs. W. Thomas Brockman
(Bernice Wood)

Sally Lunn

1 yeast cake (envelope or
    powdered)
1/2 cup lukewarm water
1 1/2 cups sweet milk
1/2 cup shortening
1/2 cup sugar

3 eggs
4 cups flour
1 teaspoon salt
1 heaping teaspoon baking
    powder

Soak yeast in 1/2 cup lukewarm water. Scald 1 1/2 cups sweet milk. While hot, melt 1/2 cup shortening in it and add 1/2 cup sugar. Beat three eggs until light and when milk is cool, add eggs and yeast. Sift flour with salt and add baking powder. Add to milk mixture to make a very stiff batter. Beat until smooth. Put in well greased steeple cake pan. Allow to rise one hour in a warm place. Bake in a slow oven for one hour. While hot, cut in wedges and put butter between them. If any is left over, it makes delicious toast.

Mrs. Mason L. Carroll
(Blanche Lindsay)

Garlic Bread

1 loaf French bread
1/2 pound corn oil margarine
1 teaspoon Peacock's garlic
  juice

Parmesan cheese
Romano cheese
Sesame seeds
Paprika

Melt together over low heat margarine and garlic juice. Slice bread lengthwise and then in slices. Dip three sides of bread (not crust) into margarine and garlic juice mixture. Place on baking sheet and sprinkle top with cheese, sesame seeds and paprika. Wrap well in tin foil and refrigerate until one hour before cooking. Take out of refrigerator at least one hour before baking in 400 degree oven until brown. Serves 6-8.

Mrs. Charles R. Duncan
(Peggy Jelks)

Indian Bread

2 cups whole wheat flour
2 cups all purpose flour
1 teaspoon salt

2 Tablespoons clarified butter
1 1/2 cups water (cold)

Sift together dry ingredients, mix in clarified butter and add enough of the water to make a stiff dough. Cover bowl and let stand for 2 or 3 hours and then knead well. Divide into 8 pieces, form into balls and flatten into circles with rolling pin or hands (like tortillas). Bake on a hot griddle or skillet. Turn and cook on other side. Eat while hot with India Curry dishes.

Buttermilk Pancakes

2 cups all-purpose flour
2 cups buttermilk
2 teaspoons baking soda
1/2 cup oil

1/3 cup sugar
1 teaspoon salt
2 eggs

Sift dry ingredients into mixing bowl. Add milk and then beat in eggs and oil. Cook on hot griddle. Serves 6-8.

Mrs. Azelee Beeks

Pan Cakes

1 1/4 cups flour	1 egg, beaten
1/2 teaspoon salt	3/4 cup milk
3 teaspoons baking powder	3 Tablespoons melted butter or
1 heaping Tablespoon sugar	bacon grease

Sift together flour, salt, baking powder and sugar. Beat egg and add to milk. Add melted shortening. Add liquid ingredients to the flour mixture. If too stiff, add a little more milk. Drop by tablespoon on hot electric frying pan or griddle which has been slightly greased. Makes about 10 pancakes.

Mrs. W. Ben Dunlap
(Martha Workman)

Hominy Spoon Bread

1 cup grits	2 Tablespoons butter, melted
2 1/2 cups milk, scalded	4 eggs
1 teaspoon salt	1 teaspoon baking powder

Add grits and egg yolks to scalded milk and cook over hot water until thick. Add salt and butter. Cool slightly. Separate eggs. Beat egg whites until stiff. Add egg whites and baking powder to grits. Put in 2 quart buttered baking dish. Bake at 350 degrees for 45 minutes. Serves 8.

Mrs. C. Douglas Wilson
(Lois Mundy)

Chicken Spoon Bread

1 can cream of chicken soup	1/2 cup cooked chicken
3/4 cup milk	1 Tablespoon butter
1/2 cup corn meal	2 eggs

Mix soup, milk, meal and chopped chicken. Heat and add butter. Cool and add egg yolks. Beat egg whites stiff and fold in mixture. Put in casserole. Place casserole in shallow pan of water and bake at 300 degrees for 45 to 60 minutes.

Mrs. Sarah F. Bates
(Sarah Bates)

Eleanor Walker's Spoonbread

1 cup yellow cornmeal
3 cups milk
2 Tablespoons butter

1 teaspoon salt
1 teaspoon baking powder
2 eggs, beaten

Combine cornmeal and milk in double boiler and cook for about a half hour or until mixture is mush. Stir in butter, salt, and baking powder. Add this to beaten eggs, slowly while beating. Fold into greased casserole. Bake 30 minutes at 375 degrees.

Mrs. Frank Halter
(Shirley Caine)

Stickies

1 recipe of roll dough
1 apple, fresh
Butter for dotting

Cinnamon and sugar for
sprinkling

Roll rather thin and cut dough as for small biscuits. Put very small piece of fresh apple in center of each biscuit. Sprinkle with sugar, cinnamon and small dots of butter. Bake at 425 degrees for 15 to 20 minutes.

Mrs. C. C. Berry
(Willie Scoville)
Berry's-on-the-Hill
Orangeburg, South Carolina

Lula's Coffee Cake

2 cups sifted plain flour
2 cups and 4 Tablespoons sugar
1 stick margarine
1 stick pure butter
1 cup sour cream
2 eggs, well beaten

1 cup chopped nuts
1 teaspoon cinnamon
1 teaspoon baking powder
1/2 teaspoon salt
1 teaspoon vanilla

Combine sugar, eggs, butter and cream well; add sour cream, flour, baking powder and flavorings. Add 3/4 cup nuts. Pour into well greased tube cake pan. Sprinkle top with remaining 1/4 cup nuts. Bake for one hour in a 350 degree oven.

Mrs. John A. Kuhne
(Lucy Simpson)

210

Nut Filled Coffee Cake

1 1/2 cups flour
1/4 teaspoon salt
3/4 cup sugar
3 teaspoons baking powder

1/4 cup shortening
1 egg
1 teaspoon vanilla
1/2 cup milk

Filling

2 Tablespoons flour
1/2 cup brown sugar
2 teaspoons cinnamon

2 Tablespoons melted butter
1/2 cup chopped nuts

Sift flour, baking powder, salt and sugar together. Cut in shortening until mixture is like corn meal. Blend in beaten egg mixed with milk. Add vanilla and blend. Pour half the batter into greased and floured 6 x 10-inch baking pan. Sprinkle with half the filling. Add the remaining batter and sprinkle remaining filling over top. Bake at 375 degrees for 25 to 30 minutes.

Mrs. Frank Olechovsky
(Olga Tasker)

Moravian Sugar Cake

Cake

3 eggs, beaten
1 package dry yeast
1 cup warm water
1 cup sugar

1/2 cup butter, softened
1 cup mashed potatoes
1/2 teaspoon salt
5 cups flour

Topping

Light brown sugar
Cinnamon

Butter

Dissolve yeast in warm water. Mix sugar, butter and potatoes. Add eggs, yeast mixture, flour and salt. Let rise 3 to 4 hours. Stir down. Pour into 2 greased, shallow pans. Spread thin. Punch holes close together (with finger) all over top of cakes. Sprinkle lavishly with light brown sugar, hunks of butter and cinnamon. Let rise about 2 hours. Bake in 350 degree oven 25 to 30 minutes.

Miss Kay McCoin

Swedish Tea Logs

I — Make the Dough the First Day

1 package dry yeast
1/4 cup very warm water
2 1/4 cups sifted flour
2 Tablespoons sugar
1 teaspoon salt

1/2 stick butter and 1/2 stick
  margarine, softened
1/4 cup evaporated milk
1 unbeaten egg

Soften yeast in warm water. Sift together flour, sugar and salt into large mixing bowl. Cut in butter and margarine. Stir in milk and then egg. Add yeast and mix well. Cover and chill overnight.

II — Next Day Make Filling

1/2 stick butter
1/2 to 3/4 cup brown sugar

1/2 to 3/4 cup chopped pecans

Cream butter and sugar and add nuts. Divide dough into thirds. Roll out one part on waxed paper, lightly floured, to a 12 X 6-inch rectangle (very thin). Spread with 1/3 of the filling. Roll up and seal edges, starting on the 12-inch side. Shape into a crescent and place on a cookie sheet, lined with foil. Make cuts along outside edge at 1-inch intervals. Twist cut pieces. Repeat with other dough. Let rise in warm place approximately 1 hour. Bake at 350 degrees 20-25 minutes.

III — Make Vanilla Glaze While Logs Bake

2 Tablespoons butter
1 cup sifted powdered sugar
1/2 teaspoon vanilla

1-2 Tablespoons evaporated
  milk

Brown butter and add sugar and vanilla. Stir in evaporated milk until spreading consistency is reached. Frost cake while it is hot. Makes 3 logs.

Mrs. G. Lee Daniel
(Virginia Kay)

Timbales

2 eggs	1 cup flour
1 teaspoon sugar	1/4 teaspoon salt
1 cup milk	2 cups Mazola oil

Mix flour, sugar and salt. Beat milk slowly into mixture. When well mixed, beat eggs in lightly. Heat oil to 370 degrees in small, deep container (such as a coffee tin) so that oil will cover iron. Heat iron in hot oil and drain. Dip iron into batter being careful not to cover top. Cook about 25 seconds or until browned slightly. Remove from iron with cheese cloth. This recipe yields about 40 timbales or rosettes.

Serve with chicken salad, creamed chicken or fruit of any kind.

Mrs. Emmett L. Reid
(Winona Ray)

Pet and Parmesan Spread for French Bread

| 1/2 cup Pet evaporated milk | Onion salt or garlic salt |
| 2/3 cup grated Parmesan cheese | Baked French bread |

Mix milk and cheese; let stand about 5 minutes to thicken. Season. Spread on bread, wrap in foil and heat in oven.

Mrs. K. D. Adcock
(Judy Liggett)

Herb Butter

| 1/4 pound butter | 2 Tablespoons herbs |

Use any one of these minced herbs: dill, garlic, parsley, mint, tarragon, basil, thyme, savory, chives or marjoram. Cream butter and herb. Put in a container and refrigerate. Use a pat of herb butter on a serving of meat.

Can be put into a food decorator for fancy designs or used as spread on bread or crackers or on baked potato.

Mrs. James H. Austin
(Elizabeth Reid)

213

Easy Sausage Dressing

1 bag Pepperidge Farm Herb
  Seasoned Stuffing
1 pound sausage, cooked
  and drained
4 slices bread, broken up
1 whole onion, chopped

2 stalks celery, chopped
1/2 apple, chopped
Milk to moisten (about
  1 to 1 1/2 cups)
Sage to taste
Salt and pepper to taste

    Mix all dry ingredients. Moisten with milk and mix. This can be used to stuff turkey, hen, goose, etc.

Mrs. Rex L. Carter
(Floride Gulledge)

Great Grandmother Newton's Chestnut Dressing

2 pounds uncooked chestnuts
1/2 pound pork sausage
1/2 pound ground beef or veal
Bouillon or broth

5 or 6 cups bread crumbs
  (part cornbread)
1 stalk celery, chopped
Seasoning to taste

    Boil nuts until tender, peel remaining husks and grind or chop fine. Cook celery in bouillon or broth. Cook ground meat and sausage in iron skillet until done, drain off fat and add cooked celery, bread crumbs and chestnuts. Add broth to soften slightly. (Liquid celery was cooked in can be added.) Add seasoning to taste. Stuff turkey or cook in patties.

Mrs. Howard Newton, Jr.
(Jourdan Jones)

Dressing

6 cups crumbled cornbread
5 cups crumbled biscuits
3/4 stick butter
1 cup chopped onion
4 eggs, slightly beaten
1 cup chopped celery

6 to 8 cups chicken or
  turkey stock
1/2 teaspoon pepper
1 1/2 teaspoons salt
2 teaspoons sage

    Mix all ingredients well. Bake in pans at 350 degrees for 1 to 1 1/2 hours. Serves 25.

214

Sausage Stuffing

1 pound Jones sausage (best to defrost day before)
1 9-inch pan cornbread, crumbled
10 slices white bread, broken up
1 egg, beaten
1 1/2 cups celery, chopped fine
1 large can mushrooms, drained
Consomme' (optional)
Butter
Salt
Poultry seasoning

Mix first six ingredients and add poultry seasoning to taste. Add consomme', if more liquid is needed, when dressing is stuck together. Stuff turkey, the inside of which has been rubbed with salt. Rub turkey on outside with butter, salt it, and cover with a greased dish cloth. At end take cloth off and let it brown. Bake in 300 degree oven approximately 20 minutes per pound, dressed, and baste every half hour with stock or turkey gravy. If there is extra dressing, put in pan to bake and remove from oven when done.

Mrs. Schuyler Campbell McPherson
(Schuyler Campbell)

Welsh Rarebit

Small amount butter
2 generous cups grated sharp New York State cheese
1/4 bottle beer
1 egg
1 teaspoon Worcestershire sauce
Salt
Pepper
Dry mustard

This should be made in top of double boiler. Line pan with small amount of butter. Add cheese. When the cheese is melted, pour in beer. After this is mixed, add beaten egg. Stir quickly. When done, pour in Worcestershire sauce. Add salt, pepper and dry mustard to taste. Serves six.

Mrs. Heyward Mahon Sullivan
(Kay Williamson)

Cheese Casserole

1/2 pound grated sharp
  cheese
8 slices bread, minus crust
  and buttered
3 or 4 eggs

2 cups milk
1/2 teaspoon salt
1 teaspoon dry mustard
Pepper

In casserole put layer of bread and one of grated cheese. Repeat layers. Beat together eggs, milk, salt, pepper and mustard. Pour mixture over bread and cheese. Chill 1 hour or overnight. Bake at 350 degrees for 35 minutes. Serves 4.

Mrs. William H. Orders
(Carolyn Lee)

Cheese Souffle

1/2 stick butter
1/4 cup flour
1 1/2 cups milk
1/2 cup grated cheese

1/2 teaspoon salt
1/8 teaspoon dry mustard
1/8 teaspoon paprika
3 eggs, separated

Make sauce by melting butter, adding flour, and then adding milk. Stir until thick, and add cheese, salt, mustard and paprika. Beat egg whites until stiff. Beat egg yolks and add to sauce. Fold in whites. Pour into large greased casserole and bake at 350 degrees for 45 minutes.

Mrs. Newton Stall, Jr.
(Kitty Williams)

Hominy Grits Souffle

3/4 cup fine grits
1 teaspoon salt
1 cup boiling water
1/4 cup butter

1 Tablespoon sugar
3 large eggs
1 3/4 cups milk

Add salt to boiling water and pour in grits. Stir constantly until grits have absorbed all water. Put in top of double boiler, add 1 cup milk and cook for one hour. Remove from heat; add butter, sugar, 3/4 cup milk and beaten eggs. Beat until lemon color. Turn into buttered 2 quart casserole. Bake at 325 degrees for 1 hour. Serves 6.

Mrs. R. A. Mattson, Jr.
(Jane MacLean)

216

Desserts

Chocolate Dessert

1 1/4 cups sugar
1 cup flour
2 teaspoons baking powder
1/2 teaspoon salt
1/2 cup milk
1 teaspoon vanilla

1 square unsweetened
  chocolate
2 Tablespoons butter
1/2 cup brown sugar
4 Tablespoons cocoa
1 cup water

Mix and sift 3/4 cup sugar, flour, baking powder and salt. Add milk and vanilla. Melt chocolate square and butter and add to first mixture. Pour into greased pan, 7x11 1/2 inches. Now mix 1/2 cup sugar, 1/2 cup brown sugar, and cocoa. Sprinkle over top of batter. Then very slowly pour 1 cup water over it. Bake in a 350 degree oven for 40 minutes. Serve topped with ice cream or whipped cream.

Mrs. Frank P. McGowan
(Gena Bryant)

Chocolate Soufflé

2 envelopes unflavored
  gelatine
2 cups milk
1 cup sugar
1/4 teaspoon salt
4 eggs, separated

12-ounce package semi-sweet
  chocolate pieces
1 teaspoon vanilla
1/2 teaspoon ground cinnamon
  (optional)
1 cup heavy cream, whipped

Sprinkle gelatine over cold milk in saucepan. Then add 1/2 cup sugar and egg yolks which have been mixed well. Add chocolate pieces. Cook over low heat, stirring constantly, until gelatine and chocolate are melted. Remove from heat; cool, stirring occasionally. Beat egg whites until thick, gradually adding the other 1/2 cup sugar, vanilla and cinnamon. Fold into thick, cooled chocolate mixture. Fold in the whipped cream. Turn into serving dish. Chill until firm. Top with additional whipped cream, if desired. Serves 10-12.

Mrs. Rex Rice
(Gladys Smith)

Jiffy Pots de Creme

3/4 cup milk
1 cup (6 ounces) semi-sweet
  chocolate bits
1 egg

2 Tablespoons sugar
1 teaspoon vanilla (or rum)
Pinch salt

Heat milk just to boiling point. Place all other ingredients in blender and add hot milk. Blend at low speed one minute. Stir with rubber spatula to remove bubbles. Pour into small cups and chill several hours. Serves 4-5.

Mrs. Charles W. Bazemore
(Nancy MacCalla)

Ruth's Chocolate Refrigerator Cake

2 bars German chocolate
1 Tablespoon water
4 eggs, separated
1 Tablespoon sugar

1 1/2 cups whipping cream
1 teaspoon vanilla
2 dozen plain lady-fingers

Melt the chocolate (over water) with water. Separate eggs. Beat yolks in large bowl with sugar. Mix chocolate with yolks. Beat whites stiff; whip cream and add vanilla. Add whites and cream to chocolate mixture. Line greased spring-form pan with lady-fingers (split) and pour in 1/2 chocolate mixture. Put another layer of lady-fingers and pour in balance of mixture. Let stand in refrigerator 24 hours. Serve with additional whipped cream (as icing on top) and toasted, slivered almonds.

This is very rich, but so delicious. It may be used as a birthday cake for a special party.

Mrs. George M. Grimball
(Dot Glover)

Mocha Mousse

1 package chocolate pudding
  mix (3 3/4 ounces)
1 teaspoon instant coffee

1 1/2 cups milk
1 8-ounce package cream
  cheese

Mix pudding mix, coffee and milk. Cook, stirring constantly, over medium heat until mixture comes to full boil. Add cream cheese, cubed. Beat until well blended. Pour into lightly oiled 1 quart mold. Place wax paper on surface to prevent film formation, and then chill. Remove paper, unmold, garnish with whipped cream and chocolate curls or grated chocolate. Serves 8-10.

Miss Inez Goldsmith

Frozen Chocolate Jubilee

3/4 box vanilla wafers, crushed
4 Tablespoons melted butter
2 cups powdered sugar
1/2 cup butter
2 squares chocolate, melted

1 teaspoon vanilla
3 egg yolks, beaten
3 egg whites, stiffly beaten
1 quart vanilla ice cream, softened
1 cup chopped nuts

Line 9x12-inch pan with wafer crumbs mixed with melted butter. Cream sugar and butter; add melted chocolate, vanilla and egg yolks. Fold in egg whites. Spread mixture on crust; chill until firm. Spread softened ice cream on top; sprinkle with nuts (slightly press into ice cream). Freeze. Cut into squares to serve. (For variety, substitute peppermint ice cream and top with shaved chocolate instead of nuts.)

Mrs. Thomas G. Hawpe
(Kitty Faulconer)

Czarina Cream

1 pint heavy cream
1 envelope Knox unflavored gelatine
1/2 cup sugar

1/4 cup blanched, slivered almonds
1 teaspoon vanilla
1/4 cup sherry

Whip cream, slowly adding sugar. Soak gelatine in 1/4 cup cold water and dissolve over hot water. Let cool and add to whipped cream. Add vanilla, sherry and slivered almonds. Put in a 1 1/2 quart ring mold and refrigerate until set. Unmold on serving plate, and in the center, place a glass or silver sauce dish of thawed frozen raspberries to spoon over the slices of Czarina Cream.

Mrs. James W. Knox
(Katherine Richards)

221

Whiskey Ice Box Cake

2 envelopes gelatine
1/2 cup cold water
1/2 cup boiling water
6 eggs, separated
8 Tablespoons whiskey, or
   1/2 cup whiskey

1 cup sugar
1 teaspoon lemon juice
1 pint whipping cream
2 1/2 packages lady fingers,
   split

Soak gelatine in cold water. Then add boiling water and dissolve. Beat egg yolks until thick. Add whiskey *very slowly*. Beat in the sugar. Add lemon juice. Stir in gelatine and chill a short time. Whip cream and fold it in. Beat egg whites and fold in. Line sides and bottom of a spring form pan (about 12 inches) with split lady fingers. Pour the mixture in slowly. When about half way, put in layer of lady fingers. Then, when filled, place a layer of lady fingers on top in a design. Chill overnight in the refrigerator.

Mrs. A. Newton Stall
(Helen Hunt)

Gypsy

1 quart milk
4 eggs, beaten together
1 cup sugar
Ladyfingers or sponge cake
   slices
Almonds

2 teaspoons vanilla
1/2 cup sherry
1 pint cream, whipped, sweetened
   and flavored to taste with
   additional sherry

Make custard by scalding milk and adding gradually to eggs and sugar which have been mixed together in double boiler. Stir over medium heat constantly until thickened. Remove from heat; add vanilla. Cool. Line a 1-quart serving bowl with lady fingers or sponge cake slices which have been stuck full of almonds which have been blanched and slivered or halved. (Better, if toasted) Sprinkle cake with sherry. Pour custard over this. Top with whipped cream. Chill overnight in refrigerator before serving.

This dessert is a special holiday dessert commonly served in Abbeville during the Thanksgiving and Christmas seasons.

Mrs. Frank Shaw
(Ellen Gibson)

Frozen Egg Nog

1 egg yolk
3 Tablespoons whiskey
1/2 pint heavy cream
1/2 cup pecans, chopped
1/2 cup vanilla wafer crumbs

1 small bottle cherries,
  chopped
1 egg white
1/4 cup sugar

Beat egg yolk until thick. Slowly add 3 tablespoons whiskey. Beat 1/2 pint heavy cream. Fold 1/2 cup chopped nuts and cherries into cream. Beat egg white until foamy and gradually add 1/4 cup sugar. Beat until holds peaks. Fold cream into yolks and then fold into whites. Line ice tray with crumbs. Spread mixture and freeze. Serve in slices.

Mrs. Kirby Quinn, Jr.
(Louise Albright)

Lemon Ice Box Cake

1 envelope gelatine
1 cup sugar
4 egg yolks and whites,
  separated

Rind of 1 lemon
Juice of 2 lemons
1 pint whipping cream
18 fresh lady fingers (plain)

Dissolve gelatine in 1/4 cup cold water. When dissolved, fill cup with warm water and stir thoroughly. Beat egg yolks and sugar together. Add juice and lemon rind to beaten egg yolks, add gelatine mixture (no longer warm), fold in stiffly beaten whites, and then stiffly whipped cream. Pour into spring form pan which has been lined with halves of lady fingers, the rounded sides turned out, the round bottoms cut off straight. In lining bottom and sides, fill all holes with pieces of lady fingers, to prevent seepage of lemon mixture. Make crumbs from remaining lady fingers, brown lightly under flame in oven and sprinkle over top, if desired. Place in refrigerator. Before serving remove sides of pan, leaving bottom of pan under cake. Serves 12.

Mrs. H. William Carter, Jr.
(Margaret Kelley)

223

Essie's Boiled Custard

1 quart milk	3 eggs
1 cup sugar	Vanilla

Beat 3 eggs in bowl and add sugar to the beaten eggs. Take about one cup of the milk and mix with the eggs and sugar. Have the remaining milk in a double boiler. Add the egg, sugar and milk mixture to the milk in the *double boiler*. Flavor with vanilla. Cook on high until water comes to a boil; then turn to medium heat for about 1 hour or until thick. Stir to keep from lumping or sticking. Serve hot or cold.

Mrs. Gordon Brown Sherard, Jr.
(Ann Cheves)

Aunt Sarah's Apple Macaroon Pudding

1 egg	1/4 teaspoon salt
3/4 cup sugar	1/4 cup chopped raw apples
5 Tablespoons flour	1 teaspoon almond extract
1/4 cup nuts	1 1/4 teaspoons baking powder

Beat egg lightly, add sugar; sift baking powder, flour and salt together and add to egg mixture. Add flavoring. Then add nuts and apples. Cook in 350 degree oven until brown. Serve with whipped cream or ice cream. This will fall and you may think it's ruined, but it's easy and good.

Mrs. Perry Earle, Jr.
(Louise Jordan)

Fruit With Honey Dressing

2 medium canteloupes, in balls	1 teaspoon orange rind, grated
1 can (1 pound 4 ounces)	Juice of one large orange
pincapple tidbits, drained	2 teaspoons lemon juice
1 cup seedless green grapes	1/4 cup pale colored honey
1 cup raspberries or	Dash of salt
blueberries	1 sprig of mint (optional)

Empty first four ingredients into a bowl. Make a sauce of the next five ingredients and add to the fruits. (This is especially good with fruits in season.) Garnish with a sprig of mint.

Mrs. B. S. Williams
(Lillian West)

224

Poached Pears in Cointreau with Cocoa Cream Fluff

9 firm pears
Juice of 1/2 lemon
4 1/2 cups water

3 cups brown sugar
1 cup cointreau

Cocoa Cream Fluff

1 pint whipped cream
6 Tablespoons powdered cocoa

2 Tablespoons powdered sugar

Peel pears — leave whole with stems. Put *at once* into deep pan of cold water that has juice of 1/2 lemon in it. (This prevents discoloration.) Make syrup of water and sugar bringing to boil and boiling a few minutes. Put pears in and cook until tender. Be careful not to overcook as they become mushy. Fill a teacup with cointreau and when pears are done, dip each into the cup for a minute or two. Continue to cook juice until moderately thick. Then add cointreau in which pears were dipped. Pour this syrup on pears and chill until served.

Cocoa Cream: To a pint of whipped cream add 6 tablespoons powdered cocoa and 2 tablespoons powdered sugar. Mix and serve separately.

Mrs. Harvey Plonsker
(Madeleine Pinsof)

Raspberry Bombe

1 quart raspberry sherbert
1 pint heavy cream, whipped
2 or more Tablespoons kirsch
(vanilla can be used)
1/2 cup chopped walnuts

1/4 cup chopped maraschino
cherries
1 1/2 cups sifted
confectioners sugar

Mix nuts, cherries, kirsch and sugar with whipped cream and line 1 1/2 quart mold with part of mixture. Freeze until firm. Place sherbert in hollow in center. Cover with rest of mixture. Cover with waxed paper and place in freezer for three hours. Place in refrigerator 45 minutes before unmolding to serve.

A very pretty Christmas or summer dessert.

Mrs. T. J. Benston
(Lyda Gerrald)

225

Raspberry Dessert

10 vanilla wafers
  (approximately)
1/4 pound butter
2 cups powdered sugar, sifted

2 eggs, beaten
1/2 pint whipping cream
1 package frozen raspberries

Grease 8x8-inch pan and line bottom with vanilla wafer crumbs. Cream butter and sugar until smooth; add eggs. Spoon onto vanilla wafer crumbs; smooth with knife. Whip cream and add drained raspberries to cream. Add this mixture on top of butter and sugar mixture. Chill for several hours before serving. Serves 9.

Mrs. John E. Johnston
(Caroline Cannon)

Cream Pineapple Cake

1 large orange chiffon cake
2 envelopes plain gelatine
1/2 cup water or orange juice
3 egg yolks, beaten
2 cups milk
1 cup sugar
3 egg whites, beaten stiff

1 No. 2 can crushed pineapple,
  drained
1 pint cream, whipped
Crushed nuts
Cherries
1/2 pint more cream, whipped

Soak gelatine in water or orange juice. Mix egg yolks, sugar and milk. Cook in double boiler until it coats spoon. Add gelatine to this mixture and cool. Add drained pineapple. Fold in beaten egg whites and whipped cream. Break cake into chunks. Put layer of cake into greased steeple pan and pour over it 3 cups of mixture. Continue until all is used (about 3 times). Refrigerate until set and then turn out. Decorate with more whipped cream, crushed nuts and cherries, if desired.

Mrs. W. M. Waters, III
(Virginia Steele)

Sherbet in Orange Cups

1/2 orange per serving
Pineapple sherbet

Fresh grated coconut
Meringue

Cut oranges in half, cross-wise, and scoop out to rind (allow 1/2 orange for each serving). To pineapple sherbet add fresh grated coconut. (Other combinations may be used.) Put in freezer until ready to use. Place scoop of meringue on top and run under broiler to brown. Serve at once.

Mrs. J. M. Gregg
(Martha Norment)

Lemon Sherbet

1 package lemon Jello
2/3 cup hot water
1 1/2 cups sugar
Juice of 3 lemons

Rind of 2 lemons, grated
Pinch of salt
1 quart sweet milk

Dissolve Jello in hot water. Add sugar, lemon juice, lemon rind, and salt. Pour milk into Jello and juice mixture. Blend well and put in freezer, stirring occasionally until frozen.

Mrs. Perry Earle, Jr.
(Louise Jordan)

Fruit Freeze

2 cups sugar
3 cups water
1 large can pineapple juice
1 1/2 cups orange juice

1/4 cup lemon juice
3 medium size ripe
   bananas, mashed

Boil water and sugar for 10 minutes and then combine ingredients and freeze in aluminum loaf pans (takes about 4 pans). To serve, fill parfait glass half full of freeze mixture and finish filling glass with chilled ginger ale. (Also good served as sherbet with ginger ale.) Garnish with fresh fruit, blueberries, strawberries, sliced banana or mint leaves with a maraschino cherry. Serve in parfait glasses with straws and spoons.

Mrs. Richard P. Coen
(Mary Catherine Reid)

Sour Cream Sherbet

1 cup sour cream
1 cup milk
1 1/2 cups sugar

1 egg, well beaten
1 cup grape juice
1/4 cup lemon juice

Combine ingredients in order listed. Beat until sugar is dissolved. Pour into two refrigerator trays and freeze until nearly firm. Turn into chilled bowl. Beat until fluffy, smooth but not melted, with chilled rotary or electric beater. Return to trays and freeze firm. Serves 6.

Mrs. B. Allston Ellis
(Virginia Hutchinson)

Lemon Ice Cream

7 lemons
2 cups sugar
1 quart milk

2 eggs
1 Tablespoon flour
1 pint cream

Slice 2 lemons as thinly as possible and let sit overnight with 1 cup sugar. Make a custard with the milk, eggs, flour, and other cup of sugar, by adding the flour and sugar to the well beaten eggs. Add milk slowly while stirring. Cook over low heat, stirring constantly, until the custard coats a spoon. Cool. Add cream, the lemon and sugar mixture, and the juice of 5 lemons. Pour into churn and churn until frozen. Serves 8.

Mrs. Earle R. Stall
(Nelle Mackey)

Home-Made Ice Cream

2 cans Eagle Brand milk
4 eggs
1 quart homogenized milk
1 quart crushed peaches

1 cup sugar
2 teaspoons vanilla flavoring
Juice of one lemon

Peel and slice peaches; let stand in sugar and lemon juice 1 hour, then crush. Beat eggs. Add Eagle Brand milk. Mix with remaining ingredients. Churn in one-gallon hand-crank or electric ice cream churn. May be made with other fruit.

Mrs. Robert N. Daniel, Jr.
(Dickie Jordan)

228

Creme de Menthe Parfait

2 ounces Bols Creme de Menthe
1/2 cup crushed pineapple
   and juice
1 cup water
1 cup sugar

1/2 cup white corn syrup
Dash of salt
1 quart vanilla ice cream
3 drops green coloring

Boil all ingredients together, except Creme de Menthe and, of course, the ice cream. When pineapple is clear, add Creme de Menthe. Let cool and make parfaits in usual manner, alternating sauce and ice cream.

Mrs. T. J. Benston
(Lyda Gerrald)

Chocolate Sauce

6 squares unsweetened baking
   chocolate
2 cups sugar
1 stick butter or margarine

1/4 teaspoon salt
1 tall can evaporated milk
1 teaspoon vanilla

Heat chocolate, sugar, margarine and salt in top of double boiler until chocolate is melted. Add milk and vanilla. Stir until smooth. May be reheated as needed.
   Delicious on ice cream.

Mrs. T. V. Howie
(Jane Satterfield)

Chocolate Sauce

3 squares chocolate
3/4 stick butter
1 cup sugar

1/2 cup *hot* water
1 teaspoon vanilla

Melt butter, chocolate and sugar together. Add hot water. Cook slowly until a little thicker than canned syrup. This burns easily. When done add vanilla. Serve hot on ice cream.

Mrs. Maye R. Johnson
(Motsy Crosland)

Caramel Sauce

1/4 cup granulated sugar
1 small can Carnation
  evaporated milk

1 cup sugar
1/3 stick margarine

Caramelize sugar in iron frying pan. Heat other ingredients and add to caramelized sugar. Put in double boiler and cook until thick.

Serve on ice cream with toasted, salted almonds, pecans or cashew nuts.

Mrs. T. C. Gower
(Kathryn Smith)

Caramel Pie

Filling

1/4 pound softened butter
5 egg yolks
4 Tablespoons flour

2 cups sweet milk — room
  temperature
2 cups sugar
1 teaspoon vanilla

Meringue

5 egg whites
5 teaspoons sugar

1 10-inch baked pie crust

Filling: Beat yolks until light. Add one cup sugar, flour, and butter. Add milk and heat to boiling point, stirring constantly. Let stand in double boiler while you caramelize one cup sugar in iron skillet. Add to mixture and cook until thick, stirring constantly. Remove from heat, add vanilla, and pour into crust.

Meringue: Beat egg whites and sugar until stiff. Cover pie with meringue. Cook at 350 degrees until lightly browned. Serves 8-10.

Mrs. Gordon B. Sherard
(Eleanor Bronough)

Macaroon Souffle

2 cups milk
1 1/2 cups crushed macaroons
3 eggs, separated
1/2 cup sugar

1 teaspoon almond extract
1 Tablespoon gelatine
1/4 cup water
Whipped cream

230

Heat milk in double boiler. Add macaroons. Beat egg yolks with sugar. Add to milk mixture. Cook, stirring constantly until thickness of thin custard. Add almond extract and gelatine, softened in water. Let get cold. Fold in stiffly beaten egg whites. Pour into mold or souffle′ dish and refrigerate to set. Serve with whipped cream.

Mrs. A. T. Odell
(Kina McGlothlin)

Tea Time Tassies

Pastry

1 3-ounce package cream cheese	1 stick margarine
	1 cup sifted plain flour

Filling

1 egg	1 teaspoon vanilla
1 cup brown sugar	Dash of salt
1 Tablespoon soft margarine	2/3 cup broken pecan meats

Pastry: Let cream cheese and margarine soften at room temperature. Blend. Stir in flour. Chill 1 hour. Shape in 2 dozen balls. Place in tiny ungreased 1 3/4 inch muffin pans. Press dough in bottom and up sides of cups.

Filling: Beat together egg, sugar, butter, vanilla and salt. Divide 1/2 the nuts among cups. Add about 1 teaspoon of filling on top of pecans and top with remaining pecans. Bake at 325 degrees for 25 minutes,until filling is set. Cool and remove from pan.

Mrs. Julian L. Wade, Jr.
(Maggie Echols)

Pecan Pie

3 eggs, beaten	1/8 teaspoon salt
3/4 cup sugar	1 teaspoon lemon juice
3/4 cup corn syrup	1/4 teaspoon maple flavoring
2 Tablespoons melted butter	1 cup pecans

Pour into unbaked pastry shell and bake in 350 degree oven for 45 minutes.

Mrs. Charles P. Scoville
(Polly Clary)

Macaroon Pie

12 double saltines,
  rolled fine
12 dates, chopped fine
1/2 cup chopped pecans

1 cup sugar
1/4 teaspoon baking powder
3 egg whites, beaten stiff
1 teaspoon almond extract

Put almond extract into egg whites and beat stiff. Fold egg whites into dry mixture and pour into well-buttered pie plate. Bake 20-25 minutes in 350 degree oven. Top with whipped cream.

Mrs. J. Philip Coyle
(Dottie Hilburn)

Maple Nut Chiffon Pie

3/4 cup maple syrup
3 eggs
Pinch salt
1 Tablespoon plain gelatine

4 Tablespoons cold water
6 Tablespoons sugar
Graham cracker crust pie shell
Chopped pecans

Separate eggs. Heat syrup, beaten egg yolks and salt in double boiler until mixture thickens, stirring constantly. Soak gelatine in cold water, add to hot mixture and stir until dissolved. Cool. Beat egg whites until frothy. Add sugar. Fold egg whites into above mixture and put in pie shell. Chill. When ready to serve, sprinkle with chopped pecans. Serves 6-8.

Mrs. Walter S. Griffin, Jr.
(Nelle Mills)

Egg Custard Pie

3 eggs
1/2 cup sugar
1 cup milk

Vanilla
Nutmeg
2 Tablespoons butter

Mix eggs, sugar, milk, vanilla, and butter and pour into unbaked pie shell. Sprinkle with nutmeg. Bake at 350 degrees until golden on top — about 45 minutes.

Mrs. Allen Armstrong
(Randolph New)

Black Bottom Pie

Crust

1 1/2 cups crushed Zwieback	6 Tablespoons melted butter
1/4 cup powdered sugar	1 teaspoon cinnamon

Crust: Mix these ingredients well and place in deep pie pan or spring form pan and pat along the sides and bottom to make crust. Bake in moderate oven for 15 minutes.

Filling — Step 1

1 Tablespoon gelatine	1 cup sugar
2 cups rich milk	4 teaspoons cornstarch
4 egg yolks, beaten	1/2 teaspoon vanilla
until light	1 teaspoon almond extract
1 1/2 ounces melted chocolate	

Filling — Step 1: Soak gelatine in 1/2 cup cold water. Scald milk. Combine beaten egg yolks, sugar and cornstarch, gradually stir in the milk, and cook over hot water until custard will coat a spoon. Take out 1 cup of custard and add chocolate to it. Beat until well blended and cool. Add vanilla and pour into pie shell. Dissolve gelatine in remaining custard, cool, but do not permit to stiffen, and stir in almond flavoring.

Filling — Step 2

3 egg whites	1/4 teaspoon salt
1/4 cup sugar	1/4 teaspoon cream of tartar

Filling — Step 2: Beat egg whites and salt until blended, add cream of tartar and beat until stiff, gradually add sugar, fold in remaining custard and cover chocolate custard with almond flavored custard. Chill and set.

Filling — Step 3

1/2 pint heavy cream	2 Tablespoons powdered sugar

Filling — Step 3: Whip cream; add powdered sugar and spread over pie. Serve.

High Hampton Inn
Cashiers, North Carolina

Grasshopper Pie

Butter (about 1 stick)
Chocolate wafers (enough
  for crust)
20 marshmallows
1/2 cup milk

2 cups whipped cream
1 1/2 ounces white Creme
  de Cocoa
1 1/2 ounces Creme de Menthe

Make crust by crushing wafers and adding melted butter. Stand wafer halves around edge of pan to form side crust. Dissolve marshmallows in warm milk and cool. When cool, add Creme de Menthe and Creme de Cocoa. Fold in whipped cream and pour into pie shell. Put in freezer. May also make a peach brandy pie using the same ingredients, but substituting peach brandy (3 ounces) for other liqueur and adding 1 cup fresh chopped peaches. Pie cuts easily when frozen.

Mrs. Irving K. Wise
(Madge Edney)

Sherry Pie

1/2 cup pecans, chopped
1 cup flour
1 stick butter
1/4 cup light brown sugar

1/2 cup sherry
1/2 pound marshmallows
1/2 pint whipping cream

Mix pecans, flour, butter and brown sugar. Spread in shallow pie pan. Place in 370 degree oven and bake 15 minutes until brown. Mix sherry and marshmallows. Melt in top of double boiler. Refrigerate until ice cold, stirring often. Fold in whipped cream and pour into cool crust. Chill for 6 hours. Save some of crust mixture to sprinkle on top.

Mrs. Howard Newton, Jr.
(Jourdan Jones)

Chess Pie

1 stick butter
1 1/2 cups sugar
4 eggs
2 Tablespoons cornmeal
2 Tablespoons milk

1 Tablespoon vinegar
1 1/4 Tablespoons lemon juice
1/8 teaspoon salt
1 deep unbaked 9-inch pie shell

234

Cream sugar and butter. Add eggs one at a time. Add milk, corn meal, vinegar, lemon juice and salt. Pour into unbaked pie shell and bake at 375 degrees for 10 minutes, reduce heat to 325 degrees and bake until set — about 35 minutes.

Mrs. C. W. Rosson
(Martha Dunlap)

Vinegar Pie

3 slightly beaten eggs
1 1/2 cups white sugar
2 Tablespoons flour
2 Tablespoons vinegar

1 Tablespoon vanilla
1 stick melted butter
1 uncooked pie shell

Mix all ingredients and pour into uncooked pie shell. Bake in oven at 300 degrees for about 1 hour.

Mrs. Peter Lowe (Janet Lyons)
The Jarrett House
Dillsboro, N. C.

Chocolate Chiffon Pie

1 envelope gelatine
1 cup sugar
Pinch salt
1 cup milk

2 1-ounce squares chocolate
2 cups whipped cream
1/2 square shaved chocolate
Graham cracker crumb pie shell

Combine gelatine, sugar and salt in double boiler. Add milk and the 2 squares of chocolate which have been cut into small pieces. Stir until melted. (The mixture will be chocolate flecked.) Chill, stirring occasionally, until it begins to thicken. Fold in whipped cream. Pour into chilled Graham cracker pie crust. Sprinkle with shaved chocolate. (Use large 10-inch pie pan.) Make the day before serving. Serves 10.

Mrs. James G. Nance
(Martha Mitchell)

235

Chocolate French Silk Pie

Meringue

2 egg whites
1/8 teaspoon salt
1/8 teaspoon cream of tartar

1/2 cup sugar
1/2 cup broken pecans
1/2 teaspoon vanilla (or rum)

Filling

1 square unsweetened chocolate
1/4 pound butter
2/3 cup sugar
2 eggs

1 teaspoon vanilla
1/2 pint whipping cream
Grated chocolate

Meringue: Beat egg whites until foamy. Add the salt and cream of tartar. Add sugar gradually, and then beat until very stiff. Fold in pecans and vanilla. Grease pie pan with butter. Arrange meringue as crust. Bake in 300 degree oven for 55 minutes.

Filling: Melt chocolate and let cool. Cream butter and add sugar gradually. Add eggs one at a time, beating 5 minutes after each egg is added. Add chocolate and vanilla. Put into pie shell. Chill overnight. When served, top with whipping cream and grate chocolate over top.

Mrs. Robert L. Chickey
(Gail Gonce)

Coffee Ice Cream/Oreo Pie

24 Oreos, crushed
1/2 stick butter, melted

1 quart coffee ice cream
Bitter chocolate, shaved

Make crust of crushed Oreos and melted butter. Press into 9-inch pie pan. Chill until firm and fill with softened coffee ice cream. Garnish top with shaved chocolate curls. Freeze. Remove from freezer for a few minutes before cutting.

An easy dessert to do ahead of time.

Mrs. J. M. Shoemaker
(Polly Sloan)

Brownie Pie

1 stick butter
1 square semi-sweet chocolate
2 eggs, beaten
1 cup sugar

1/2 cup sifted flour
1 teaspoon vanilla
1/2 cup chopped pecans

Melt chocolate and butter. Add sugar and eggs. Add flour, vanilla and pecans. Put in greased pie pan. Bake in oven at 325 degrees for 30-40 minutes. Serve with vanilla ice cream or whipped cream on top.

Mrs. Braxton B. Comer
(Charlene Holloway)

Chocolate Ice Box Pie

Crust

2 cups crushed vanilla wafers
1/3 cup soft butter

Filling

1 large package Nestlé's
  semi-sweet chocolate bits
1 whole egg
2 egg yolks

1 teaspoon rum
1 pint whipping cream
2 egg whites

Crust: Combine wafer crumbs and butter and press into a spring form pan or deep pie pan.

Filling: Melt chocolate bits over simmering water in double boiler. Beat 1 whole egg and 2 egg yolks well and add to melted chocolate bits, then add rum. Whip 1/2 pint cream and beat egg whites stiff. Fold both into chocolate mixture. Pour into crust and freeze for several hours.

Top with other 1/2 pint cream, whipped, before serving. To decorate for company, put cream through a pastry tube, and top with grated chocolate. The pie can be returned to freezer. The cream will freeze and keep.

Mrs. Harvey Plonsker
(Madeleine Pinsof)

Graham Cracker Crumb Crust Pie

Crust

3 egg whites	1 cup nuts, chopped
1 cup sugar	1 teaspoon vanilla
1 cup graham cracker crumbs	

Filling

1/2 pint whipping cream	1 teaspoon vanilla
1 teaspoon powdered sugar	Baker's German Sweet Chocolate

Crust: Beat egg whites until stiff. Slowly add sugar. Add other ingredients. Put into 10-inch ungreased aluminum pie pan and bake 30 minutes at 350 degrees. Cool thoroughly and fill.

Filling: Whip cream and add sugar and vanilla. Pour into pie crust and leave in refrigerator several hours. Shave chocolate over top before serving. May be made the day before.

Mrs. H. E. Runge
(Gertrude Thompson)

Heavenly Pie

4 large egg whites	1 cup cream
1/4 teaspoon salt	Almond extract
1 1/2 cups sugar	Strawberries, raspberries,
1 teaspoon vanilla	or peaches
1 teaspoon vinegar	

Grease well a 9-inch pie plate (grease right to the edge). Sprinkle on a complete coating of flour, shake off. Beat whites of eggs with the salt until stiff but not too dry. Add gradually 1 cup of sugar, beating between each addition. Add vanilla and other sugar gradually, alternating with vinegar, beating continuously. Put meringue into pie plate. Bake 1 hour (30 minutes at 275 degrees and 30 minutes at 300 degrees). Cool. Whip cream stiff, sweeten to taste and flavor with almond extract. Spread cream on pie. Cut up desired fruit and arrange on cream.

Mrs. Maye R. Johnson
(Motsy Crosland)

Kanuga Angel Pie

Meringue Pie Shell

4 egg whites
1/2 teaspoon cream of tartar

1 cup granulated sugar

Filling

4 egg yolks (beaten slightly)
Juice of one lemon

1/2 cup sugar
2 teaspoons lemon rind, grated

Pie Shell: Beat eggs until stiff but not dry. Add cream of tartar and sugar. Beat 10 minutes at high speed in electric mixer. Pour into 1 inch deep pie pan. Smooth with knife. Bake 1 hour at 250 degrees. Leave in oven with door open to cool.

Filling: Beat eggs, lemon juice and 1/2 cup sugar until the sugar is dissolved. Cook in top of double boiler until thick, stirring constantly. Add rind and let cool. When shell and filling are both cool, whip cream and add 2 teaspoons sugar. Spread half the cream on meringue pie shell. Next spread the filling, and then top with remaining cream. Keep in refrigerator 24 hours before serving. (Can be made in individual servings by putting large spoonfuls of meringue on cookie sheet instead of in pie pan.)

Mrs. James H. Austin
(Elizabeth Reid)

Yum Yum Pie

1 8-ounce package cream
  cheese (room temperature)
1 can Eagle Brand condensed
  milk
1/3 cup lemon juice

1 can blueberry or cherry pie
  filling
2 graham cracker pie shells
Dream Whip

Blend cheese, condensed milk and lemon juice until smooth. Divide mixture and pour into each pie shell. Divide blueberry or cherry pie filling and pour over cheese. Cover with Dream Whip and place in refrigerator for several hours or overnight preferably.

Yum Yum, as the name implies.

Mrs. George Bogle
(Elizabeth Leach)

239

Hawaiian Pie

1 stick butter, melted
1 cup sugar
3 eggs

1/2 cup raisins
1/2 cup coconut
1/2 cup pecans, chopped

Mix well and pour into uncooked pie shell. Bake in moderate oven, 325 to 350 degrees, for 30 to 40 minutes.

Mrs. John Coble
(Alma Presnell)

Lemon Pie

1 large or 2 small pie shells,
  slightly baked
2 sticks margarine
2 cups sugar

2 Tablespoons corn meal
3 Tablespoons plain flour
Juice and rind of 2 lemons
5 eggs

Cream margarine and sugar. Beat eggs into this, and add meal, flour, lemon juice, and rind. Pour into shells. Cook at 375 degrees for 10 minutes, and then lower oven to 325 degrees for 30 minutes more. Good with whipped cream or meringue on top. Makes 1 large pie or 2 small pies.

Mrs. David Quattlebaum
(Mary Jane Galloway)

Lime Pie

1 cup sugar
1 package lime Jello
1 cup boiling water
1 large can Carnation milk

Pinch of salt
Juice of two lemons
1 box vanilla wafers

Dissolve Jello in boiling water and stir in sugar. Cool and whip until light. Chill milk and whip. Fold in whipped Jello. Slowly fold in lemon juice and salt. Line two pie pans with vanilla wafers. Pour in mixture. Top with whipped cream and sliced cherries. Makes 2 pies. Serves 12.

Mrs. Julian L. Wade, Jr.
(Maggie Echols)

Lemon Tarts

Crust

1 stick margarine
1 cup flour

1 3-ounce package cream
cheese

Filling

1 cup sugar
Grated rind of 1 lemon
1/4 stick butter

2 eggs, beaten
Juice of 2 lemons

Crust: To make tart shells, cream together margarine and cream cheese and add flour. Mix well and shape into small balls. Shape these into tart pans or small muffin tins.

Filling: Cream together sugar and butter. Add lemon rind, and the beaten eggs, and then the lemon juice. Pour into shells and bake at 350 degrees for 20 or 25 minutes. Serves 9 to 12.

Mrs. James M. Stewart
(Rita Duggeth)

Nantucket Cranberry Pie

Filling

2 cups raw cranberries
1/2 cup sugar

1/2 cup chopped walnuts

Batter

1 cup sugar
3/4 cup melted margarine
1 cup flour

1 teaspoon almond extract
2 beaten eggs

Grease 10-inch pie plate. Wash and drain cranberries, and place on bottom of plate. Sprinkle one-half cup sugar and nuts over cranberries. For batter, mix sugar and margarine and add rest of ingredients. Pour over cranberries. Bake at 325 degrees 35 to 40 minutes. Serve with whipped cream or ice cream. Serves 6 to 8.

Mrs. Henry Truslow
(Gretchen Smith)

241

Grape Pie
(An adaptation of an old Vienna recipe)

2 cups (scant) plain flour
1 stick plus 2 Tablespoons
  butter

1 Tablespoon rum
2 Tablespoons sugar
1 egg yolk

Filling

1 pound whole seedless grapes
3/4 cup sugar
1/2 cup ground pecans

2 egg whites, stiffly beaten
Grated rind of 1 small lemon

Work flour, butter, rum, sugar and egg yolk together with fingers, and then divide into two parts. Chill slightly. Press half of dough into pyrex pie dish. Combine filling and place in unbaked shell. Form lattice top by rolling bits of remaining dough between palms, working strips in criss-cross design. Bake at 350 degrees until brown — about 45 minutes.

Mrs. Kenneth Edgar
(Josephine Beasley)

Pumpkin Chiffon Pie

1 Tablespoon plain gelatine
1/4 cup cold water
3 slightly beaten egg yolks
1 cup sugar
1 cup canned pumpkin
1 1/2 cups milk
1/4 teaspoon salt

1/4 teaspoon ginger
1/4 teaspoon cinnamon
1/4 teaspoon nutmeg
3 well beaten egg whites
Whipping cream
Graham cracker pie shell

Soak gelatine in cold water for 5 minutes, and add to the following mixture: slightly beaten egg yolks, 1/2 cup sugar, pumpkin, milk, salt, and spices. Cool. When this begins to thicken, fold it into the well beaten egg whites to which has been added the remaining sugar, while beating. Pour into a graham cracker shell. Chill and cover with whipped cream to serve.

Mrs. Owen W. Pittman, Jr.
(Susan Stovall)

Pawley's Island Cobbler

Crust

1/4 cup butter	2 teaspoons baking powder
1/2 cup sugar	1/4 teaspoon salt
1 cup sifted flour	1/2 cup milk

Filling

Fruit and juice	Sugar

Crust: Cream butter and sugar; add milk and dry ingredients. Pour batter into 2-quart greased casserole. Place fruit, sugar and juice over batter *in that order.* Bake at 375 degrees for 45 minutes or until batter rises to top, browns and cobbler is bubbly.

Filling: Use enough fresh fruit of any kind, sugared, to cover bottom of 2-quart casserole or No. 2 can of cherries, blackberries, blueberries, etc. If using canned fruit use 1/4 cup of sugar and 1 cup juice.

Mrs. Frank Halter
(Shirley Caine)

Peach Quiche

Pre-baked 10-inch pastry shell	3 eggs
6 medium peaches (ripe)	1 cup whipping cream
1 cup sugar	2 Tablespoons bourbon
1 cup water	3/4 cup chopped almonds
1 1/2 teaspoons vanilla	(optional)

Blanch unpeeled peaches for a minute in boiling water. Peel, cut in half, then in quarters. Bring 1/2 cup water and 1 teaspoon vanilla to a boil. Poach peaches in this syrup until they are cooked but still firm. Sprinkle almonds over bottom of pastry shell (optional). Drain peaches and arrange in shell. Beat eggs lightly and stir in cream, bourbon and the remaining vanilla and sugar. Bake in a 350 degree oven until the custard is set. Cool on a rack. Serves 6-8. This is very rich. Small portions are recommended.

Mrs. Heyward Mahon Sullivan
(Kay Williamson)

Strawberry Pie

1 pint fresh strawberries
1 cup sugar
1 cup water
3 Tablespoons cornstarch

4 Tablespoons strawberry Jello
  (powder)
1 baked pie shell — cooled,
  or Pet-Ritz frozen shell

Arrange berries (whole or if large, halved) in pie shell. Cook cornstarch, sugar and water until thick and clear. Add a few drops of red food coloring. Stir in Jello until all dissolved. Pour this over strawberries and chill. Serve topped with sweetened whipped cream. For company you may want to garnish with a few berries.

Mrs. William Kehl
(Libby Adams)

Jersey Peach Pie

6-8 medium peaches (peeled and
  halved)
1/4 cup butter
3/4 cup sugar

1/3 cup flour
4 Tablespoons water
Nutmeg or cinnamon
1 unbaked pie crust

Line a pie plate with pastry. Make a crumb-like mixture of the butter, sugar and flour (use pastry blender or fork). Sprinkle half over crust. Lay peaches on this, cut side down. Sprinkle lightly with water and spice. Sprinkle remaining crumb mixture over the top. Bake at 350 degrees for 40-45 minutes.

Mrs. Henry Truslow
(Gretchen Smith)

Fresh Peach Glaze Pie

1 baked and cooled 9-inch pie
  shell
1 1/2 cups crushed peaches
1 cup sugar
1/4 teaspoon salt

1/2 cup water
3 Tablespoons corn starch
1 Tablespoon butter
Sliced peaches

244

Combine crushed peaches, sugar, salt, water and corn starch in a saucepan and boil for 2 or 3 minutes. Into baked pie shell, slice fresh peaches nearly to top. Slightly cool crushed peach mixture and add butter. Pour over sliced peaches in pie shell. Serve at once topped with whipped cream or ice cream if desired.

Mrs. Henry E. Barton
(Sarah Guess)

Apple Pie

Pastry for 2 crust pie	1/2 teaspoon cinnamon
1 can pie-sliced apples	1/4 teaspoon nutmeg
1 cup brown sugar	2 Tablespoons flour
1/2 cup granulated sugar	1/4 teaspoon salt
1 teaspoon white vinegar	2 Tablespoons butter

Combine all ingredients, except butter, with well drained apples. Pour into unbaked pie shell and dot with butter. Place top crust on pie and make slits in top. Bake at 425 degrees for 10 minutes. Reduce heat to 350 degrees and continue to bake 30 to 40 minutes or until crust is golden brown.

Mrs. Herbert H. Provence, Jr.
(Anne Foster)

Apple Strudel

4 cups cooking apples	3/4 cup flour
1 teaspoon cinnamon	1 cup sugar
1 teaspoon salt	1/3 cup butter or margarine
1/4 cup water	

Place mixture of apples, cinnamon, salt, and water in 10 x 6 buttered baking dish. Mix remaining ingredients until crumbly. Spread over apples. Bake at 350 degrees for 40 to 50 minutes. Serves 6.

Good plain or with whipped cream or ice cream.

Mrs. George E. Welborn
(Kate Marett)

Meringue Shells

3 egg whites   3/4 cup sugar
1/4 teaspoon cream of tartar

Preheat oven to 275 degrees. Butter 9-inch pie pan. Have the egg whites room temperature. Beat egg whites and cream of tartar in small bowl of mixer at speed 7 for 1 minute. Continuing at speed 7, gradually add sugar, beating for 5 minutes, or until the egg whites are stiff. Spread on bottom and sides of prepared pan, or drop from spoon onto a cookie sheet. Bake 1 hour. Cool.

Note: If it is not convenient to make mayonnaise with egg yolks at the time you make meringues, carefully put yolks, unbroken, into plastic covered container and slowly add cold water to cover them. Drain off water when ready to use.

Mrs. A. Newton Stall
(Helen Hunt)

Never Fail Pastry

	9-inch Single Crust	9-inch Double Crust
Sifted flour	1 1/2 cups	2 1/4 cups
Salt	1/2 teaspoon	1 teaspoon
Shortening	1/2 cup	3/4 cup
Water (cold)	3 Tablespoons	4 Tablespoons

Sift flour and salt into bowl. Remove 3 tablespoons of flour and combine with water to make a paste (a little more for large crust). Cut shortening into remaining flour until pieces are the size of small peas. Stir flour and water paste into this mixture until it all sticks together. Shape dough into a flat, round mass with no breaks in the edge. Roll out about 1/8 inch thick.

Butterscotch Toll House Candy

2 6-ounce packages   1 cup, dry roasted peanuts
  butterscotch morsels   1 can chow mein noodles

Melt butterscotch morsels in top of double boiler. Add noodles and peanuts. Stir well. Drop on wax paper with teaspoon. Let cool.

Miss Eyleen Runge

246

Divinity

2 cups white sugar
1/3 cup white Karo syrup
2/3 cup water

2 egg whites, beaten stiff
Pecan halves

Boil sugar, Karo and water until mixture forms a hard ball in cold water that will crack on cup. (Do not stir while cooking or candy might be grainy.) Add this syrup slowly to the egg whites, beating constantly until hard enough to drop from spoon. Arrange on waxed paper and press 1/2 pecan on top of each piece. Makes 5 dozen pieces.

Mrs. David M. Adams
(Helene Elizabeth Mitchell)

Pulled Mints

1 cup boiling water
3/8 stick margarine

2 cups sugar
6 drops oil of peppermint

Heat water and margarine, add sugar and stir until dissolved; then cover pan and cook for 3 minutes. Uncover and cook without stirring to 260 degrees. Pour on marble which has been greased with Wesson oil. Add oil of peppermint. When it is cool enough to handle, flour or grease tips of fingers and pull until it holds its shape and no longer looks clear; then cut. Let stand until cold (do not refrigerate), and place in tightly covered tin can. Should cream in about 2 days.

Mrs. T. C. Gower
(Kathryn Smith)

Vanilla Sugar

1 pound granulated sugar

2 vanilla beans

Pour sugar into glass jar. Add vanilla beans. Use after one week. Sugar may be added from time to time. Add a new bean every six months. Use in lieu of vanilla flavoring for a rich vanilla taste. One tablespoon of vanilla sugar equals 1/4 teaspoon vanilla flavoring.

Mrs. James H. Austin
(Elizabeth Reid)

Chocolate Fudge

3 cups light brown sugar
6 1/2 ounces of milk (small
  can or 3/4 cup)
9 ounces of semi-sweet
  chocolate drops

1/4 pound butter
5 ounces marshmallow cream or
  whip
1 1/2 teaspoons vanilla
1 cup chopped nuts, if desired

Boil sugar and milk over low heat for ten to eleven minutes, stirring constantly. Burns easily. Immediately after removing from heat, pour over other ingredients. Stir until everything is melted and pour into greased pan. Cut when hard. In damp weather mixture should be boiled a minute longer.

For variety, mix white and brown sugar. For smoother fudge, substitute 2 1/2 cups white sugar for brown sugar. In this case, nine minutes of boiling is usually sufficient. For variety also, rum flavoring may be substituted for vanilla.

Miss Choice McCoin

No-Cook Fudge

1 box confectioners sugar
2 blocks semi-sweet chocolate
4 Tablespoons milk
1 cup chopped nuts

3/4 stick margarine
  (6 Tablespoons)
1 Tablespoon vanilla

Melt all ingredients but nuts together in top of double boiler; then add nuts. Pour into greased pan. Refrigerate.

Mrs. William Y. Quarles, Jr.
(Patricia Gibson)

Fudge

1 1/2 cups sugar
1/2 cup milk
2 ounces bitter chocolate
  squares

2 Tablespoons butter
1 teaspoon vanilla
3/4 cup nuts

248

Place sugar, milk and chopped up chocolate in pot and boil very slowly for 6 minutes. (Don't time until boiling; don't stir.) Add butter and boil very slowly for another 6 minutes. Test for a soft ball. Remove from stove; beat until creamy. Add nuts, chopped not too fine, and vanilla. Pour on greased platter. Cool and cut. Makes about 30 small pieces.

Mrs. William B. Long, Jr.
(Ann Shields King)

High Brow Chocolate Candy

4 cups sugar	1 jar marshmallow cream
1/4 pound butter	1 teaspoon vanilla
1/4 pound bitter chocolate	1 cup nuts, chopped
1 cup milk	

Cook first four ingredients in a heavy pot until a soft ball forms in a cup of cold water. (Boil about 5 minutes, stirring constantly.) Whip in one jar of marshmallow cream. (Mix with electric mixer for one minute.) Add one teaspoon vanilla and one cup of nuts. Pour in heavy "lard" platter. Cool.

This keeps well in the refrigerator to slice for quick treats.

Lawton-Wyman Family Recipe
Mrs. E. E. Stone IV
(Barbara McCready)

Whiskey Pralines

2 1/2 cups sugar	1/2 cup milk
Lump of butter	Pinch soda
(approximately 1-ounce)	2 Tablespoons whiskey
1/4 cup white syrup	2 cups chopped pecans

Cook sugar, butter, syrup, milk and soda very slowly until soft ball is formed. Add whiskey. Stir, but do not beat, until thick. Stir in pecans. Drop by teaspoonfuls on waxed paper. Do not let mixture become too thick before dropping. Yields 50.

Mrs. H. R. Stephenson, Jr.
(Kitty Lawder)

Mrs. Bender's Applesauce Cake

1 cup butter
2 cups sugar
3 eggs
2 cups applesauce
3 cups flour
1 teaspoon soda
1 pound white raisins

2 cups chopped pecans
1/2 cup watermelon preserves
  or citron
1 cup preserved cherries
1 teaspoon each: nutmeg,
  cinnamon, cloves

Cream butter and sugar, beat in eggs and add applesauce. Sift dry ingredients into large bowl, add fruits and nuts and then add applesauce mixture. Batter should be stiffer than ordinary cake. Line the bottom of a greased tube pan with wax paper. Bake about 2 1/2 hours in slow oven at 300 degrees.

Mrs. Wake H. Myers, Sr.
(Mary Louise Bender)

Fresh Apple Cake

2 1/2 cups flour
2 cups sugar
1 teaspoon cinnamon
2 teaspoons baking powder
1 teaspoon salt

4 eggs
1 1/2 cups cooking oil
1 teaspoon vanilla
3 cups chopped raw apples
1 cup chopped pecans

Mix all dry ingredients. Add eggs. Slowly pour in cooking oil, beating constantly. Add vanilla. Fold in apples and pecans. Bake in oven in a greased tube pan for one hour at 350 degrees.

Mrs. William H. Johnson, Jr.
(Becky Cashwell)

Rene's Sour Cream Pound Cake

1 cup sour cream
1/2 pound butter
3 cups sugar
6 eggs
3 cups flour

1/4 teaspoon baking soda
1 teaspoon water
1 jigger bourbon
  (1 1/2 ounces)

Cream butter, add sugar. Add eggs, one at a time, beating well. Sift flour with baking soda and add alternately with sour cream. Add water and bourbon. Bake in oven in greased and floured tube pan for 1 1/2 hours at 350 degrees.

Mrs. Ralph Bailey
(Pappy Godbey)

Easy Pound Cake

2 cups flour
2 sticks butter
2 cups sugar
5 eggs

2 teaspoons flavoring as
desired (vanilla, lemon peel
or extract, orange peel,
almond extract or
1 teaspoon nutmeg)

Cream butter and sugar and add eggs, one at a time. Add flour and flavorings. Bake in 350 degree oven in greased and floured pan for 1 hour.

Mrs. Raymon Reece
(Jeannette Hendricks)

Old Fashioned Pound Cake

1 pound butter
3 cups sugar
4 cups plain flour
1 teaspoon baking powder

Pinch of salt
2 teaspoons vanilla
6 eggs
1/2 cup milk

Let butter and eggs sit at room temperature one hour. Sift flour and measure 4 cups. Sift flour, baking powder and salt 3 times. Beat eggs well. Cream butter and sugar. Add eggs and beat well. Add dry ingredients alternately with milk. Add vanilla. Cook in preheated 300 degree oven on middle rack. Cook 2 hours in greased and floured large tube pan. Do not open door while cooking. Turn out on plate as soon as done.

Mrs. David Quattlebaum
(Mary Jane Galloway)

Chocolate Pound Cake

Cake

5 eggs
2 sticks butter or margarine
1/2 cup shortening (Crisco or Snowdrift)
3 cups sugar
1 teaspoon vanilla
1 cup sweet milk

3 cups flour (measure after sifting)
1/2 cup cocoa (more if desired)
1/2 teaspoon baking powder
1/4 teaspoon salt

Icing

1/2 cup marshmallow bits
2 squares chocolate
1 stick Nucoa margarine
1 egg

1 box 10X confectioners sugar
1 teaspoon vanilla
Salt
Milk (if necessary)

Cake: Beat eggs. Let stand. Cream butter, sugar, Crisco. Add eggs and vanilla. Sift together 4 times the flour, cocoa, baking powder and salt or use a triple sifter. Add to egg mixture alternately with milk. Grease pans and put wax paper in bottoms. Use 2 loaf pans or a *large* tube or Bundt pan. Pour batter into pans and bake 1 hour and 20 minutes at 325 degrees. When done, remove from oven and let stand 25 to 30 minutes before removing from pans.

Icing: (if desired) Melt chocolate with margarine and marshmallows in double boiler. Remove from heat and with electric beater, beat in the egg, sugar, salt and vanilla. Add milk, if necessary to make right spreading consistency.

Ice cake. When icing cools, grate German chocolate over it.

Mrs. R. L. Cashwell
(Mary West)

Sherry Sauce

1 cup sugar
2 eggs
1/2 cup sherry

Lump of butter
Pinch of salt

Beat eggs and sugar together; add other ingredients. Cook in double boiler until thick. Serve warm over pound cake.

Mrs. H. T. Williams
(Catherine Hudson)

Martha's Brown Sugar Pound Cake

1 cup butter
1/2 cup shortening
1 cup white sugar
1 pound light brown sugar
5 large eggs

3 cups flour
1/2 teaspoon baking powder
1 cup milk
1 teaspoon vanilla
1 cup chopped nuts

Remove all lumps from brown sugar by rolling on wax paper with rolling pin. In a large bowl cream butter and shortening. Add sugar and cream again. Add eggs. Sift dry ingredients and add alternately with milk. Add vanilla and nuts. Bake in large greased and floured tube pan 1 1/2 to 1 3/4 hours at 325 degrees. Cool in pan.

Mrs. Ben C. Thornton
(Anne Wallace Marshall)

Bourbon and Walnut Pound Cake

2 cups walnuts, finely chopped
1 cup bourbon
3 1/2 cups flour
1 1/2 teaspoons baking powder
1/2 teaspoon salt
1/2 teaspoon nutmeg
1/2 teaspoon cinnamon

1/4 teaspoon ground cloves
2 cups butter
2 1/2 cups sugar
8 eggs, well beaten
1 teaspoon vanilla
Cheesecloth

Combine walnuts and 1/2 cup bourbon, and let stand. Sift dry ingredients. Cream butter and sugar. Beat in eggs and vanilla until batter is thick and fluffy. Beat in dry ingredients. Stir in walnut mixture. Pour into 10-inch tube pan, and bake at 350 degrees for 1 hour and 10 minutes. Soak cheesecloth in 1/2 cup bourbon. Wrap cake in cheesecloth and refrigerate for several days.

Mrs. John E. Johnston
(Caroline Cannon)

Cheesecake

Cake

1 1/4 cups graham cracker
  crumbs
1/4 cup sugar
1/4 cup melted margarine
5 packages (8 ounces each)
  cream cheese
1 3/4 cups sugar

1 can of apricot halves
1 can of pineapple wedges

Syrup from apricots and
  pineapple
1 Tablespoon lemon juice

3 Tablespoons flour
Grated rind of 1 lemon
Grated rind of 1/2 orange
5 whole eggs
2 egg yolks
1/4 cup heavy cream

Fruit

Strawberry halves
Grapes

Glaze

1 Tablespoon cornstarch
2 Tablespoons cold water
Yellow food coloring

Cake: Mix cracker crumbs, sugar and butter. Butter a 10 inch springform pan and press crumb mixture onto bottom and sides of pan. Let cake ingredients, except last 2, reach room temperature. Beat cheese until fluffy. Mix sugar and flour; gradually blend into cheese. Add grated rinds. Add eggs and egg yolks one at a time, beating well after each. Stir in cream. Turn into crust. Bake in hot oven (500 degrees) 10 minutes. Reduce heat to 200 degrees and bake one hour longer. Remove from oven and place away from drafts until cooled. Refrigerate until cold, then remove sides of pan and put cake on serving plate. Top with fruit and glaze. Refrigerate until serving time. Cake is better if made the day before but fruit and glaze should be put on the day it is served.

Fruit and glaze: Arrange fruit on chilled cake, 4 or 5 canned apricot halves around center, surrounded by a circle of canned pineapple wedges, and a border of halved strawberries and grapes. To make glaze, combine pineapple and apricot syrup drained from fruit to make 3/4 cup. Add 1 tablespoon lemon juice. Combine 1 tablespoon cornstarch with 2 tablespoons cold water. Add to juices and cook in a double boiler, stirring until thickened. Yellow food coloring may be added. Spoon over fruit. Refrigerate again for 2 hours before serving.

Mrs. William H. Johnson, Jr.
(Becky Cashwell)

Mrs. MacLean's Angel Food Cake

12 egg whites, or 1 1/2 cups
  egg whites
1/4 teaspoon salt
1 1/4 teaspoons cream
  of tartar

1 1/2 cups sugar
1 cup cake flour
1 teaspoon vanilla extract
1/2 teaspoon almond extract

Add salt to egg whites and beat until frothy. Then add cream of tartar and beat until stiff or until whites stand in peaks. Add sugar slowly, a little at a time, beating until all sugar is used. Add flour in the same manner, slowly, beating all the while. Add vanilla and almond flavorings and blend.

Turn into ungreased angel cake tube pan. Turn on oven to 325 degrees a minute or two before putting cake in oven. Cook for 1 hour. Remove cake from oven and invert over neck of bottle or 3 inverted teacups. Allow to cool before removing from pan.

Mrs. R. A. Mattson, Jr.
(Jane MacLean)

Chocolate Angel Food Cake

3/4 cup flour
1/4 cup cocoa
1/2 teaspoon salt
1 1/2 cups egg whites
  (room temperature)
1 1/2 cups sugar

1 1/2 teaspoons cream of
  tartar
1 1/2 teaspoons vanilla
1 pint whipping cream
  (sweetened to taste)

Sift flour and salt. Add cocoa and 1/2 cup sugar. Sift 6 times. Beat egg whites with wire whip to a froth, add cream of tartar and continue beating until stiff but not dry. Add 1 cup sifted sugar, folding in gently 2 tablespoons at a time and then add vanilla. Fold in the mixture of sugar, flour, salt and cocoa slowly turning bowl as you fold. Spoon into large tube pan. Put in cold oven, set at 350 degrees and cook until crusty on top — 40 to 50 minutes. Remove from oven and turn upside down and do not remove until cold. Divide into 3 layers and spread layers and top with whipped cream seasoned to taste with sugar and vanilla.

Mrs. T. C. Gower
(Kathryn Smith)

Carrot Cake

Cake

2 cups sugar	3 cups plain flour
4 eggs	2 teaspoons soda
1 cup Wesson oil	1 teaspoon cinnamon
3 cups grated carrot	1 teaspoon salt

Icing

1 8-ounce package cream cheese	1 teaspoon vanilla
1/2 stick margarine	1 cup slivered pecans, toasted but not salted
1 box confectioners 10x sugar	

Cake: Cream first 3 ingredients together and then add carrots. Sift together flour, soda, cinnamon and salt. Add this to mixture. Bake in three 9 or 10-inch cake pans at 350 degrees.

Icing: Cream the cream cheese, margarine and sugar. When they are well mixed, add vanilla and pecans. Ice cake.

Mrs. J. Philip Coyle
(Dottie Hilburn)

Party Rum Cake

(A moist, heavy cake that must be made exactly by the recipe with ingredients at room temperature. Use a ten inch non-fluted tube pan.)

1 cup margarine, non-whipped	1 teaspoon soda
2 cups granulated sugar	1 cup buttermilk
Rind of 2 large oranges, grated	1 cup pecans, chopped
Rind of 1 lemon, grated	Juice of 2 large oranges
2 1/2 cups flour (sifted all purpose)	Juice of 1 lemon
2 eggs	3/4 teaspoon salt
2 teaspoons baking powder	2 Tablespoons rum
	1/2 cup confectioners sugar
	24 pecan halves

256

Beat butter until fluffy and gradually add granulated sugar, beating constantly. Add rind and eggs, one at a time, still beating. In another bowl, sift flour that has been measured after first sifting and add baking powder, soda and salt to sifter. Add flour mixture to butter mixture, alternately with one cup of buttermilk in small amounts. Beat after each addition. Fold in chopped nuts. Grease pan and pour in batter. Bake at 375 degrees for 1 hour or until cake shrinks from pan edges. As cake cooks, combine juice, sugar and rum, bringing mixture to a boil before pouring over cake when it is done. Let cake stay in pan for 30 minutes to absorb juices and then remove. Mix confectioners sugar with enough milk to spread. Roll pecan halves in this mixture until coated. After dry, press onto sides of cake. This cake will stay for 2 weeks in the refrigerator if wrapped in foil. Freezes well.

Mrs. Frank Halter
(Shirley Caine)

Cupcakes

Cake

1/2 cup butter	1/2 teaspoon soda
1 cup sugar	1 teaspoon baking powder
2 eggs	1 cup dates, chopped
2/3 cup buttermilk	1 cup pecans, chopped
2 cups flour	

Sauce

Juice of 2 oranges	1 1/2 cups sugar
Rind of 1 orange	

Cream butter and sugar, add other ingredients having sifted flour with soda. Bake at 350 degrees for 15 minutes in a greased muffin tin or cups. While cakes are baking, boil sauce and pour over cupcakes while hot.

Mrs. H. William Carter, Jr.
(Margaret Kelley)

Magic White Cake

2 cups flour
1 1/3 cups sugar
1/2 cup shortening
1 teaspoon salt
2/3 cup milk

3 1/2 teaspoons double acting
  baking powder
4 unbeaten egg whites
1/3 cup milk
1 teaspoon vanilla

Mix flour, sugar, salt, shortening and milk. Blend for two minutes, stir in baking powder, add egg whites, milk and vanilla. Mix for two minutes. The batter will be smooth and thin. Pour into two greased 9-inch layer pans. Bake 25-30 minutes at 360 degrees.

Mrs. Gary Hiott, Sr.
(Eunice Biggerstaff)

Master Cake

1 stick butter
1 cup sugar
1 teaspoon vanilla
2 eggs

2 cups flour
1/2 teaspoon salt
3 teaspoons baking powder
2/3 cup milk

Cream together butter and sugar. Then add vanilla and eggs, beating until blended. Sift together flour, salt and baking powder and add to mixture alternating with milk. Beat after each addition. Bake in 2 greased layer pans 25-30 minutes in 350 degree oven.

Mrs. Newton Stall, Jr.
(Kitty Williams)

Prune Cake

Cake

1 cup Wesson oil	1/2 teaspoon nutmeg
1 1/2 cups sugar	1/2 teaspoon allspice
3 eggs	1/2 teaspoon salt
1 cup buttermilk	1 teaspoon vanilla
1 teaspoon soda	1 cup chopped nuts
2 cups plain flour	1 cup prunes (16 cooked and
1/2 teaspoon cinnamon	cut up)

Icing

1 cup sugar	1 Tablespoon white Karo syrup
1/2 cup buttermilk	1/2 stick butter
1/2 teaspoon soda	1 teaspoon vanilla

Cake: Cream oil and sugar. Add eggs and alternate flour and buttermilk to which soda has been added. Add spices, salt and vanilla. Fold in nuts and prunes that have been floured. Bake in greased and floured tube pan 1 hour and 20 minutes at 325 degrees.

Icing: Make icing while cake bakes. Add soda to buttermilk and then mix all ingredients together. When mixture begins to boil, cut down. Icing should be done when cake is done, if you start making it when cake begins to cook. Pour icing over cake before you remove cake from pan.

Mrs. Julian L. Wade
(Maggie Echols)

Mocha Cakes

1 plain layer cake	Almond flavoring to taste
1 cup butter	2 cups blanched, browned
2 cups powdered sugar	almonds

Make a plain layer cake in a square pan. When cool, preferably the next day, cut into small squares. Cream butter with powdered sugar, adding almond flavoring. Crush nuts very fine with rolling pin. With knife, spread butter and sugar mixture on all sides of cake squares and roll in crushed almonds.

Mrs. E. S. McKissick
(Jean Reamsbottom)

Chocolate Cake

2 cups sugar
1/2 cup cocoa
1 1/2 cups sour milk or
   buttermilk
1/2 cup butter
2 eggs

2 cups flour
1 teaspoon soda
1/2 teaspoon salt
1 teaspoon vanilla
1 pint cream

Part one: Mix 1 cup sugar, cocoa and 1/2 cup sour milk. Beat and set aside.

Part two: Cream butter and 1 cup sugar. Beat in eggs, one at a time. Add sifted dry ingredients alternately with 1 cup sour milk. Add vanilla. Fold in part one. Bake in two 9-inch cake pans at 375 degrees for 30 to 35 minutes. Cool. Split layers and fill with whipped cream. Top with chocolate icing.

Chocolate Icing

1 pint half and half
1/2 cup butter
2 1/4 cups granulated sugar

1/8 teaspoon salt
4 ounces chocolate
1 teaspoon vanilla

Mix half and half, butter, sugar and salt. Start on low heat and stir until sugar is dissolved. Cook gently until it makes a soft ball when dropped in cold water – 230 degrees. Pour over broken chocolate. Beat. Add vanilla and beat until thick enough to spread.

Mrs. Juanita S. Groff
(Juanita Sikes)

Chocolate Picnic Cake

Cake

2 cups flour
2 cups sugar
1/4 teaspoon salt
2 sticks margarine
   (Fleischman's)
4 heaping Tablespoons cocoa

1 cup water
2 eggs
1/2 cup buttermilk
1 teaspoon soda
1 teaspoon vanilla

Fudge Icing

1 stick margarine
4 heaping Tablespoons cocoa
6 Tablespoons sweet milk
1 box confectioners sugar

1 cup chopped pecans
Pinch salt
1 teaspoon vanilla

Cake: Mix flour, sugar and salt. Melt margarine, cocoa and water together. Mix with flour mixture. Add remaining ingredients. Mix well. Pour into greased 11 X 14-inch pan. Bake 20 minutes in 400 degree oven. Don't overcook.

Icing: Melt margarine, milk and cocoa together. Bring to a boil. Stir in sugar, then nuts and vanilla. Pour on cake while still warm — right out of oven.

Mrs. W. Ben Dunlap
(Martha Workman)

Chocolate Roll

5 eggs
3/4 teaspoon baking powder
1/4 teaspoon salt
1 cup sugar
3/4 cup sifted cake flour

2 Tablespoons cocoa
1 1/2 pints whipping cream
1/2 teaspoon vanilla
Confectioners sugar

In the bowl of an electric mixer, combine eggs, baking powder, and salt. Beat the mixture until it is pale and thick. Gradually add 1/2 cup of the sugar, beating the batter vigorously for about 10 to 15 minutes or until it rises in bowl. Fold in by hand the sifted cake flour and cocoa. Grease a jelly roll pan, line it with wax paper, and grease the paper. Spread the batter in the pan and bake it in a hot oven, 400 degrees, for about 13 minutes or until the cake pulls away from the sides of the pan. Turn out on wax paper sprinkled with confectioners sugar. Roll the cake lengthwise in the wax paper and let the cake cool. Beat whipping cream stiff with remaining 1/2 cup sugar and vanilla. Unroll the cake and spread the cream mixture over the cake. Reroll gently. Slip onto platter or jelly roll board. Serve sliced with hot chocolate sauce.

Mrs. James Austin Neal
(Leonette Dedmond)

261

German Chocolate Cake

1 1/2 sticks butter	3/4 cup milk
1 1/2 cups sugar	2 1/4 cups plain flour
1 teaspoon vanilla	2 1/4 teaspoons baking powder
3 eggs	1 package German chocolate

Filling

4 egg yolks	1 teaspoon vanilla
1 can evaporated milk	1 cup chopped pecans
(13-ounce size)	1 cup grated coconut
1 1/2 cups sugar	1 stick butter

Cream butter and sugar and add vanilla. Beat eggs and add to milk. Sift flour and baking powder. Add milk and eggs and flour to sugar and butter. Blend in chocolate that has been melted with 1 tablespoon water. Bake in 2 rectangular layer pans, 7 by 11 inches, for 25 minutes at 350 degrees.

Filling: Beat egg yolks and mix with milk and sugar, add vanilla, nuts, coconut and butter. Cook over low heat until thick enough to spread on cake.

Mrs. Ralph Ellis
(Frances Moore)

White Chocolate Cake and Icing

1/4 pound white chocolate, melted	1 cup angel flake coconut
1 cup butter	2 3/4 cups sifted cake flour
2 cups sugar	1 teaspoon vanilla
4 eggs	1 teaspoon baking powder
1 cup buttermilk	1/2 teaspoon soda
	1 cup chopped nuts

Icing

2 cups white sugar	2 sticks butter, melted
1 small can evaporated milk	

262

Cake: Cream butter and sugar well. Add eggs one at a time. Add vanilla. Reserve 2 tablespoons flour. Sift remaining flour, baking powder and soda. Add chocolate. Add flour mixture alternately with buttermilk. Stir in pecans mixed with 2 tablespoons of flour, and then add coconut. Makes two 8 or 9 inch layers. Grease pans. Bake 350 degrees for 25 minutes.

Icing: Mix well and let stand 1 hour; stir several times. Cook to soft ball stage on medium heat. Cool. Beat to a good spreading consistency.

Mrs. Sidney B. Paine
(Elaine Brooks)

Red Velvet Cake

Cake

1 cup Crisco or butter or	2 level Tablespoons cocoa
1 stick butter and	1 teaspoon soda
1 stick margarine	Pinch salt
1 1/2 cups sugar	2 1/2 cups flour
2 eggs	1 teaspoon vanilla
1 1/2 bottles red food	1 cup buttermilk
coloring	1 Tablespoon vinegar

Frosting

2 Tablespoons cornstarch	1 cup sugar
1 cup water	1 teaspoon vanilla
1 cup butter	

Cake: Cream together shortening, sugar and eggs. Make a paste of coloring and cocoa and add this to butter mixture. Add everything else except the vinegar and soda. Beat. After beating, add vinegar and soda. Mix well and pour into two layer pans that have been greased and floured. Bake at 350 degrees for 30 minutes. (Three small pans can be used and ice only the cake tops.)

Frosting: Mix cornstarch with water and cook until thick. Cool. Cream butter, sugar and vanilla for approximately 10 minutes. Add to cornstarch mixture and beat with beater. Spread over layers.

Mrs. Gordon R. Vinson
(Carolyn Godwin)

Nut Fudge Cake

Cake

1/4 cup butter	1 teaspoon baking powder
2 eggs	1 cup sugar
2 squares chocolate, melted	1/4 cup milk
1 cup flour	1 teaspoon vanilla
2/3 cup nuts	1/2 teaspoon salt

Filling

1/2 cup white sugar	1 Tablespoon white Karo syrup
1/2 cup brown sugar	1/3 cup milk
1 1/2 squares chocolate	1/4 teaspoon salt
1/4 stick butter	

Cake: Cream butter and sugar. Add eggs, and then milk and dry ingredients alternately. Bake in 350 degree oven for 15 minutes. Makes 2 layers.

Filling: Bring all ingredients to a boil. Cook until drop of mixture forms a ball in cold water. Beat until right consistency for icing.

Berry's-on-the-Hill
Orangeburg, S. C.

Gingerbread

1 cup Grandma's molasses	1/2 teaspoon soda
1/2 cup sugar	1 cup boiling water
1/2 cup melted margarine	2 1/2 cups sifted flour
2 teaspoons ginger	2 well beaten eggs
2 teaspoons cloves or allspice	

Put molasses in a bowl, add sugar, melted shortening, ginger and cloves. Dissolve soda in boiling water and add to first mixture. Then add flour and eggs. Batter will be very thin. Do not fill the pan more than one-half full. Cook for 30 minutes in a 375 degree oven. Stored in a covered tin, it will keep indefinitely.

Mrs. E. L. Smith
(Edith Bryant)

Gingerbread Sauce

1 cup sugar
1 Tablespoon flour
1 cup boiling water

Juice and rind of 1 lemon
2 Tablespoons butter

Mix first three ingredients and let this come to a boil. Boil several minutes. Add lemon juice and rind. When slightly thick, take off stove and add butter.

Mrs. E. L. Smith
(Edith Bryant)

Chess Cakes

3/4 cup butter or margarine
1 1/2 cups all-purpose flour, sifted
3 Tablespoons sugar
3 eggs, separated

2 1/4 cups brown sugar, firmly packed
1 cup pecans, chopped
1 1/2 teaspoons vanilla
Powdered sugar

Heat oven 350 to 375 degrees. Work butter until creamy soft; then work flour in gradually. Add white sugar and continue working until batter is smooth. Pat into 11 1/2 x 7 1/2 x 1 1/2-inch ungreased baking pan about 1/4-inch thick. Bake 20 to 30 minutes, or until crust is golden brown. Beat egg yolks until foamy, then add brown sugar gradually and beat until thick and spongy. Stir in chopped pecans and vanilla extract. Next beat egg whites until they stand in points. Then mix gently into sugar and nut mixture. Spread over crust, return to oven and bake 25 to 30 minutes longer, or until set. Sprinkle with powdered sugar and when cool, cut into 24 squares, 1 1/2 inches apiece.

Mrs. A. Welling LaGrone
(Martha Dunson)

Surprise Cake

1 angel food cake, store
  bought and slightly stale
1 envelope Knox gelatine
1 cup cold water
5 egg yolks
3/4 cup powdered sugar
1/2 cup hot milk

1/2 pint heavy cream, whipped
1 large jigger sherry or
  bourbon or any other
  flavoring desired
Whipped cream, sweetened
Almonds, slivered and toasted

Dissolve gelatine in water. Beat yolks and add sugar. Add milk to egg mixture and then add the softened gelatine. Cook in double boiler until mixture coats spoon, stirring constantly. *Cool.* When cool, add flavoring and whipped cream. When it starts to hold its shape, put into a scooped out angel food cake. Top with cake pieces and let it stand 5 or 6 hours. Ice with whipped cream, flavored, and sprinkle with almonds. (Or ice with white frosting made from egg whites.)

Mrs. W. M. Webster, III
(Langhorne Tuller)

Orange Cake

Cake

3/4 cup butter
1 cup sugar
3 eggs
1 cup buttermilk
3 cups flour
1/2 teaspoon salt

1/2 teaspoon soda
1 cup chopped dates
1 cup pecans, chopped
  and floured
Grated rind of 2 oranges

Topping

Juice of 2 oranges
1 cup sugar

Cream butter and sugar, add eggs, flour and buttermilk. Then, add other ingredients. Pour into a well greased and floured Bundt cake pan or steeple pan. Bake at 350 degrees for 1 hour. When cake is done, remove from pan and immediately pour topping (which has been mixed without heating) over cake to form a crusty glaze.

Mrs. James H. Austin
(Elizabeth Reid)

266

Grandmother's Fruit Cake

1/2 pound butter
1/2 pound sugar
4 cups flour
1 grated nutmeg
6 eggs
1 pound shelled pecans

1 pound candied cherries
1 pound candied pineapple
1/2 cup bourbon or sherry
1/2 teaspoon salt
1 teaspoon baking powder

Soak cherries and pineapple overnight in the bourbon or sherry. Cream butter and sugar. Add nutmeg. Add one egg at a time, beating constantly until 4 eggs have been added. Add a little flour and then alternate adding the remaining eggs and flour which has been mixed with the salt and baking powder. Fold in the nuts, cherries, and pineapple soaked in the bourbon or sherry. Pour into 2 loaf pans which have been lined with greased brown paper. Bake for 2 hours at 250 degrees. Place a small pan of water in the oven during baking to prevent drying. If cakes seem dry, spread with a little bourbon or sherry. These fruit cakes keep for a long time in a cool place.

Mrs. Earle R. Stall
(Nelle Mackey)

English Fruit Cake

1 3/4 cups chopped cherries
1 3/4 cups chopped pineapple
3 cups pecans
1 pound white raisins
6 Tablespoons brandy
1 cup margarine
2 1/4 cups sugar

6 eggs
4 cups flour
1 1/2 teaspoons salt
1/2 teaspoon baking powder
1 1/2 teaspoons cinnamon
1 teaspoon nutmeg

Cream margarine and sugar, beat in eggs, one at a time. Sift dry ingredients — divide in half. Stir half of flour in egg mixture with brandy. Stir other half of flour into fruit and nuts. Then mix with the batter. Bake at 275 degrees for 3 3/4 hours in 10-inch tube pan, lined with brown paper. Cool before turning out.

Mrs. J. R. Freeman
(Kathryn O'Dell)

Mincemeat Squares

1/2 cup shoftening (half
  Crisco and half margarine)
1 cup brown sugar
1 1/2 cups flour
1 teaspoon soda
1 teaspoon salt

1 3/4 cups Quaker oats
  (not instant)
1 package dried mincemeat or
  jar of prepared mincemeat
Rum or sherry

Prepare mincemeat according to directions of package; flavor with rum or sherry. Work first five ingredients together. Add Quaker oats. Put 1/2 mixture in slightly greased oblong pan. Spread with mincemeat. Use rest of crumb mixture for the top. Bake at 350 degrees. When done, cut in squares and sprinkle with confectioners sugar.

Mrs. C. C. Withington, Jr.
(Hamlin McBee)

Merry Christmas Cookies
(Fruit Cake)

1 cup butter
1 cup brown sugar
3 well beaten eggs
4 cups cake flour (reserve
  1 cup for flouring fruit)
1 teaspoon soda
1 teaspoon cinnamon
1 cup whiskey (milk or juice)
1 pound white raisins

2 cups chopped dates
  (1 small package)
6 slices candied pineapple
  (2 each, red, yellow
  and green)
2 cups candied cherries
  (red and green)
6 to 7 cups pecans

Cream butter and sugar. Add beaten eggs. Add, alternately, dry ingredients and whiskey. Mix well. Mix reserved flour with chopped fruits. Add fruit and pecans to cake mixture. Use teaspoon and drop on greased cookie sheet. Bake in slow oven at 250 degrees for about 20 minutes. Yields approximately 12 dozen. These will keep indefinitely in air-tight container.

Mrs. Walter G. King
(Mary Louise Bouchillon)

Fruit Cake Cookies

1/2 box light brown sugar
1 stick butter
2 eggs
1 cup sifted flour
1 teaspoon vanilla

Pinch salt
2 cups pecans
1/2 pound candied cherries
1/2 pound candied pineapple

Cream butter and sugar, add eggs, beaten lightly, fold in flour, salt and add vanilla. Grease 13 x 8 inch pan. Sprinkle chopped nuts on bottom, add batter and sprinkle chopped fruit over batter. Bake for one hour at 300 degrees. Cut while hot. Remove from pan when cooled.

Miss Margaret T. Bates

Seafoam Icing

1 cup brown sugar
1 cup white sugar
1 cup cold water
3 egg whites

15 marshmallows
1 cup crushed nuts
Vanilla

Cook brown sugar, white sugar and water until it spins a thread. Remove from burner. Chop 15 marshmallows into mixture. Fold in stiffly beaten egg whites. Beat until cool. Add nuts and few drops of vanilla.

Mrs. Henry Sullivan
(Mary Barr Prince)

Brown Sugar Caramel Icing

1 cup dark brown sugar
2 cups white sugar
1/2 cup milk
1/2 cup evaporated milk

3 Tablespoons Karo syrup
1 teaspoon vanilla
1/2 stick butter
1/8 teaspoon soda

Mix together all ingredients except butter and vanilla and boil rapidly, stirring constantly until soft boil (231 degrees F.). Remove from heat and add butter and vanilla. Beat until proper consistency to spread. (Will ice a 2 layer cake.)

Mrs. Newton Stall, Jr.
(Kitty Williams)

269

White Icing

2 1/4 cups sugar
1/2 cup water
1/4 cup white Karo syrup
2 egg whites

1/2 teaspoon baking powder
1 teaspoon vanilla or
   almond flavoring

Put sugar, water and Karo into saucepan and boil until candy thermometer registers 246 degrees. Beat egg whites, and add baking powder, beating until very stiff. Pour hot syrup over egg whites, add 1 teaspoon vanilla and beat until it holds peaks and is ready to spread.

Mrs. Newton Stall, Jr.
(Kitty Williams)

Krispie Balls

2 sticks butter
2 cups brown sugar
2 packages dates (1 pound)
1 can coconut

4 cups Rice Krispies
2 cups nuts (chopped)
Powdered sugar

Melt butter and add sugar. Cook over low heat 6 minutes. Add dates and coconut. Stir in Rice Krispies and nuts. Let cool, roll in small balls and then in powdered sugar. Store in jar in refrigerator. Keeps well.

Good to have on hand at Christmas time.

Mrs. T. R. Easterby
(Margaret West)

Swedish Balls

1/2 pound butter or margarine
1 1/2 cups granulated sugar
1/2 cup *strong,* cold
   coffee (instant)

2 teaspoons vanilla
1 cup cocoa
4 cups quick rolled oats
   (uncooked)

270

Cream together butter and sugar. Add coffee, vanilla and cocoa, and mix well. Add rolled oats and mix. Shape into balls about 1 inch in diameter and roll in granulated sugar. Place on cookie sheet in refrigerator to dry overnight. Store in tight container at least 24 hours before serving. Makes over 5 dozen.

A delicious confection to serve at Christmas (or any time) and to give as gifts in decorated tins.

Mrs. C. D. Bessinger, Jr.
(Jane Prevost)

Cheese Date Goodies

Pastry

1 stick butter	1 teaspoon salt
2 cups sharp cheese	Dash of red pepper
1 1/2 cups flour	

Filling

1 8-ounce package dates	1/4 cup water
1/2 cup brown sugar	1/2 cup chopped nuts

Grate cheese and mix with other pastry ingredients until dough can be rolled. Cut with small biscuit cutter. Cut dates into pieces, mix with other filling ingredients and cook until thick and fairly dry. Cool. Add nuts. Put small amount of filling on half the cheese biscuit. Fold over other side and mash edges together. Bake at 325 degrees for 15-20 minutes. Yields 2 to 3 dozen.

Mrs. Newton Turrentine
(Elizabeth Horton)

Grandma's Tea Cakes

1/2 pound butter	1 teaspoon soda
2 cups sugar	1 teaspoon cream of tartar
2 eggs	1 teaspoon vanilla
5 cups flour	

Cream butter; add sugar gradually. Then add beaten eggs. Add flour, soda, cream of tartar and vanilla. Mix well, roll thin and cut with cookie cutter. Bake at 350 degrees in a preheated oven.

Miss Unity Brock

Crescents or Tea Biscuits

4 Tablespoons sugar
1/2 pound butter
3 cups sifted flour

1/4 teaspoon salt
1 cup chopped nuts

Cream sugar and butter. Add flour and salt. Add nuts. Shape into crescents and place on greased cookie sheets. Chill 2 hours. Bake at 350 degrees until brown. Roll in powdered sugar after baking.

Mrs. W. H. Johnson
(Ruth Southerlin)

Sugar Cookies

1 cup butter
1 cup sugar
2 eggs
1 teaspoon vanilla

1/2 teaspoon soda
1/2 teaspoon salt
2 1/2 cups flour

Cream butter and sugar. Add eggs one at a time and blend. Add vanilla and sifted dry ingredients. Dough will be loose and sticky. Refrigerate overnight. Roll thin on lightly floured board. Cut and sprinkle with sugar. Bake in 350 degree oven for 8 to 10 minutes on ungreased cookie sheet.

Mrs. J. D. Galloway, Jr.
(Feeny Dunlap)

Quick Sugar Cookies

2 1/2 cups Bisquick (do
   not sift)
1 1/2 cups sugar

2 eggs
1 teaspoon vanilla
1/2 cup corn oil
Pecan halves

Mix all ingredients well, except nuts. Drop by 1/2 teaspoons on cookie sheet. Flatten a bit, sprinkle with sugar, and place 1/2 nut meat on top of each cookie. Bake 4-5 minutes at 350 degrees.

Mrs. Dillon Myer

Pecan Dreams

1 stick butter or margarine
1/8 cup sugar
1 cup flour

1 cup ground pecans
1 teaspoon vanilla

Thoroughly blend butter and sugar. Then add flour, vanilla and nuts. Drop by teaspoons on cookie sheet. Cook at approximately 325 degrees for about 12 minutes. Do not overcook. Yield: Approximately 40 cookies.

Miss Marie Mahon

Butter Nut Cookies

1 stick butter
1 stick margarine
1 cup sugar
1 egg yolk
1 egg white

2 cups flour
2 teaspoons vanilla
1 cup pecans (may substitute
    almonds), broken

Cream butter, margarine and sugar. Add egg yolk, flour and vanilla. Spread thinly on a 10 by 13-inch jellyroll pan. Brush top with slightly beaten egg white. Sprinkle with pecans. Bake in oven at 275 degrees for 45 minutes. Makes 4 to 5 dozen.

Mrs. Edward H. Stall
(Betty Peace)

Forgotten Cookies

2 egg whites
3/4 cup sugar
1/2 cup nuts, crushed

1 6-ounce package semi-sweet
    chocolate bits

Preheat oven to 375 degrees. Beat egg whites until peaks form. Add sugar and continue beating until very stiff. Fold in chocolate bits and nuts. Drop by *level* tablespoonfuls onto greased cookie sheets. Place in oven and turn off heat. Let remain in oven until cookies cool to room temperature. (May be left in oven overnight and removed in the morning.) Store in airtight container.Yields 2 to 2 1/2 dozen.

Mrs. Harold Stuckey
(Leila Barr Sullivan)

273

Pecan Cookies

1/2 pound creamery butter
1 cup brown sugar
1 cup white sugar
1 scant cup flour
1 teaspoon baking powder

1/4 teaspoon salt
1 1/2 cups pecans, broken into
   small pieces
2 eggs, well-beaten
1 teaspoon sherry flavoring

Melt butter in saucepan and add sugar. Mix and add flour, sifted with baking powder and salt. Add eggs, pecans and flavoring. Mix well and spread thinly with spatula in well-greased, large, flat pan. Cook in 350 degree oven until brown. Remove from oven, cool slightly, cut into small squares and remove from pan.

Mrs. Charles Mayes
(Jessica Crawford)

Glorified Brownies

Brownies

1 cup sugar
1/2 cup butter
2 eggs
3/4 cup flour, sifted

3 Tablespoons cocoa, scant
1 cup nuts
Pinch of salt

Icing

1/8 cup butter
2 cups confectioners sugar
3 Tablespoons cocoa, scant

Miniature marshmallows
3 Tablespoons milk

Brownies: Cream butter and sugar. Add eggs. Beat until fluffy. Sift flour and cocoa together and add to egg mixture. Add salt and nuts. Bake 18 to 20 minutes in 350 degree oven in rectangular 1 1/2 quart pan. *Do not cook too long.*

Icing: Make icing while brownies are cooking. Heat milk and melt butter in it. Add sugar and cocoa. Make sure that sugar melts. Cover brownies with marshmallows as soon as you take from stove; then pour icing on. Cool in pan before cutting.

Miss Emma Major

Drop Cookie Supreme

1 cup butter
1 cup brown sugar
1 cup white sugar
2 eggs
2 cups plain flour
1/2 teaspoon soda
Pinch of salt

1 teaspoon baking powder
1 cup uncooked quick oatmeal
3 cups corn flakes
1 cup shredded coconut (dry)
1 cup chopped pecans
1 teaspoon vanilla

Cream butter and sugars; add eggs one at a time and beat. Sift flour, baking powder, salt and soda, and add to creamed mixture. Stir in corn flakes, coconut, oatmeal, nuts and vanilla. Drop by teaspoon on greased cookie sheet. Bake at 325 degrees or in slow to moderate oven. Makes about 140 small cookies, or can be dropped to make larger cookies.

Mrs. Charles H. Lawton
(Caroline Lauchman)

Dropped Cookies

1 cup brown sugar
1/2 cup margarine
2 squares melted bitter
    chocolate
1 egg
1/2 cup milk

1 1/2 cups flour
1/4 teaspoon salt
1/2 teaspoon soda
1 teaspoon baking powder
1 teaspoon vanilla
1 cup chopped nuts

Cream margarine and sugar. Add chocolate and beaten egg. Sift dry ingredients together and add alternately with milk. Add vanilla and stir in nuts. Drop by teaspoon on greased baking sheet. Bake at 350 degrees for 15 to 20 minutes.

Mrs. H. B. McBee
(Ava Ferguson)

Coconut Nut Bars

1 stick butter

1 cup flour

2 eggs

1 1/2 cups brown sugar

1 cup pecans

1 Tablespoon brown sugar

Topping

1 cup coconut

1 1/2 teaspoons vanilla

1 teaspoon baking powder

Cut butter, flour, and brown sugar together with a fork, spread thinly in a brownie pan and bake 20 minutes at 300 degrees.

Topping: Combine all ingredients, spread on top of previously baked base and bake 30 minutes at 300 degrees.

Mrs. B. H. Peace
(Dorothy Pedrick)

Date and Nut Bars

3/4 cup plain flour

1/2 teaspoon baking powder

1/2 teaspoon salt

2 eggs

1 cup brown sugar

1/2 cup chopped pecans

1/2 pack sliced dates

Sift dry ingredients. Beat eggs and stir in sugar gradually. Add dates and nuts. Stir in dry ingredients. Spread mixture in shallow pan which has been greased and floured. Bake in 350 degree oven 30 minutes. Cut in squares. Roll in powdered sugar when cooled.

Mrs. James B. Gowan
(Ella Zachary)

Oatmeal Cookies

3/4 cup shortening

2 cups sugar

2 eggs

2 scant cups quick oatmeal

1 cup raisins

1/2 cup nuts

2 scant cups sifted flour

1 teaspoon soda

1 teaspoon salt

276

Cream together shortening and sugar. Beat eggs and add. Grind together raisins and nuts and add them and oatmeal to mixture. Sift together flour, soda and salt; add to mixture and stir thoroughly. Shape into small balls, roll in granulated sugar, and flatten slightly with prongs of fork as you place on cookie sheet. Bake at 350 degrees for 10-12 minutes.

Mrs. George Bogle
(Elizabeth Leach)

Brown Sugar Surprises

3/4 cup margarine or butter	1 teaspoon baking powder
2 cups brown sugar	1 teaspoon vanilla
2 eggs, beaten	3/4 cup broken nut meats
1 cup cake flour, sifted	Confectioners 4X sugar

Cream together thoroughly margarine and brown sugar. Add 2 beaten eggs. Then fold in cake flour which has been sifted with baking powder. Add vanilla and nut meats. Pour in greased pan and bake at 350 degrees for 1/2 hour. Will rise and then fall. Let cool thoroughly before cutting into bars. Roll bars in 4X sugar.

Mrs. J. Robert Stogner, Jr.
(Pat Everton)

Butterscotch Bites

2 eggs, beaten	3/4 cup plain flour
1 cup brown sugar	1 teaspoon baking powder
1 teaspoon orange peel, grated	1/4 teaspoon salt
2 Tablespoons butter, melted	1 cup pecans, chopped
1 cup corn flakes	

Combine eggs and sugar in top of double boiler. Cook over boiling water, stirring constantly for 15 minutes. Add orange peel and butter and mix thoroughly, then set aside to cool. When thoroughly cool, mix in all other ingredients and spread in a greased 8X8X2-inch pan. Bake at 350 degrees for 20 minutes. Cool and cut into bite size pieces or bars. Yields 2 dozen.

Mrs. Hugh Z. Graham
(Hessie Morrah)

Ice Box Cookies

1 cup butter (1/2 pound)
2 cups brown sugar
3 eggs, beaten
3 1/2 cups flour

1/2 teaspoon soda
1/2 teaspoon salt
1 1/2 cups pecans, cut fine
2 teaspoons vanilla

Cream butter and sugar. Mix flour, salt and soda. Gradually add dry ingredients and eggs, alternately. Add vanilla and nuts. Make into two rolls and put in refrigerator over night. Slice thin and cook in 350 degree oven for 10 to 12 minutes.

Mrs. Vardry Ramseur, Jr.
(Eleanor Mullinnix)

Seven Layer Cookies

1 stick butter
1 cup graham cracker crumbs
1 cup coconut
1 6-ounce package chocolate
  chip morsels

1 6-ounce package
  butterscotch morsels
1 can sweetened condensed milk
1/2 cup chopped pecans

Melt butter. Put in 13 X 9-inch pan. Spread graham cracker crumbs on butter; then spread the coconut, the chocolate chips and the butterscotch morsels. Drizzle milk over this and add nuts on top. Do not mix. Bake at 350 degrees for 25-30 minutes.

Mrs. Roger W. Smith
(Mary Jane Peter)

Spritzgeback (German Cookies)

2 1/2 sticks butter
1 1/4 cups sugar
2 eggs

Pinch of salt
4 cups flour
1 teaspoon baking powder

Cream butter and add sugar. Add eggs and salt. Slowly add sifted flour and baking powder. Using a cookie press, fix dough on greased cookie sheets. Bake 10 to 20 minutes at 375 degrees. Decorate with colored sugar or crystalized cherries. Yields 8 dozen.

Mrs. William H. Johnson, Jr.
(Becky Cashwell)

Pickles and Preserves

Dilly Beans

Green beans
2 teaspoons crushed red pepper
   or 4 red pepper pods
   (optional)
4 cloves garlic

4 teaspoons dill
2 cups cider vinegar
2 cups water
1/4 cup salt

Wash and steam beans no longer than 10 minutes and pack 35 per sterile pint jar. Add to each jar 1/3 amount of pepper, garlic and dill. Heat vinegar, water and salt to boiling point. Pour over beans. Let stand 2 weeks. (Carrots and okra can also be used.) Makes 3 pints.

Mrs. James R. Jacobs
(Beryl Martin)

Bullard Pickle

1 dozen green peppers (seeded)
6 hot red peppers
1 quart green tomatoes
2 heads cauliflower
1 quart celery
2 quarts vinegar
2 quarts sugar
1 3/4 ounces mixed pickling
   spice

1/4 cup salt
2 medium jars of mustard
1 cup flour
1 box turmeric
4 quarts commercial sweet
   mixed pickles
1/2 gallon thinly sliced
   artichokes

Cut peppers, tomatoes, cauliflower and celery into small pieces. Add vinegar, sugar, pickling spice, salt, and mustard, and simmer for 30 minutes. Combine flour and tumeric, beat with a little of the pickle juice and add to mixture, stirring well. Add sweet pickles, and simmer for 10 minutes. Add artichokes. Put in sterile jars and seal when artichokes are hot.

Mrs. Earle R. Stall
(Nelle Mackey)

Uncooked Artichoke Pickle

Step I

1 large white cabbage
  (7 to 8 pounds)
1 dozen white onions
1 dozen green peppers
  (optional)

1 dozen big cucumber
  dill pickles
2 quarts artichokes, peeled
Cauliflower (optional)
2 cups salt

Cut the vegetables as fine as you like and sprinkle with 2 cups salt. Let stand 12 hours and squeeze dry.

Step II

Vinegar

Cold water

Cover vegetables with vinegar and cold water, using half and half. Let stand 24 hours and squeeze dry.

Step III

Vinegar
1/4 pound Coleman's
  dry mustard
3 ounces celery seed

1 ounce tumeric
4 pounds white sugar
1/4 pound mustard seed

Cover vegetables with vinegar in which has been dissolved dry mustard, celery seed, tumeric, sugar and mustard seed. (It takes a good gallon of vinegar to cover this amount.) Put in a cold place in a 3-gallon crock. Keep covered. It is ready to use in a week or 10 days.

Mrs. Augustus W. Smith
(Frances Poole)

Artichoke Pickle

4 quarts artichokes
3 cauliflower
1 quart green and red peppers
1 pint celery
1 quart onions
1/2 cup salt
2 pounds sugar

1 cup flour
2 Tablespoons dry mustard
2 Tablespoons tumeric
5 Tablespoons salt
1 gallon vinegar
1 Tablespoon celery seed
1 Tablespoon allspice

282

Cut vegetables into small pieces. Soak overnight in cold water and 1/2 cup salt. Drain and rinse thoroughly with cold water. Mix sugar, flour, vinegar and spices. Bring to boil. Add vegetables, cook for five minutes and put in sterilized jars and seal.

Mrs. George H. Edwards
(Martha Scoville)

Jerusalem Artichoke Pickle

4 quarts artichokes	1 Tablespoon tumeric
4 large onions	3 Tablespoons salt
3 pints vinegar	2 Tablespoons white
2 1/2 cups brown sugar	mustard seed

Wash and scrape artichokes. Put artichoke and onion through food chopper. While grinding the vegetables, have other ingredients cooking. Combine all and let boil slowly for 20 minutes. Pour in jars and seal while hot.

This belonged to my grandmother, Mrs. James Ferguson.

Mrs. C. C. Withington, Jr.
(Hamlin McBee)

Chow-Chow Pickle

1 peck green tomatoes	2 pounds white sugar
1 large cabbage	1 box celery seed
12 green peppers (1 or 2 red for color)	2 boxes mustard seed
	1 box dry mustard
12 onions	1 Tablespoon pickling spice
2 quarts artichokes	2 teaspoons tumeric
1 gallon light vinegar	2 cups salt

Grind tomatoes, cabbage, peppers and onions (saving juices to add to pickle before cooking). Sprinkle with salt and let stand several hours. Put in sack to drain over night. (Add vinegar, sugar, spices and some of the vegetable juice (about 1 quart). Put vegetables in and cook until done (about 45 minutes). Just before removing from stove, add artichokes which have been scraped and cut in pieces. Cook 5 minutes and then pack in pint jars.

Mrs. Alfred T. Smith
(Sammie McCall)

283

Crystal Pickle

25 cucumbers (dill size)	1-ounce alum
	Brine
1 cup salt	8 cups water
	Syrup
1 quart vinegar	Cinnamon
2 quarts sugar	Whole cloves

Wash cucumbers and put in brine. Weight down and let stand two weeks. (Don't worry about the mold which forms on top). Wash the cucumbers, cut into slices about 3/8 inch thick, cover with fresh water and add one ounce alum. Let stand over night, drain and wash again. Make syrup and a spice bag of cinnamon and cloves. Bring syrup to a boil and pour over the pickles for three mornings in succession. Use a fresh spice bag each day to put in syrup. On the fourth morning heat the pickles and seal while hot. Yields 6 pints.

Miss Margaret H. Spencer

Green Tomato Chow Chow

5 quarts green tomatoes	1 quart onions
2 large cabbages	11 green peppers
1 quart cucumbers or sweet pickle (optional)	1 cup salt
	Sauce
1/2 gallon vinegar	2 Tablespoons mustard seed
3 cups sugar	1 Tablespoon celery seed
1 1/2 cups flour	2 Tablespoons tumeric
2 Tablespoons dry mustard	

Grind vegetables medium fine, saving juice, and mix vegetables, juice and salt. Soak over night. Cook until tender, about 10 minutes. Dip off some juice but leave thick. Mix flour, sugar and mustard with enough vinegar to make a paste. Add rest of vinegar gradually. Add mustard and celery seed. Bring to a boil and add tumeric. Mix with vegetables. Bring to boil. Seal in sterilized jars.

Mrs. Ralph McPherson
(Julia Russell)

284

Sweet Pickled Peaches

14 pounds peaches
10 pounds sugar
2 quarts vinegar

4 Tablespoons cloves
4 Tablespoons allspice
2 sticks cinnamon

Make syrup of sugar and vinegar. Tie spices in cloth sack and boil in syrup. Drop in peeled peaches and cook until tender. Pack in sterile jars and cover peaches with hot syrup.

Mrs. Alfred T. Smith
(Sammie McCall)

Cucumber Pickle

7 pounds cucumbers
2 gallons water
3 cups lime
3 pints vinegar

5 pounds sugar
1 Tablespoon whole cloves
1/2 teaspoon celery seed

Slice and soak cucumbers in lime and water solution (2 gallons water, 3 cups lime) for 24 hours. Drain. Rinse and soak in clear water (change water once each hour for four hours). Mix remaining ingredients, bring to a boil and pour over cucumbers. Let stand overnight. Bring to a slow boil and cook 45 minutes or until fruit turns green.

This makes 11 pints of the best cucumber pickle you have ever put in your mouth!

Miss Grace Littlejohn

Pear Chutney

1/2 pound onion, sliced
4 pounds pears, cut up
2 pounds Sultana raisins
1/2 teaspoon ground mace
1/2 teaspoon ground cinnamon
1/2 teaspoon ground cloves
1 1/2 teaspoons ginger

1 1/2 teaspoons paprika
1 1/4 teaspoons cayenne
2 ounces chopped garlic
2 ounces salt
3 1/4 pounds sugar
3 quarts dark cider vinegar
2 pounds candied dried ginger

Combine all ingredients. Simmer for 3 hours. Pour into jars and seal. Makes 12 pints.

Mrs. E. S. McKissick
(Jean Reamsbottom)

Spiced Pears

5 pounds firm pears (14-16)
2 cups white vinegar
1 1/2 cups water
5 cups sugar

6 2-inch sticks whole
  cinnamon
1 Tablespoon whole cloves
1 Tablespoon whole allspice

Wash fruit, pare and cut in halves or quarters; remove stemmed cores. Measure vinegar, water and sugar in 5-quart saucepan. Add spices tied in piece of clean cheesecloth. Boil for 5 minutes. Add half of pears and boil gently about 10 minutes until tender but still firm enough to hold their shape. Pack fruit in hot sterilized jars. Put remaining fruit in syrup and boil for 5 to 10 minutes. Remove bag of spices and pour syrup over pears to fill jars. Seal. Makes 4 or 5 pints.

Gugga's Pear Relish

1 dozen green bell peppers
1 dozen red bell peppers
1/2 dozen hot bell peppers
1 peck (or 2 dozen large)
  green pears
1 dozen medium sized onions

1 quart white vinegar
4 Tablespoons salt
4 Tablespoons celery seed
4 Tablespoons mustard seed
2 cups sugar

Wash and cut peppers in two. Peel pears and onions and cut. Grind all together. Add vinegar, salt, celery seed, mustard seed and sugar. Boil about 45 minutes and seal in jars.

Mrs. H. T. Williams
(Catherine Hudson)

Pepper Relish

12 red peppers (medium size
  or large)
12 green peppers (medium size
  or large)
12 medium onions

12 pods hot pepper
3 cups sugar
3 cups vinegar
3 Tablespoons salt

286

Remove seeds and veins from peppers. Chop peppers and onions with meat grinder. Cover mixture with boiling water and let stand at least 5 minutes. Drain well. Add sugar, vinegar and salt. Boil gently 5 to 10 minutes. Put in sterilized jars and seal. Makes approximately 6 half pints.

H. E. Runge

Iced Green Tomato Pickle

7 pounds green tomatoes	1 teaspoon cloves
2 gallons water	1 teaspoon ginger
3 cups powdered lime (use	1 teaspoon allspice
plain yard lime)	1 teaspoon celery seed
5 pounds sugar	1 teaspoon mace
3 pints vinegar	1 teaspoon cinnamon

Soak sliced tomatoes in lime water 24 hours. Drain, soak in fresh water for 4 hours, changing water every half hour. Drain well to be sure all lime is removed. Make a syrup of sugar, vinegar and add spices. Bring syrup to a boil (green food coloring may be added, if desired) and pour over tomatoes. Let stand overnight. Next morning boil for 1 hour or until tomatoes are clear. Seal in jars while hot. Yields 7 pints.

Sweet Pickles

1 gallon sour pickles	5 pounds sugar
6-8 garlic sections, chopped,	4 sticks cinnamon, broken into
depending on size to taste	pieces
1/2 box whole black pepper	1 box mustard seed
corns	

Pour out pickle juice. Cut off pickle ends and slice in one inch rounds. Return to jug (or 2 jugs). Add rest of ingredients. Mix by turning jug every day for about 5 days or until sugar is dissolved. Chill to serve.

Mrs. J. Larry Jameson
(Addie Welborn)

Watermelon Pickle

4 pounds watermelon rind (outer
   green peeled and pink pulp
   removed.)
2 quarts cold water
1 Tablespoon slake lime
2 Tablespoons whole allspice

2 Tablespoons whole cloves
1 quart vinegar
1 quart water
3 1/2 pounds sugar
6 pieces stick cinnamon

Remove all pink pulp from rind and peel. Weigh. Cut in 1 inch cubes. Combine cold water and lime; pour over rind. Let stand 1 hour. Drain. Cover with fresh cold water. Simmer 1 hour or until tender. Drain. Tie spices in cheesecloth. Combine vinegar, remaining water and sugar. Heat until sugar dissolves. Add spice bag and rind. Simmer gently 2 hours. Add green vegetable color to your taste. Pack rind in hot sterile jars. Fill with boiling hot syrup. Seal. Yields approximately 12 half pints.

Mrs. Deas Richardson, Jr.
(Emily Bull)

Ginger Pear Preserves

10 pounds hard pears
7 pounds sugar
3 lemons

1 box root ginger
1 1/2 cups water

Peel pears and slice in fairly large slices. Add sugar. Add thinly sliced lemons and root ginger. Add water to dissolve sugar. Cook slowly over low heat until syrup is thick and an amber color, around two hours. Put in prepared jars.

Mrs. Wade H. Stephens, Jr.
(Genevieve Wilkins)

Hot Pepper Jelly

3/4 cup chopped hot peppers
   (about 20 peppers)
3/4 cup chopped bell peppers
   (4-6 medium peppers)

6 1/2 cups sugar
1 6-ounce bottle Certo
Red or green food coloring
1 1/2 cups vinegar

Put vinegar and chopped peppers in blender and chop fine. Bring this mixture to a rolling boil. Stir in sugar until dissolved. Remove from heat. Strain through mesh sieve. Wait 5 minutes. Add Certo and food coloring, stir. Seal in jars with wax. Serve with cream cheese and crackers or with meat.

This is good and different — very hot!

Mrs. Phil Wilmith
(Harriet Perkin)

Spiced Grapes

8 pounds grapes (purple)   4 sticks cinnamon
4 pounds sugar   1 ounce whole cloves
3 cups vinegar   2 blades mace

Remove and set aside the skin of the grapes. Cook the pulp in vinegar with the spices (tied in cheesecloth) until the grapes are soft. Pass as much pulp as possible through a fine sieve, keeping back the seeds. Put the skins through a food chopper. Add chopped skins to the pulp and return to stove. When boiling, put in sugar and bag of spice. Cook until thick. Then put in jars and seal.

Mrs. W. S. Adams
(Lucy Boyd)

Cranberry Sauce

4 cups cranberries   2 cups sugar
2 cups boiling water

Boil berries in water for 20 minutes or until berries are soft. Rub through sieve and cook 3 minutes. Add sugar and cook 2 minutes. Put in hot jelly glasses.

Mrs. C. Douglas Wilson
(Lois Mundy)

Mammy's Cranberries

2 cups cranberries   1 pound sugar
Juice of 1 large orange

Wash berries; do not use any water except the water that clings to berries. Let sugar, orange juice, and berries stand a few minutes. Stir with a fork until berries are coated. Put on very low heat; when berries reach a boil, let cook 3-5 minutes. These should look like beautiful crystallized cherries. A large flat pan is best to use for these.

Mrs. Otis Garrison
(Ann Massey)

Strawberry Butter

1 cup butter, room temperature   3 Tablespoons confectioners
3/4 cup frozen strawberries,   sugar
  drained

Put butter into blender. Add remaining ingredients. Blend until smooth. Delicious on hot rolls.

Mrs. J. Carter Latimer
(Gladys Ayers)

Strawberry Preserves

1 quart berries   Juice 1/2 lemon, optional
3 cups sugar

Pour boiling water over berries and let drain. Put into large boiler and add 2 cups sugar and lemon juice. Boil hard 1 minute and then add the other 1 cup sugar and cook 10 minutes. Pour into large platter to cool. Fill jars and seal next day.

Mrs. Newton Stall, Jr.
(Kitty Williams)

Beverages

Spiced Tea

1 dozen cloves
1 stick cinnamon
2 quarts water
4 teaspoons tea

1 cup unsweetened orange juice
6 Tablespoons lemon juice
1 3/4 cups sugar

Boil cloves and cinnamon in one quart water for 15 minutes. Remove cloves and cinnamon. Make tea in other quart of boiling water, strain and add to spiced liquid. Add juices and sugar. Serves 16.

Mrs. II. Elliott Batson
(Salley Langley)

Easy Spiced Tea

Pot of tea
4 or 5 cloves
Fresh orange juice

Sugar
Cinnamon sticks

Brew a pot of tea with 4 or 5 cloves added. Serve with a pitcher of fresh orange juice, sugar and cinnamon sticks. Each person may sweeten and add orange juice to taste and stir with the cinnamon stick.

Mrs. Philip G. Hill
(Marjorie Ellen Fyfe)

Russian Tea

2 cups Tang
3/4 cup instant tea
3/4 to 1 cup sugar
1 teaspoon ground cloves

1 envelope Lemonade Twist
(mix)
1 teaspoon cinnamon

Mix all ingredients well. Serve 2 or 3 teaspoons of mix to one cup of hot water.
Good for a Christmas present or as a gift for a sick friend.

Miss Ann Dunson LaGrone

Irish Coffee

1 jigger Irish whiskey
Coffee
1 1/2 teaspoons whipped cream

Sugar
Hot water

Make coffee, heat whiskey and warm Irish coffee mug over Sterno. Dip rim of mug into very hot water and then into sugar to coat rim. Immediately pour warm whiskey into hot mug and tilt over fire of Sterno to flame for 1/2 minute. Drop whipped cream onto flaming whiskey. Fill with hot coffee. Serves 1.

Chris Macaluso

Coffee Punch

1 pint milk
2 quarts strong coffee, cooled
2 1/2 teaspoons vanilla
1/2 cup sugar

1 cup heavy cream, whipped
1 quart ice cream: vanilla,
  chocolate or coffee
Nutmeg

Mix milk, coffee, vanilla and sugar together in a pitcher and chill for at least one hour. Place ice cream in a punch bowl, break into chunks with a spoon and pour the coffee-milk mixture over it. Cover the top with whipped cream; sprinkle with nutmeg. Serve in punch cups. Serves 10.

Mrs. John Roberts
(Celeste Hamrick)

Plantation Eggnog

4 eggs
3 jiggers bourbon
1 jigger rum

1/2 pint heavy whipping cream
4 teaspoons sugar
Nutmeg

Separate eggs. Mix liquors with yolks gradually. Beat whites until stiff. Whip cream. Mix sugar, yolks and whiskey together. Blend mixture with whites. Fold in whipped cream. Garnish with nutmeg. Serves 6.

Spoons necessary!

Mrs. Howard Newton, Jr.
(Jourdan Jones)

Cola Punch

24 Tablespoons lemon juice   5 pints water
3 cups sugar   6 Coca-Colas

Mix lemon juice, sugar and water and let stand over night. Add Coca-Colas when ready to serve.
Inexpensive and zippy and serves a lot of people.

Mrs. C. Heyward Morgan
(Nancy Perry)

Catawba Wine Punch

1 gallon sauterne   1 quart Catawba wine
1 quart gin   2 quarts soda

Mix all but soda, adding this just before serving.

Mrs. William Bradford Dunson
(Liza Leman)

Luncheon Apertif

1 quart pale dry sherry   1 small can frozen lemonade
  or sauterne   or limeade

Mix together at least a day ahead and serve chilled in sherry glasses. Makes 10 glasses.

Mrs. Victor N. Shepherd
(Sarah Thompson)

MacCalla's Punch

1 quart orange *ice*   1 quart bourbon, chilled
1 quart Rhine wine, chilled   1 quart soda water, chilled

Place orange ice in punch bowl. Pour wine, bourbon and soda over orange ice. Stir once or twice gently, serve and beware!

Mrs. Charles W. Bazemore
(Nancy MacCalla)

Punch for 75

2 big cans Hawaiian punch
2 big cans pineapple juice
2 big cans apple juice
2 quarts water

4 cups sugar
2 cups fresh lemon juice
1 quart ginger ale to each
quart of fruit mixture

This can be poured into quart cartons and frozen. Thaw several hours before serving. Add ginger ale right before serving. The beauty of this is that no extra ice is used. Makes three gallons.

Mrs. N. B. Hudson, Jr.
(Mary Lou Kincannon)

Sangría

Sangría is a Spanish wine punch, served with the meal. This recipe came from the Spanish Pavilion Restaurant, via the Jockey Club, Madrid.

1 bottle of a good dry
red wine
1/2 cup of cognac and a
smaller portion of
Cointreau

2 lemons, sliced
2 oranges, sliced
1 dash sugar
1 small bottle club soda

Mix all ingredients in 1/2 gallon stoneware jug.

Mrs. Wade H. Stephens, Jr.
(Genevieve Wilkins)

Frozen Daiquiri

1/2 jigger Daiquiri Mix or
juice of 1 1/2 limes
1 jigger rum

1 iced teaspoon sugar
1 cup cracked ice

Put all ingredients in blender and blend on maximum speed until even consistency is obtained. Serves 1.

Newt Stall, Jr.

296

Planter's Punch

1 part simple syrup   3 parts Myers Dark Jamaica Rum
2 parts lemon juice   Cointreau (optional)

Shake first 3 ingredients vigorously with crushed ice and pour without straining into Collins glasses. Pack glasses to the top with crushed ice and add a generous splash of Cointreau, if desired. Bottled lemon juice may be used but fresh is better. Sugar and water may be used if no simple syrup is on hand.

Charles W. Bazemore

Simple (or Sugar) Syrup

3 cups sugar   1 cup water

Add the sugar to cold water in saucepan, heat to boiling and allow to boil for a few minutes. Cool the syrup and bottle. This will keep indefinitely.

Simple syrup can be used in all cocktails and drinks calling for sugar. Be certain to add to other ingredients before adding alcohol.

Charles W. Bazemore

Mint Julep

12 or more tender mint leaves   1 Tablespoon simple syrup or
Bourbon   heaping teaspoon granulated
Crushed ice   sugar and little water

For each julep place 1 tablespoon simple syrup (or sugar and water) in bottom of silver julep cup or hi-ball glass and add the tender mint leaves. Bruise the mint gently with a muddler and blend the ingredients by stirring and pressing gently for several minutes. (Do *not* crush the leaves for this releases the bitter, inner juices.) Pack the glasses with crushed ice and add bourbon to cover. Stir with a long bar spoon and churn the contents up and down for a few minutes. Add more bourbon if necessary. Insert long straws or silver sippers, and if time permits, place drink in refrigerator for 5 to 10 minutes at least. Do not touch glass with hands as this will "disturb" the frost on the glass. Garnish with a sprig of mint and serve with cocktail napkin around bottom of glass.

Charles W. Bazemore

Old Fashioned Cocktail

1 teaspoon or 1 lump sugar	2 ounces bourbon
2 dashes bitters	Orange slice
Water	Cherries

Place sugar in an Old Fashion glass and add bitters and enough water to cover sugar. Mix well. Add ice and bourbon. Stir again and decorate with orange slice and cherry. Serves 1.

Robert L. Chickey

Mary Ellen's Whiskey Sours

1 small can sweetened frozen lemonade	2 cans bourbon
	2 cans soda water

Blend in blender undiluted lemonade with bourbon measured in the lemonade can. Use same can to measure two cans soda water. Add soda water, stirring in by hand — otherwise you will have whiskey sour all over the kitchen. This is a good quick method and easy to fix at the last minute. Serve over crushed ice.

Mrs. A. Welling LaGrone
(Martha Dunson)

Sherry Martini

1 3/4 ounces dry gin	Lemon twist
1/4 ounce pale dry cocktail sherry	Olives or cocktail onions (optional)

Chill 3-ounce stemmed cocktail glass to the point of frost. Fill Martini pitcher with cracked (not crushed) ice. Pour the gin into the pitcher first. The gin should smoke as it settles over the ice. Then pour in the sherry. Stir briskley until the drink is very cold. Strain at once into frosted glass. A twist of lemon adds a special touch. Add olive or cocktail onion, if preferred. Serves 1.

Robert L. Chickey

298

Helpful Hints

Oven Heats

250 degrees	- Very slow
300 degrees	- Slow
325 degrees	- Moderately slow
350 degrees	- Moderate
375 degrees	- Moderately hot
400 degrees	- Hot
450 degrees to 500 degrees	- Very hot

Occasionally have your oven regulator tested for accuracy.

Weights and Measures

In adapting a foreign recipe it may be necessary to experiment a little, since the ingredients may be slightly different from American ones.

Few grains, pinch, dash (dry)	= less than 1/8 teaspoon
A dash (liquid)	= a few drops
3 teaspoons	= 1 Tablespoon
2 Tablespoons	= 1/8 cup (1 ounce)
4 Tablespoons	= 1/4 cup
5 1/3 Tablespoons	= 1/3 cup
8 Tablespoons	= 1/2 cup
8 ounces	= 1/2 pint or 1 cup
2 cups	= 1 pint
2 pints	= 1 quart
4 quarts (liquid)	= 1 gallon
8 quarts (dry)	= 1 peck
4 pecks (dry)	= 1 bushel
1 jigger	= 1 1/2 fluid ounces (3 Tablespoons)
1 large jigger	= 2 fluid ounces (1/4 cup)

Temperature Definitions

180 degrees	-	Simmering point of water
212 degrees	-	Boiling point of water
234 degrees to		
240 degrees	-	Soft ball stage for syrups
255 degrees	-	Hard crack stage for syrups
320 degrees	-	Caramel stage for syrups
220 degrees	-	Jellying point for jams and jellies

At altitudes above 3000 feet, lower air pressure causes differences in the boiling point of water and syrups. Consult government bulletins for details.

Equivalents

Bread crumbs
    4 ounces   =   3/4 cup less 1 Tablespoon

Butter, lard, other fats and cheese
    1 pound   =   2 cups
    1 ounce   =   2 Tablespoons
    1 stick   =   1/2 cup

Currants and raisins
    1 pound   =   2 3/8 cups

Flour
    1 pound   =   3 1/2 to 4 cups
    1 ounce   =   3 Tablespoons

Nut meats
    4 ounces   =   2/3 cup (chopped)

Rice (uncooked)
    1 pound   =   2 1/2 cups (8 cups cooked)

Brown sugar
    1 pound   =   2 1/4 cups (about)

Confectioners' sugar
    1 pound   =   3 3/4 cups (about)

Granulated sugar
    1 pound   =   2 cups

Egg whites (approximately)
    1   =   1 1/2 Tablespoons
    4 to 6   =   1/2 cup

Egg yolks (approximately)
    1   =   1 Tablespoon
    6 to 7   =   1/2 cup

Approximate Can Sizes

Can size	Weight	Contents
6 ounces	6 ounces	3/4 cup
8 ounces	8 ounces	1 cup
Number 1	11 ounces	1 1/3 cups
12 ounces	12 ounces	1 1/2 cups
Number 303	16 ounces	2 cups
Number 2	20 ounces	2 1/2 cups
Number 2 1/2	28 ounces	3 1/2 cups

Substitutions

Arrowroot
  1 Tablespoon = 2 Tablespoons flour (as thickening).
Baking powder (tartrate or phosphate)
  1 teaspoon = 2/3 teaspoon double-action type or 1/4 teaspoon
    baking soda plus 1/2 teaspoon cream of tartar.
Chocolate
  1 ounce (1 square) = 3 Tablespoons cocoa plus 1 teaspoon to 1
    Tablespoon shortening (less for Dutch cocoa).
Cornstarch
  1 Tablespoon = 2 Tablespoons flour (as thickening).
Flour
  Pastry flour. 1 cup = 1 cup all-purpose or bread flour less 2
    Tablespoons
  Potato flour. 1 Tablespoon = 2 Tablespoons flour (as
    thickening).
Milk
  Fresh, whole. 1 cup = 1/2 cup evaporated milk plus 1/2 cup
    water or 1/2 cup condensed milk plus 1/2 cup water
    (reduce the sugar in the recipe) or 1/4 cup powdered
    whole milk plus 1 cup water or 1/4 cup powdered skim
    milk plus 2 Tablespoons butter and 1 cup water.
  Fresh, skim. 1 cup = 1/4 cup powdered skim milk plus 1 cup
    water.
  Sour. 1 cup = 1 cup lukewarm fresh milk (less 1 Tablespoon)
    plus 1 Tablespoon vinegar. Let stand 5 minutes.

White Sauce

Ingredients	Thin	Medium	Thick
Butter or shortening	1 Tablespoon	2 Tablespoons	3 Tablespoons
Flour	1 Tablespoon	2 Tablespoons	3 Tablespoons
Milk	1 cup	1 cup	1 cup

Melt butter or shortening, remove from heat and blend in flour
until smooth. Slowly stir in milk. Cook until thick, stirring
constantly. Season to taste with salt and pepper.

Index

307

308

309

311

312

313

314

315

300 YEARS OF CAROLINA COOKING
The Junior League of Greenville, Inc.
P. O. Box 8703, Station A
Greenville, South Carolina 29604

Please send _____ copies of *300 Years of Carolina Cooking* @
$4.50 per copy (plus 50-cents postage per copy) to:
(S. C. Residents Please Add 18-cents Per Copy Sales Tax)

Name . . . .

Address . . . .

City . . . .

State . . . . Zip . . . .

300 YEARS OF CAROLINA COOKING
The Junior League of Greenville, Inc.
P. O. Box 8703, Station A
Greenville, South Carolina 29604

Please send _____ copies of *300 Years of Carolina Cooking* @
$4.50 per copy (plus 50-cents postage per copy) to:
(S. C. Residents Please Add 18-cents Per Copy Sales Tax)

Name . . . .

Address . . . .

City . . . .

State . . . . Zip . . . .

300 YEARS OF CAROLINA COOKING
The Junior League of Greenville, Inc.
P. O. Box 8703, Station A
Greenville, South Carolina 29604

Please send _____ copies of *300 Years of Carolina Cooking* @
$4.50 per copy (plus 50-cents postage per copy) to:
(S. C. Residents Please Add 18-cents Per Copy Sales Tax)

Name . . . .

Address . . . .

City . . . .

State . . . . Zip . . . .